HUMAN RIGHTS

Third Edition

Michael Freeman

Polity

First edition published in 2002 by Polity Press
This edition published in 2017 by Polity Press

Reprinted 2018, 2019

Polity Press
65 Bridge Street
Cambridge CB2 1UR, UK

Polity Press
350 Main Street
Malden, MA 02148, USA

ISBN-13: 978-1-5095-1027-6
ISBN-13: 978-1-5095-1028-3(pb)

A catalogue record for this book is available from the British Library.

Library of Congress Cataloging-in-Publication Data

Names: Freeman, Michael, 1936- author.
Title: Human rights / Michael Freeman.
Description: Third edition. | Cambridge ; Malden, MA : Polity, 2017. |
    Series: Key concepts | Includes bibliographical references and index.
Identifiers: LCCN 2016055252 (print) | LCCN 2016058072
    (ebook) | ISBN 9781509510276 (hardback) | ISBN
    9781509510283 (paperback) | ISBN 9781509510306
    (Mobi) | ISBN 9781509510313 (Epub)
Subjects: LCSH: Human rights. | BISAC: POLITICAL SCIENCE /
    Political Freedom & Security / Human Rights.
Classification: LCC JC571 .F675 2017 (print) | LCC JC571 (ebook) |
    DDC 323–dc23
LC record available at https://lccn.loc.gov/2016055252

Typeset in 10.5 on 12 pt Sabon
by Toppan Best-set Premedia Limited
Printed and bound in Great Britain by TJ International Ltd, Padstow

For further information on Polity, visit our website:
politybooks.com

Contents

Preface to the Third Edition   vi

Acknowledgements   viii

1   Introduction: Thinking About Human Rights   1

2   Origins: The Rise and Fall of Natural Rights   15

3   After 1945: The New Age of Rights   38

4   Theories of Human Rights   63

5   Putting Law in its Place: The Role of the
    Social Sciences   90

6   Universality, Diversity and Difference:
    Culture and Human Rights   120

7   The Politics of Human Rights   162

8   Globalization, Development and Poverty:
    Economics and Human Rights   183

9   Conclusion: Human Rights in the
    Twenty-first Century   210

References   222

Index   251

Preface to the Third Edition

Each edition of this book has been written under the shadow of a human-rights dilemma. The first was completed in 2001, shortly after NATO had conducted a bombing campaign against Serbia to protect the human rights of ethnic Albanians in Kosovo. Since this action had not been authorized by the UN Security Council, it raised the question as to the conditions under which outside powers had the right, or the duty, to intervene militarily in the affairs of a sovereign state to protect the human rights of some of its citizens – the so-called doctrine of 'the responsibility to protect'.

The second was completed in 2010, after the election of Barack Obama as President of the USA, and the ambiguous 'ending' of the 'global war on terror'. The Obama presidency failed to resolve dilemmas about how to fight terrorism while defending human rights or the responsibility to protect.

This third edition, completed in 2016, was written under the shadow of the terrible civil war in Syria, and the challenge of massive refugee flows. These constitute a kind of crisis for the human rights movement. 'Crisis' has been a theme of some recent academic writings on human rights: Michael Ignatieff (1999) has announced the 'midlife crisis' of human rights; Stephen Hopgood (2013) their 'endtimes'; and Eric Posner (2014) 'the twilight of human rights law'. In the second half of 2016 human-rights supporters were alarmed by the rise of extreme nationalism in several Western democracies, as expressed, for example, in the referendum vote for the United Kingdom to leave the European Union, the election of Donald Trump as President of the USA, and the increasing influence of right-wing governments and parties in continental Europe. Despite these developments, this book offers a defiantly, though cautiously, optimistic alternative to this fashionable pessimism.

This edition updates, revises and hopefully improves the second edition. In particular, chapter two takes into account the several excellent books on the Magna Carta written to mark its 800th anniversary in 2015, and recent contributions to Kant scholarship; chapter three updates the story of human rights through the Obama presidency to the current civil war in Syria; chapter six has been substantially rewritten to reflect recent thinking about the relation of human rights to 'culture', and includes, for the first time, sections on the human rights of persons with disabilities, refugees and migrant workers. Chapter eight brings the story of climate change up to the Paris Conference of November–December 2015. There are also updates and revisions in the other chapters.

This edition is dedicated, with admiration, to the democrats of Syria; with respect to all those seeking to struggle for human rights in a sustainable environment; and with love to Atala, Emilio and Ada.

Michael Freeman
University of Essex
November 2016

Acknowledgements

One evening in the autumn of 1977, Nick Bunnin, then teaching in the Department of Philosophy at the University of Essex, invited me to accompany him to a meeting of Amnesty International in Colchester. I agreed, reluctantly (for no reason other than laziness), but ended that evening as Chairperson of the newly formed Colchester Group of Amnesty International. This book would never have been written were it not for Nick Bunnin and my colleagues – local, national and international – at Amnesty. I would like to remember particularly the late Peter Duffy, whose moral commitment and intellectual rigour made him an exemplary human-rights activist.

I hesitate to list those to whom this book owes an intellectual debt, for fear of omitting many unfairly. I would, nevertheless, like to thank Onora O'Neill, Sheldon Leader, Nigel Rodley, Françoise Hampson, Geoff Gilbert, Paul Hunt, Brian Barry, Alan Ryan, Albert Weale, Tom Sorell, Deborah Fitzmaurice, Matthew Clayton, Marcus Roberts, Andrew Fagan, David Beetham, Peter Jones, Simon Caney, Hillel Steiner, Bhikhu Parekh, Brenda Almond, Paul Gilbert, Peter Baehr, David Forsythe, Jack Donnelly, Rhoda Howard-Hassmann, Joseph Chan, Julia Tao, Will Kymlicka, Barry Clarke, Hugh Ward, John Gray, David Robertson, Richard Claude, Stan Cohen, Richard Wilson, Wiktor Osiatyńksi, Saladin Meckled-Garcia and Basak Çali.

I have learned a great deal from students in the Department of Government and the Human Rights Centre at the University of Essex, far too numerous to mention. I have been invited to teach and learn about human rights in many countries, from China to Brazil, from Sweden to South Africa, and cannot emphasize too much how important the ensuing cross-cultural dialogue has been.

None of the above is, of course, responsible for the errors in this book, which I have managed on my own. The book is dedicated to June, Saul and Esther with love and admiration. Without them, especially, it would not have been possible.

Michael Freeman
University of Essex
November 2016

1
Introduction
Thinking About Human Rights

Realities

On a visit to Darfur, a region of western Sudan, Nicholas Kristof, a journalist on the *New York Times*, arrived at an oasis where, he reports, several tens of thousands of people were sheltering under trees after having been driven from their villages by *Janjaweed* militia, supported by the government of Sudan. He describes what he saw there.

> Under the first tree, I found a man who had been shot in the neck and the jaw; his brother, shot only in the foot, had carried him for forty-nine days to get to this oasis. Under the next tree was a widow whose parents had been killed and stuffed in the village well to poison the local water supply; then the Janjaweed had tracked down the rest of her family and killed her husband. Under the third tree was a four-year-old orphan girl carrying her one-year-old baby sister on her back; their parents had been killed. Under the fourth tree was a woman whose husband and children had been killed in front of her, and then she was gang-raped and left naked and mutilated in the desert. (Kristof 2006: 14)

This report will arouse various emotions in those who can bear to read it: horror, sympathy, outrage. We may struggle to find words adequate to express our emotions. These are 'atrocities', we may say, or 'crimes against humanity'. We may demand that someone should stop them, although we may well not be clear who should do what to bring this about. We may ask why such things happen.

These terrible events are the product of complex historical, political and economic processes. Darfur is composed of many ethnic groups, all Muslim. It has suffered from economic and social neglect since colonial times. Nevertheless, it was relatively stable until recently, even though a long and brutal civil war had been waged between the government of Sudan and the Muslim north of the country against the mainly Christian south. The peace of Darfur was unsettled by a number of different factors: increased competition between farmers and nomads for land resources that were diminishing as a result of desertification; the emergence of a racist ideology in Sudan distinguishing supposedly superior Arabs from supposedly inferior Africans; expansionist policies by Libya's Colonel Gaddafi in neighbouring Chad that destabilized the Sudan–Chad border with movements of insurgents and refugees; and the intrusion of southern Sudanese rebels. Darfurian self-defence organizations developed into a number of rebel forces. The Sudanese government sought to repress these rebellions by a savage counter-insurgency, employing Arab militias known as the *Janjaweed* ('evil horsemen'). A peace agreement was signed on 5 May 2006 by the Sudanese government and the largest rebel group, but not by other rebels. It has been estimated that at least 200,000 people were killed in the period 2003–6, more than two million displaced, and more than four million have suffered deprivation on both sides of the Darfur–Chad border (Reeves 2006). (The population of Darfur is approximately six million).

Many people in many countries have been victims of state violence in recent times. Government forces massacred more than half a million civilians in Indonesia in the mid-1960s in an attempt to suppress Communism. Estimates of the number of people killed by the Khmer Rouge regime of Pol Pot in Cambodia are as high as 2.2 million people, or between one-quarter and one-third of the entire population. More than 9,000 people 'disappeared' under the military government in Argentina in the late 1970s. During the rule of Idi Amin in Uganda from 1972 to 1978 more than 250,000 people were killed. Hundreds of thousands of civilians were murdered by security forces in Iraq during the 1980s. Between 1980 and 1992 almost 2 per cent of the population of El Salvador is estimated to have died as the result of 'disappearances' and political killings during the civil war (Amnesty International 1993: 2). In 1994 between 500,000 and 1,000,000 people were killed in the government-directed genocide in Rwanda (Glover 1999: 120). This list is far from complete. It does not include Bosnia, Chechnya, Kosovo, East Timor, Sri Lanka, Yemen and Syria.

The concept of human rights provides a way of thinking about such events. As you read these words, there will probably be reports in the newspapers, and on radio, television, the internet and other 'new media', of similar cruelties and injustices elsewhere. These are stories about the violation of human rights. These events are all too real, but 'human rights' is a *concept*. It is a device for thinking about the real, and expressing our thoughts. If we are to understand the discourse of human rights, we must analyse this concept. It is, however, easier to respond with sympathetic emotion to stories like those of the Darfurians than to analyse our concepts so that they are clear, precise and coherent. The understanding of concepts is the goal of the philosophical discipline of conceptual analysis. The concept of 'human rights', however, presents a challenge to this discipline. Concepts are abstract, and *conceptual analysis* is an abstract discipline. It can seem remote from the experiences of human beings. The analysis of the concept of human rights, therefore, must be combined with a sympathetic understanding of the human experiences to which the concept refers.

If conceptual analysis is both necessary and problematic for understanding human rights, so is statistical analysis. R. J. Rummel has calculated that governments murdered at least 169,202,000 persons in the twentieth century. According to his estimates, more than 45,000,000 political murders occurred between 1945 and the early 1990s (Rummel 1994: chapters 1–2). These statistics are important, but they can easily numb our sense of the human suffering involved. Human-rights violations are facts that can sometimes be best expressed in terms of numbers, but there is an uneasy relationship between our knowledge of the numbers and our understanding of what they mean.

We do not need the concept of 'human rights' to know and to say that these things are wrong. We do, however, need a *reason* to oppose them. If reality violates human rights, why should we take the side of human rights, and not that of reality? How do we know that there are any human rights? Such questions were posed, to challenge us, by the philosopher Jean Améry, who survived the Nazi extermination camp at Auschwitz. Perhaps, he considered, the Nazis were right because they were the stronger. Perhaps people had no rights. Perhaps all moral concepts were mere fashions. Was this not the reality of history? After all, classical Greek civilization was based on slavery and massacre. Was Nazi Germany different (Glover 1999: 40)?

Glover has suggested that, for most people, most of the time, the virtues that matter are personal and narrow in scope. In everyday life, ordinary kindness is more important than human rights (Glover 1999: 41). Ordinary people, however, are sometimes not permitted an everyday life. They may get terror, massacres, mass rapes and 'ethnic cleansing'. The concept of human rights becomes relevant to ordinary people when the relative security of everyday life is absent or snatched away. It has been said that human rights are most needed when they are most violated. Where they are generally well respected, we tend to take them for granted, and may consequently underestimate their importance.

The concept of human rights is, to a considerable extent, though not wholly, *legal*. It first appeared on the international agenda when the United Nations Charter declared in 1945 that the UN was determined 'to reaffirm faith in fundamental human rights, in the dignity and worth of the human person, in the equal rights of men and women and of nations large and small'. The fountainhead of human-rights law is the Universal Declaration of Human Rights (UDHR), which was adopted by the UN General Assembly on 10 December 1948. This Declaration has, according to Morsink, 'profoundly changed the international landscape, scattering it with human rights protocols, conventions, treaties, and derivative declarations of all kinds'. There is now 'not a single nation, culture or people that is not in one way or another enmeshed in human rights regimes' (Morsink 1999: x). The Declaration was adopted in the aftermath of the victorious war against

Fascism, and in a spirit of idealism. It was proclaimed to be 'a common standard of achievement for all peoples and all nations'. All human beings, Article 1 affirms, 'are born free and equal in dignity and rights'. Everyone, Article 2 states, 'is entitled to all the rights and freedoms set forth in this Declaration without discrimination of any kind, such as race, colour, sex, language, religion, political or other opinion, national or social origin, property, birth or other status'.

There is obviously a wide gap between the promises of the 1948 Declaration and the real world of human-rights violations. In so far as we sympathize with the victims, we may criticize the UN and its member governments for failing to keep their promises. However, we cannot understand the gap between human-rights ideals and the real world of human-rights violations by sympathy or by legal analysis. This requires investigation by the various social sciences of the causes of social conflict and political oppression, and of the interaction between national and international politics. The UN introduced the concept of human rights into international law and politics. The field of international politics is, however, dominated by states and other powerful actors (such as multinational corporations) that have priorities other than human rights. It is a leading feature of the human-rights field that the governments of the world proclaim human rights but have a highly variable record of implementing them. We must understand why this is so.

Concepts

The concept of human rights raises further difficulties because it stretches well beyond cases of extreme cruelty and injustice. Article 1 of the Universal Declaration, for example, states that all human beings are equal in rights. Article 18 says that everyone has the right to freedom of religion. How should we define the right to freedom of religion of those whose religion denies that all human beings are equal in rights? How can we make sense of human rights if the implementation of some human rights requires the violation of others? Here the problem of implementing human-rights ideals derives, not from lack of political will or conflicts of political interests, but from the fact that human rights may not be 'compossible', that is, the implementation of one human right may require the violation of another, or the protection of a human right of one person may require the violation of the *same* human right of another. If a religious group, for example, forbids its members, on the basis of its religious beliefs, to change their religion, then the religious freedom of the group will conflict with that of any members who wish to change their religion. If we support human rights that are not compossible, our thinking must surely be confused.

The problem of compossibility has been aggravated by what has been called 'rights inflation', that is, the extension of the concept of human rights to an ill-defined number of causes. There are controversial human rights even in the UDHR, such as the right to 'periodic holidays with pay'. If the concept of human rights is to be useful, we must distinguish human rights from other social demands. Courts may decide rather precisely the legal rights of those who appear before them. Human rights are rather vaguely worded, and their meaning is not always settled in courts of law. The determination of the meaning of human rights is a continuing *social* process that involves not only legal professionals (such as judges, UN experts and academic lawyers) but also various 'stakeholders' (such as governments, inter-governmental organizations, non-governmental organizations (NGOs), non-legal academics and citizens). If the concept of human rights is to be useful, we must distinguish *human* rights from the *legal* rights of particular societies, and from other desirable social objectives.

What are 'rights', and how do 'human rights' differ from other kinds of rights? The concept of 'rights' is closely connected to that of 'right'. Something is 'right' if it conforms with a standard of rightness. All societies have such standards, but it is often said that many cultures have no conception of people 'having rights'. The idea of everyone having 'human rights' is said to be especially alien to most cultures. MacIntyre has argued that human rights do not exist. Belief in human rights is like belief in witches and unicorns; it is superstition (MacIntyre 1981: 67).

MacIntyre's mistake is to think of 'human rights' as 'things' that we could 'have' as we have arms and legs. This mistake is admittedly embedded in the language of rights, for we do speak of our 'having' rights. Rights are, however, not mysterious *things* that have the puzzling quality of not existing, but *just claims* or *entitlements* that derive from moral and/or legal rules. This conception of rights defeats MacIntyre's objection because, unlike witches and unicorns, these moral and legal rules exist in numerous treaties and other agreements, and in values shared by many, if not by all. It is not superstitious to believe that human beings ought to *have* a certain kind of respect. The problem of 'believing in' human rights is not whether or not they exist, but whether there are sufficiently good *reasons* for supporting them and seeking to implement them. This requires a justificatory philosophical theory of human rights.

The social sciences

Social scientists neglected human rights until recently. The aspiration to be 'scientific' marginalized the legal and moral conceptions of human rights. However, the increasing importance of the concept of human rights in national and international politics has stimulated the interest of some social scientists. The explanation of variations in respect for human rights in different societies has been accepted as a proper object of social-scientific investigation. It is sometimes said that gross human-rights violations – such as genocide – are 'irrational' and beyond scientific explanation. There is, however, a body of knowledge about state behaviour, ethnic diversity, repression, rebellion and social conflict that may explain a great deal about such actions. There is much controversy about theories and methodology in the social sciences, but there is no reason why behaviour that violates or respects human rights should be less explicable than other complex social phenomena.

The academic study of human rights has been dominated by lawyers. This may be explained by the fact that the concept has been developed to a large extent through national and international law. The field of human rights has become a technical, legal discourse, and lawyers dominate it because they are the technical experts. Law appears to provide 'objective' standards that 'protect' the concept of human rights from moral and political controversy. This appearance is, however, illusory, for the meaning and application of human-rights standards are legally and politically very controversial. International human-rights law is made by governments that act from political motives. The extent to which they implement human-rights law is influenced by political factors. NGOs, which have come to play an increasingly important role in the making of human-rights law, monitoring its implementation and campaigning for improved human-rights performance by governments, are political actors, even if they appeal to legal standards. Major human-rights changes, such as those which took place in the Communist societies of central and eastern Europe, in Latin America, South Africa and elsewhere towards the end of the twentieth century, were primarily political events.

The study of international politics has been dominated by the theory of Realism, which is primarily concerned with the interests and power of states rather than with such ethical issues as those of human rights. The academic discipline of International Relations has recently shown some interest in human rights (Forsythe 2012), but the topic remains marginal. Some International Relations scholars challenge the Realist school by emphasizing the role of ideas in general, and of human-rights ideas in particular, in international politics (Risse, Ropp and Sikkink 2013). The study of human rights in international politics has, however, with a few notable exceptions, fallen between international law, which is not systematically empirical, and International Relations, which has neglected human rights for the supposed 'realities' of state power.

The neglect of human rights by the social sciences and the domination of human-rights studies by lawyers distort the concept of human rights. Two different conceptions of contemporary human rights challenge the legal approach. The first conceives of human rights as fundamental *moral* rights and then proceeds to consider that they may need legal and/

or political protection (Wellman 2011). The second holds that human rights are *political* constructions and do not derive from any particular moral philosophy (Beitz 2009). International human-rights law is concerned primarily with the obligations of governments and the rights of citizens. Political theory is the discipline that seeks to explain and evaluate the relations between governments and citizens. Political science is the discipline that describes and explains the variations in the degree to which governments respect their citizens' rights. The contribution of political science to the study of human rights has, however, been limited until recently. The study of human-rights issues has sometimes been carried out with the use of related concepts such as 'dictatorship', 'totalitarianism', 'authoritarianism', 'repression', 'state terror' and 'genocide'. There is also much work in political science on democracy that is relevant to understanding the current state of human rights. The desire of political scientists to be 'scientific', however, has led them to neglect a concept that appears at worst moralistic, and at best legalistic. Slowly, this neglect is being overcome (Landman 2005b).

The Western tradition of political theory has produced many formidable critics of such rights. This presents a strong challenge to the political science of human rights, especially since the classical critics are echoed by contemporary theorists. Underlying any social sciences of human rights, therefore, are a number of controversial philosophical assumptions. This does not, however, distinguish the social science of human rights from other branches of social science, such as the politics of democracy or the sociology of inequality. Nevertheless, it requires the social scientist of human rights to be aware of these philosophical controversies.

Sociologists and anthropologists have recently begun to contribute to human-rights studies (Morris 2013; Frezzo 2015; Goodale 2009). The impact of the global economy on the protection of human rights is increasingly becoming a subject of study (Pogge 2008). This has been accompanied by an interest in 'the human-rights movement' as a transnational social movement (Brysk 2013). There are, therefore, signs that the social science of human rights is beginning to wake up.

Beyond human-rights law

International law was traditionally concerned with regulating the relations among states with the primary aim of maintaining international peace. The leading concept of this project was that of *state sovereignty* that forbade states from interfering with each other's internal affairs. The UN introduced the concept of human rights into international law without altering the concept of sovereignty. This legal framework is, however, subject to intense political pressures, as states and other actors seek to realize their interests and their principles in the international arena. The implementation of human rights by the UN is, therefore, highly politicized, and this leads to selective attention to human-rights problems, political bargaining and delays. The UN is not a utopian realm above politics, and the political character of human-rights implementation is unavoidable. The politics of human rights is not, however, always harmful to human rights, for governments may raise genuine human-rights issues from political motives, and, when political motives lead to a narrow and selective concern for human rights, appeals are sometimes made to human-rights principles that can be applied more widely.

The implementation of the UN's human-rights principles was seriously delayed and distorted for many years by the politics of the Cold War. The UN proclaimed human rights, but did little to implement them. The cost of proclaiming human rights is low, and many governments, in the conditions of the Cold War, thought that they had much to lose by respecting the human rights of their sometimes highly discontented citizens. In this context, what is at first sight surprising is the development, albeit slow, of international human-rights law, and of a movement of NGOs to campaign for its implementation. In this situation, the UN stood in an ambiguous position. It was, on the one hand, the author and guardian of international human-rights standards, while, on the other hand, it was an association of governments that were often serious human-rights violators. The UN has, therefore, been the central institution where international human-rights law and politics meet, and often clash, and where the gap between human-rights ideals and realities is especially apparent.

The political character of human rights has philosophical implications. The lawyers who dominate human-rights studies sometimes rely, explicitly or implicitly, on the philosophy of *legal positivism*, which says that human rights are what human-rights law says they are. Human rights are, however, made and interpreted by a political process. The provisions of the UDHR were the subject of intense debates, and the final text was produced by a long series of votes (Morsink 1999). It is *politically* important that human rights have been codified in international and national law. It is a mistake, however, to believe that the legalization of human rights takes the concept out of politics.

The legal-positivist approach to human rights not only misrepresents their character, but also has dangerous implications. The *point* of human rights has historically been to criticize legal authorities and laws that violate human rights. Legal positivists sometimes say that the only rights are those that are legally *enforceable*. It may be desirable that human rights should be legally enforceable, but it is not necessary that they should be so. The concept of human rights implies that they are often not. If human rights were legally enforceable, one could, and normally would, appeal to one's *legal* rights, and would not need to appeal to one's human rights. One appeals to human rights precisely when legal institutions fail to recognize and enforce them. If legal positivism were true, an important basis for criticizing unjust legal systems would be eliminated.

The principal philosophical problem of human rights is to show how they can be justified, if they derive neither from law nor culture, both of which can be criticized on the ground that they violate human rights. There is an historical reason why there is a problem about the 'source' of human rights. The first systematic human-rights theory, presented by John Locke, assumed that God was the 'source' of human rights. Locke could assume agreement with and among his readers that this source provided the ultimate validation of such rights: God was the source both of what exists and of value. The problem faced by the United Nations in proclaiming the UDHR was that, precisely because it claimed that these rights were universal, it could not base them on any particular religious belief. The justificatory basis of human rights had to be *abstracted* from particular religious and ideological beliefs, but the character of that abstraction was not clear. The UDHR says little about the source of these rights, apart from some large and unsubstantiated claims in the preamble that recognition of human rights is 'the foundation of freedom, justice and peace in the world', and that disregard for human rights has resulted in 'barbarous acts which have outraged the conscience of mankind'. These claims may contain important truths, but they do not give a clear account of the source or justification of human rights.

The idea of the 'source' of human rights contains an important and confusing ambiguity. It can refer to the *social origins* or the *ethical justification* of human rights. Social scientists have studied the social origins of rights in, for example, popular political protest, and, important though such studies may be for an historical understanding of the discourse of rights, we must be careful not to confuse social origins with ethical justifications, since there are social origins of evil as well as of good. The social-scientific approach to rights, by its preference for avoiding ethical questions, sometimes falls into this confusion. There are, therefore, two distinct questions about the 'sources' of human rights that we need to answer. Why *do* we have human rights? Why *ought* we to have human rights?

Another set of philosophical questions concerns the relations between human rights and other values. Do human rights occupy the whole space of moral and political theory, or are there other important values? If there are other important values, how are human rights related to them? The UDHR claims that human rights are the foundation of freedom, justice and peace, but does not say how these values are related, conceptually or empirically. It is important to determine as clearly as possible the *limits* as well as the *value* of human rights. It is common to say that human rights establish *minimum standards* of good government. Claiming too much for human rights may make it harder to defend them against their critics, and thereby weaken their appeal and effects. We need to be clear, therefore, whether the concept of human rights supports a *comprehensive* or a *minimum-standards* political philosophy.

There is a huge gap between the experiences of the Darfurians and the world of the UN. This gap has been filled to a large extent by law and legal studies. These studies are certainly important. The gap is, however, also filled by politics, and by social, cultural and economic forces. These may be more important, but they have been relatively neglected in academic discourse. The aim of this book is to make a contribution to rectifying this neglect.

Conclusion

The study and, to a considerable extent, the practice of human rights have been dominated by lawyers. The cause of human rights owes a great debt to them. There is a danger, however, that excessive attention to human-rights law distorts our understanding of human rights. This book seeks to put law in its place by adopting an interdisciplinary approach. The concept of human rights has a history marked by philosophical controversies. Knowing that history and understanding those controversies illuminate the state of human rights today. In the past half-century, the concept has been incorporated into a large body of international and national law, but it has also been at the heart of political conflicts. The law is important, but understanding human rights requires us to understand its politics. Law and politics do not exhaust the human-rights field. The other social sciences – such as sociology, anthropology and economics – are essential to our appreciation of human-rights problems and their possible solutions. Human rights is an interdisciplinary concept *par excellence*.

We begin this inquiry by tracing, in chapter two, the historical emergence of human rights. The story continues in chapter three by examining its gradual acceptance by the international community. Chapter four investigates the principal theoretical justifications of and debates about the concept. The distinctive contribution of the social sciences is then surveyed in chapter five. In chapter six, much-debated questions about the supposed universality of human rights and its relation to actual human differences are addressed, with particular emphasis on cultural minorities, indigenous peoples, and the rights of women, children, sexual minorities, disabled persons, migrants and refugees. In chapter seven the place of human rights in national and international politics is analysed, and the respective roles of international institutions, governments and NGOs evaluated. The political economy of human rights forms the subject of chapter eight, with special attention to development, globalization, business corporations, international financial institutions and climate change. We conclude, in chapter nine, with reflections on the history of human rights, their current status, and their likely future. One of the few certainties is that understanding human rights will be essential to understanding the world that we live in for a long time to come.

2
Origins
The Rise and Fall of Natural Rights

Why history? Which history?

The history of human rights can be studied for its own sake and to understand better the contemporary concept of human rights. Before we can study the history of human rights, however, we must know what it is the history of. Until recently, there were two main views about the history of human rights. On one view, human rights had little history before the establishment of the United Nations (UN) in 1945. Another view was that human rights had a much longer history. Both views have been challenged recently by Samuel Moyn, who maintains that the concept of human rights refers to a global morality that became significant only in the 1970s. Earlier concepts of rights were addressed to different problems and thus had different meanings. These earlier concepts could not therefore be the source of the later one (Moyn 2010).

Moyn rightly notes that human rights achieved unprecedented influence in the 1970s, but is wrong to claim that this was discontinuous with previous concepts. There is continuity and change in the concept of human rights from the ancient Greeks to the present.

Some say that the concept of human rights has a *universal* history. The Code of Hammurabi (c.1792–1750 BC), king of Babylon, is said to be the oldest surviving text establishing the rule of law. Cyrus the Great (died 529 BC), king of Persia, proclaimed a policy of religious toleration and abolished slavery. The Buddhist King Ashoka of India (c.264–238 BC) also promoted religious toleration, provided for the health and education of his people, and appointed officials to prevent wrongful punishments (Weeramantry 1997: 7–8). Thus principles now associated with human rights can be found in ancient times in many cultures. These examples weaken the claim that the concept of human rights is Western. However, they appear to be evidence of benevolent rulers rather than of human rights as such.

Others maintain that the concept of human rights originated in the West, and was universalized only recently. Some argue that, if the *history* of the concept is Western, its *validity* cannot be universal. Others say that the history of a concept is irrelevant to its validity: there may be good reasons for universalizing a concept that has a particular history.

MacIntyre has claimed that there is no expression in any language correctly translated by our expression 'a right' before 1400. He doubts whether human beings could have had rights if they could not have expressed them in their language (MacIntyre 1981: 66–7). He suggests that the fact that there was no concept of 'rights' before 1400 means that the concept of universal human rights is invalid.

Some have argued that there could be no concept of individual rights in ancient times, because individuals were considered to be subordinate parts of the social whole. This idea was weakened by increasing social complexity that undermined roles and identities, creating the rights-bearing individual. This historical sociology of individual rights is supposed to discredit the concept of universal human rights. But is it true?

On rights and tyrants

The contemporary concept of human rights is intended primarily to protect individuals from the abuse of power by governments. Whether or not the ancient Greeks had a concept of 'rights', they certainly had the concepts of power and its abuse. This was expressed in the concept of tyranny, which was a form of government in which the ruler governed in his own interest and treated his people unjustly. It was possible, however, for the Greeks to think about tyranny without talking about rights. In Sophocles' play *Antigone*, for example, the king forbids Antigone to bury her dead brother because he had been a rebel. Antigone defies the king's order, but on the ground that she has a religious *duty* to bury her brother, not on the ground that she has a *right* to do so. We might see this as a human-rights drama about freedom of religious practice, but Sophocles did not express it this way.

There are reasons, however, for rejecting MacIntyre's view that the ancient Greeks had no language of rights. Aristotle had a conception of rights and a language in which to express it. He believed that constitutions could assign rights to citizens. Citizens' rights might include rights to property and to participation in public affairs. When these rights were violated, the laws determined compensation or punishment. Citizens' rights would be distributed differently in different political systems. Aristotle used a range of expressions that we can properly translate as 'a right'. In particular, he used the expression *to dikaion* to mean a just claim, which we could translate as a right. He had no conception of *human* rights, however, as he believed that rights derived from constitutions, and that some men were slaves by nature (Miller, F. 1995).

Justice and rights

Roman law provides the main link between classical Greek thought about rights and modern conceptions through its influence on medieval ideas. The French historian Michel Villey initiated a debate on the distinction between *objective right* (that which is right) and *subjective rights* (personal entitlements). Villey argued that Roman law had no conception of subjective rights: the Latin word *ius* referred to objective right (Tuck 1979: 7–9; Tierney 1988: 4–6, 15). Villey's view has been questioned on the ground that Roman law conceived of justice as rendering to each his right (*suum ius*). Whether *ius* was objective or subjective, it was *legal*, and not *natural* (Tuck 1979).

The Stoic philosophers believed in a universal moral community, governed by a common natural law. It is, however, doubtful whether they had the concept of human rights, although there is some scholarly disagreement on this point (Sorabji 1993; Mitsis 1999: 176–7).

The Stoic philosophy influenced early Christianity, which provided a new basis for the unity underlying the diversity of peoples. Christians saw the salvation of *the individual soul* as the highest good. The *duty* to seek salvation presupposed the autonomy of the individual will, which derived its dignity from the will of God. However, although Christianity separated the demands it made of the individual from those made by society, St Paul preached obedience to secular political authority. Christianity also preached the 'love of the poor'. Although salvation might be available only to an elite, all humans were morally equal in that each was a candidate for salvation: women as well as men. The Christian author Tertullian wrote around 217 AD that it was 'a basic human right that everyone should be free to worship according to his own convictions' (Wiles and Santer 1977: 227). Eventually, the idea emerged that secular laws were not legitimate if they contravened the laws of God. The Church, however, largely conformed to the norms of society, accepting existing social hierarchies, the patriarchal family, and slavery.

A clear shift from objective right to subjective rights took place in the late Middle Ages. According to Tierney, medieval people had the concept of rights, and a language in which to express it, at least as early as the twelfth century (Tierney 1989: 626, 629). These rights were rights of particular persons, statuses, collectivities or classes: kings, lords, bishops, communities, etc. They were not natural rights. However, according to one conception of natural law, natural right was what natural law permitted. Natural rights might be rights of individuals, but they derived, not from the nature of the individual, but from the right order of society (Tierney 1989).

Gratian's *Decretum* (c. 1140), an encyclopaedia of Church law, however, referred to the *iura libertatis* (rights of liberty) that could never be lost (Coleman 1993: 109–10). The thirteenth-century writer Henry of Ghent held that everyone had a natural right to self-preservation and property in his body. The canonistic vocabulary of the thirteenth century was rich in terms that could be translated as 'right': *libertas* (liberty), *potestas* (power), *facultas* (faculty), *immunitas* (immunity), *dominium* (lordship) and others (Tierney 1992: 63–7; 1997: 262).

One source of late medieval natural-rights theory was the dispute between the Dominicans and the Franciscans, who championed the life of poverty, thereby questioning the legitimacy of private property. The Franciscans claimed to renounce their will and their material possessions to devote themselves to God. This challenged the Church, which was committed to the compatibility of Christian virtue and private property. The Dominicans argued that the Franciscans could not renounce their will, and they could not entirely renounce property, as they were necessarily the proprietors of the food and drink that was necessary to their survival. In 1328 Pope John XXII declared that God had granted to Adam *dominium* over temporal things. Property was therefore sanctified by divine law. By the fourteenth century it was also possible to argue that to have a right was to be the lord of one's moral world (Tuck 1979; Brett 2003).

The Magna Carta (1215) recognizes 'subjective' rights by such terms as 'his right' (*jus suum*) (Holt 1965: 96, 100, 104). The concept of rights was, however, at that time embedded in customary law. The Magna Carta was, furthermore, a text whose purpose was to provide remedies for specific grievances. It was, therefore, not a charter of the rights of Englishmen, still less of human rights. Yet its reputation as a precursor of modern human-rights texts is not wholly unmerited. Article 39, for example, says that no free man shall be arrested, imprisoned, expropriated, exiled or in any way ruined, except by the lawful judgement of his peers or by the law of the land (Roshwald 1959: 361–4; Holt 1965: 1–2, 327). This article was more limited than it might appear, as the category of 'free men' was created by royal prerogative. However, Parliament in 1354 applied the principle of this article to all men 'of whatever estate or condition' (Coleman 1993: 113–14).

The Magna Carta was later transformed from a limited political and legal agreement into a national myth. From seventeenth-century struggles against monarchical rule in England to various claims to rights for the oppressed around the world, the myth of Magna Carta has been invoked in causes associated with civil and human rights. Eleanor Roosevelt described the UN Universal Declaration of Human Rights as 'the international Magna Carta' (Holt 1965; Breay 2002; Melton and Hazell 2015; Jones 2014).

Natural rights

There is no direct line from medieval conceptions of *ius* to early modern conceptions of rights. The humanist lawyers of the Renaissance, for example, were concerned, not with natural rights, but with *civil* rights (Tuck 1979). However, medieval conceptions of natural law had the most influence on the modern concept of natural rights.

In the fourteenth century William of Ockham argued that all men knew intuitively that they had a natural power to make choices. Men possessed, therefore, certain liberties that could never be alienated to church or state, and they had a natural right to the necessities of life, and to consent voluntarily to the creation of a system of laws. Positive law was required to coerce fallen men when they did not act according to their natural knowledge of what was morally right. However, the social individual possessed certain inalienable rights and duties prior to any incorporation into a political system (Coleman 1993: 116–17; McGrade 1974).

In the fifteenth century, Conrad Summenhart maintained that Man had right over himself and his body. 'Here', Brett comments, 'Summenhart introduces a notion of negative liberty which is very close to elements of the modern language of rights' (Brett 2003: 42). The association of right and freedom was developed further by Spanish thinkers of the sixteenth century. Domingo de Soto, for example, held that the proper dignity of man was to live according to reason, for through that he was free and existed for the sake of himself, *sui juris* (autonomous). The political community had the right to exercise power over its members, so that each could live well, but that public right extended to the individual only as a member of the community rather than as a separate individual. Beyond that, man must not only have his rights as an individual; he must also have their exercise within his own control: that is, he must be *sui juris* (Brett 2003).

The Spanish conquest of America raised important questions for Catholic theology and international politics. The debate on its legitimacy is a largely neglected moment in the history of human rights. Those who justified the conquest employed Aristotle's doctrine of natural slavery to deny any rights to the native Americans. They were opposed by Bartolomé de Las Casas, a Dominican priest, who argued that the Indians were in all essential respects human and therefore entitled to their land and to self-government. He sought to demonstrate that the Indians had complex cultures and that the Spanish treatment of them showed that the Spanish, not the native Americans, were the barbarians. He defended the collective cultural rights of the Indians rather than the idea of individual human rights, and, in that, anticipated the modern idea of indigenous rights.

Vitoria argued that the cities of the Mexica and the Inca proved that they were not natural slaves, but rational, and consequently had a right to their lands. The Spaniards had natural rights to trade and settle in America, preach the gospel, and intervene to prevent Indian rulers from exercising tyranny over their subjects. If the Indians tried to prevent the Spanish from exercising these rights, they would commit an act of war. The Spaniards could then exercise their war rights, including plunder, enslavement, deposition of native rulers and the institution of new ones (Vitoria 1991).

The Spanish Dominicans developed the philosophy of Aquinas with a doctrine of subjective rights. Neither Vitoria nor Las Casas doubted the right of Spain to exercise sovereignty over the New World or the rightness of attempting to convert the Indians to Christianity. Only late in his life did Las Casas come to believe that it might be better for the native Americans to remain heathens, with their distinctive cultures, than to be brought to Christianity by force. The practical advocacy of Las Casas and the more academic philosophy of Vitoria provided an important link between Thomist philosophy and later theories of rights. They both showed that the concept of natural rights could be used both to condemn and to justify European imperialism (Pagden 1982; Carozza 2003; Talbott 2005: 84–5).

By the beginning of the seventeenth century there were two principal traditions of thinking about rights. The first emphasized natural, subjective, individual rights. The second emphasized objective right and/or civil rights (Tuck 1979: 54–7; Tierney 1989: 621). The Dutch jurist Hugo Grotius was a crucial figure in transforming medieval ideas into the modern concept of rights. He began with the proposition that the will of God was law, and was known through man's sociability, which was the basis of all other laws of nature. Men had natural rights, but these were transformed by society. He conceived of *ius* as what is just and as the ability of a person to have or do something justly. The law of nature concerned the maintenance of rights, the subject-matter of justice. 'Rights', Tuck says in his discussion of Grotius' ideas, 'have come to usurp the whole of natural law theory, for the law of nature is simply, respect one another's rights' (Tuck 1979: 67). Everyone should enjoy his rights with the help of the community, which was required to defend our lives, limbs, liberties and property. Grotius held that moral obligations were owed not only to members of one's own society, but also to mankind as such. He also maintained that his theory of natural law did not logically require belief in the existence of God, providing thereby the basis for a secular theory of natural rights. Like Vitoria, Grotius argued that there was a natural right to free trade, and, if anyone violated that right the aggrieved party had the right to wage war against the violator. Grotius made this argument in support of Dutch commercial imperialism (Tuck 1979; Tierney 1989: 621–2; Van Ittersum 2006).

In seventeenth-century England Thomas Hobbes drew a sharp distinction between right (*jus*) and law (*lex*). Since right was liberty, and law was restraint, right and law not only differed from each other, but they were opposites. In the natural condition of mankind, everyone had the natural right to do anything that was conducive to their preservation.

There was both an obligation under the law of nature and a natural right to preserve oneself. The natural condition of mankind was one of war of each against everyone else, and therefore one of great insecurity. Reason required men to authorize a sovereign to act on their behalf. All men were obliged to obey this sovereign, provided that he did not threaten their preservation (Tuck 1979: 126–31).

We are so familiar with the use of the concept of human rights to limit the powers of government that we may be surprised to learn that most early modern natural-rights theorists argued that rational individuals would give up their natural rights to absolute rulers for the sake of social order. However, in the English Civil War the Levellers adopted the concept of individual, inalienable rights and maintained that Parliament was violating them. Richard Overton argued that all governments were trusts, because by nature everyone had a 'self propriety' which could not be invaded or usurped without his consent. The concept of 'self propriety' entailed freedom of conscience, equal rights in law, and the right of at least the majority of men to vote. John Wildman thought that the concept of natural rights entailed the principle of universal suffrage. The Levellers held that persons were prior to estates, which justified the right to subsistence and the legitimation of some redistribution of wealth (Roshwald 1959: 369; Tuck 1979: 148–50; Ashcraft 1986: 155, 160–3; McNally 1989: 35–7).

By grounding rights in the law of nature, the Levellers emancipated such claims from historical precedents. Overton maintained that reason had no precedent, for reason was the fountain of all just precedents. Arguments from reason were, however, mixed with arguments from history, including references to the Magna Carta. This mixture of natural-law and historical argument created some ambiguity as to whether the rights claimed were those of Englishmen or universal human rights. Roshwald suggests that their practical emphasis was on the rights of Englishmen, but their logic was universalistic. The Bill of Rights (1688) was concerned with vindicating the ancient rights of Englishmen, not human rights (Roshwald 1959: 366–70; Griffin 2008: 13).

The deep ground for opposition to political absolutism in seventeenth-century England was the Protestant belief that

God had made human beings rational so that each could determine their own way to salvation. The Protestant conception of reason entailed freedom of the will, the legitimacy of independent action and dissent from authority. Religion, on this view, required conscientious action that could oppose the individual to authority. This argument claimed to be based on what was common to all men and represented rational individuals as having been created in a state of equality and freedom. No one was, therefore, subject to the absolute will of any other person. Rational individuals constituted a natural moral community, since they lived under a framework of moral obligations that were owed to each other and to God. By the use of their reason, they were able to discover these obligations contained in the law of nature. This law not only imposed duties on but also accorded rights to individuals, including, especially, the right to follow the dictates of one's conscience (Ashcraft 1986: 49, 66–7).

In his *Essay on Toleration* Locke argued that man was a rational and active creature. Religious faith, therefore, must be active, and required liberty of action. The political authorities ought not to interfere with religious beliefs, since they concerned only the relation between the individual and God. The individual had a natural right to freedom of religion, both because salvation was infinitely more important than any political relation, and because political authorities were fallible in matters of religion (Ashcraft 1986: 88, 93–6).

Locke held that each individual had a responsibility to God to observe the law of nature. Every man was rational in that he could know the law of nature. God willed the preservation of mankind, and this imposed on everyone the obligation not to harm the lives, health, liberty and possessions of others. In 'the state of nature', in the absence of government, everyone had the right to self-defence and to enforce the laws of nature. Since everyone was judge in their own cause, they would be partial to themselves, and this would lead to conflict. Rational individuals would therefore agree to live under a government that was entrusted to enforce the law of nature, protect the natural rights of all through the rule of law and to promote the public good. Governments that breached this trust, and that systematically and persistently violated the rights of the people, were tyrannies, lost authority to rule, and might be resisted by the people by force if necessary (Locke [1689] 1970). Locke's political theory entails a rejection of the 'Magna Carta' or 'ancient constitution' ground for resisting unjust government.

Locke is usually interpreted as a theorist of a strictly *individualist* conception of natural rights. This interpretation is supported by Locke's belief that each individual had fundamental obligations to God, was endowed with reason, and had a natural right to freedom, which was limited only by the obligation to respect the natural rights of others. Nevertheless, he also held that God's will for mankind could be achieved, and the natural rights of men could be protected, only in a political community, and that this community should be governed for the public good. There is, therefore, an unresolved tension in Locke's political theory between the natural rights of individuals and the collective good of society. The foundation of Locke's theory in the will of God and the reason of Man supported his belief that individual rights and public good were mutually compatible.

Locke argued that each individual had a property in himself, in his labour and in the products of his labour. Labour was the basis of the right to private property. Locke's theory of property has been the subject of prolonged controversy. C. B. Macpherson interpreted Locke as a defender of 'possessive individualism' and of the interests of the bourgeois class (Macpherson 1962). Critics have pointed out that Locke's theory of rights was set in a Christian natural-law framework, and that property rights were subject to a set of moral obligations designed to provide for the common good and the benefit of mankind. Locke's theory of property clearly allows considerable inequality of wealth, but accords to everyone the natural right to subsistence, and imposes on those who have excessive wealth the obligation to aid those who cannot meet their subsistence needs by their own efforts. Locke's attitude to women was ambiguous: women might acquire property through their labour and had certain rights in marriage. Men had ultimate authority in the family, however, because they were 'abler and stronger'. It is not clear whether women could participate in politics (Tully 1980, 1993; Ashcraft 1986; Waldron 1988; Hirschmann and McClure 2007).

Several scholars have linked Locke's defence of property with his support for British colonialism. Tully interprets Locke as believing that America was a state of nature. Europeans had productive agricultural practices, modern states and property laws, while native Americans had none of these. Europeans had the right, therefore, to appropriate American land without the consent of the natives (Tully 1993: 129, 141–5, 151–64). On this view Locke used the concept of natural rights to justify European imperialism. Locke rejected the Aristotelian doctrine that some human beings were slaves by nature, but, like Vitoria, argued that those who resisted the right of Europeans to cultivate land conducted an unjust war and might be enslaved. The wives and children of the aggressors, however, might not be enslaved. Locke's theory might justify the enslavement of native Americans – on a questionable view of the facts – but it could not be used to justify enslavement of Africans (Hinshelwood 2013).

The age of revolutions

After the Glorious Revolution of 1689 the Lockean principles of constitutional monarchy and the rights to life, liberty and property became part of Whig (liberal) ideology, although the radical, egalitarian thrust of natural-rights theory was muted. In the later eighteenth century, however, radical Whigs appealed to the right of the people to reform or remove a government that did not protect their rights. The natural right to freedom of conscience was held to entail the principle that the state should not discriminate against anyone on the ground of religion, and that consequently everyone should be an equal citizen in a secular state. A few radicals, led by Mary Wollstonecraft, argued for the natural rights of women (Dickinson 1977).

The concept of natural rights was pervasive in eighteenth-century America. Americans linked the defence of religious liberty with the struggle for political freedom. American perceptions of the tendency of the British government towards tyranny and the fact that they were not represented in that government made it easier to justify resistance (Bailyn 1992;

Dickinson 1977: 225). Although Locke was only one among many influences on the American revolutionaries, the American Declaration of Independence (1776) certainly expressed Lockean ideas.

> We hold these truths to be self-evident, that all men are created equal, that they are endowed by their creator with certain unalienable rights, that among these are life, liberty and the pursuit of happiness – that to secure these rights, governments are instituted among men, deriving their just powers from the consent of the governed. That whenever any form of government becomes destructive of these ends, it is the right of the people to alter or abolish it.

The Virginia Declaration of Rights included specific liberties that were to be protected from state interference, including freedom of the press, the free exercise of religion and the right not to be deprived of freedom except by due process of law. In 1791 the Bill of Rights was enacted as a set of amendments to the US Constitution, and included rights to freedom of religion, the press, expression and assembly, protection against unreasonable search and seizure, the right not to incriminate oneself, and the right to due process of law. These rights were based on historical precedents, the rights of Englishmen, but were justified by appeal to natural rights grounded in the laws of God. Notwithstanding the reference to God, however, the Declaration of Independence almost secularized the concept of natural rights. The Americans were also strongly constitutionalist, believing that the constitution, with its separation of powers, was the foundation of liberty. The American conception of natural rights at the time of the Revolution did not include the rights of women, and was generally considered compatible with the institution of slavery. It also offered little protection for the native peoples of the country (Bailyn 1992; Becker 1966; Dickinson 1977; Griffin 2008: 13).

When the French Revolution broke out in 1789, the newly formed National Assembly proclaimed the Declaration of the Rights of Man and the Citizen in order to lay down the principles upon which the new constitution of France was to be founded. The Declaration stated that the preservation of the natural Rights of Man was the aim of every political association. These rights were those of liberty, property, security and resistance to oppression. It affirmed equality before the law, freedom from arbitrary arrest, the presumption of innocence, freedom of expression and religion, the general freedom to do anything that did not harm others, and the right to property. The rights that it declared were qualified repeatedly by restrictions and conditions, and made subject to the rule of law. This ambivalence between individual natural rights and the requirements of social order reflected deep ideological differences among the revolutionaries (Baker 1994: 192–3).

The French Declaration of Rights was an act of revolutionary power carried out in the name of the popular will. The revolutionary governments faced, of course, many practical problems that threatened the stability of the new order. However, the degeneration of the Revolution from the declaration of the Rights of Man to the reign of terror had theoretical as well as practical sources. In the face of serious practical challenges, the ideological mixture of individual natural rights, popular sovereignty and commitment to the public good was insufficient to protect any of these values.

The ideology of the French Revolution was expressed in egalitarian terms. The theoretical concept of equal rights had, however, to be implemented in a society in which various forms of inequality existed. Yet in three respects the French Revolution was more egalitarian than the American. During the Revolution economic and social rights – such as those to work, education and social security – were proclaimed. The question of the rights of women was raised, especially by Olympe de Gouges, who, in 1791, published a Declaration of the Rights of Woman and the Citizen. The demand for human and civil rights for women was, however, defeated in the National Assembly, and Olympe de Gouges was guillotined in 1793. The idea of women's rights was suppressed. The revolutionaries also abolished slavery, which Napoleon soon restored.

The secularization of the concept of natural rights that gradually took place during the eighteenth century created an important philosophical problem. The principles of morality and politics had to be derived from nature by reason. Late eighteenth-century secular natural-rights thinkers assumed that this could be done, but their arguments were often weak. Advocates of natural rights in the late eighteenth century tended to assert these rights without much attention to foundations or arguments. Critics of natural rights began to mock the fondness of their advocates for declarations and their lack of arguments. Attempts to derive natural rights from a cross-cultural consensus were undermined by evidence that no such consensus existed. In the late eighteenth century, therefore, the concept of natural rights enjoyed a practical triumph in the American Revolution, but rested on insecure theoretical foundations.

Immanuel Kant is often considered the most important eighteenth-century philosopher for the development of human rights. The supreme principle of his moral philosophy was the categorical imperative. One version of this required everyone to act so that they treated humanity in every person as an end, never merely as a means.

Natural rights were innate or acquired. There was only one innate right: the right to freedom. There were acquired rights to property, but these were provisional. Freedom was not secure in the state of nature, so there was an obligation to enter civil society, for freedom could be secure only under a republican constitution by which the state created legal rights and duties. The state could not make people moral, because morality required appropriate inner motives, but it could regulate external conduct by coercion. The only legitimate use of coercion was to secure freedom; it was never justified to promote happiness or meet needs. Kant never made clear what 'the innate right of freedom' entailed, but it has been interpreted to entail the usual liberal freedoms (Simmons 2001; Maliks 2014; Sangiovanni 2015).

Simmons suggests that Kant's rights were similar to human rights. Others maintain that Kant had no theory of human rights, although we might derive human rights from his theory. Kant praised the Rights of Man proclaimed in the French Revolution, but insisted that there was no right to rebel against tyranny. He supported the republicanism of the Revolution, not its violence (Simmons 2001; Flikschuh 1999; Sangiovanni 2015; Maliks 2014).

In Kant's republic each citizen would have the right to vote for representatives. Not everyone would be a citizen, however. Those who were dependent on others – women, servants, labourers – would be subject to their masters, and therefore would not vote for the public good. Kant also thought that women lacked the 'cognitive power' necessary to be active citizens. Denial of the right to vote was not deprivation of freedom because everyone would be protected by the rule of law. Some of Kant's followers believed that his philosophy should support votes for women. At that time, however, even the participation of all men in politics was associated with the radicals of the French Revolution. Kant was a classical republican who saw democracy as a threat to the rule of law and freedom. Others thought that the principle of self-government required democracy (Maliks 2014; Gilabert 2010; Kleingeld 2012).

There was no innate right to property, or even to survival. There was a natural right to acquire property, but this was provisional. In the civil condition, property rights depended on law. Since there was no natural right to subsistence, the needy had no right to assistance from the state. Weinrib argues that the state had a duty to aid the poor on two grounds: (1) it might be necessary to maintain order; (2) the authority of the state depended on a social contract by which all could be taken to agree to the law (Weinrib 2002–3). Penner counters that the only purpose of the state was to protect freedom. Kant had no solution to the problem that the poor might effectively be excluded from the benefits of society (Penner 2010). Ripstein thinks that Kantianism permits a range of public services – such as education and health – if they contribute to the public good. Kantian arguments could support the right of the poor to subsistence, even if Kant did not (Ripstein 2009).

Kant developed a concept of 'cosmopolitan right', by which individuals could be citizens of a universal state of mankind. It specified a 'right to hospitality' – the right not to be treated with hostility in a foreign country – but no modern human rights. Most commentators believe that Kant opposed the idea of a world-state on the ground that it would become tyrannical; a universal federation of sovereign republics was the ideal for international relations. Rights depended on states, and thus states had the right to non-interference. Kant's philosophy could support a non-coercive, international human-rights regime. Kant also held that international peace was necessary to state protection of rights, and he denounced the injustices of European colonialism (Simmons 2001; Maliks 2014; Sangiovanni 2015).

Kant's early writings were racist, although his later writings were not. He has also been justly charged with anti-Semitism. Some see his universalistic rationalism as hostile to cultural diversity, while others argue that Kant's value of freedom supported cultural pluralism (Bernasconi 2005; Kleingeld 2012; Rose 1992; Mack 2003; Muthu 2003).

There are conflicting interpretations of Kant; there are different views of his relation to human rights. Kant's paradox is that he provided deep and strong arguments that can be used to justify human rights, but, if we seek such justifications in the historical Kant, we may be disappointed.

Inspired by the French Revolution, English radicals adopted the concept of the Rights of Man rather than the appeal to historic rights, as they were seeking reforms for which there were no historical precedents. No one sought to universalize the significance of the French Revolution more than Thomas Paine. The Rights of Man, he maintained, promised 'a new era to the human race' (Dagger 1989: 301). They were the rights that men had by virtue of their status as human beings. They owed nothing to society or the state. The state had value, and therefore claims on the obligations of citizens, only as an instrument for the protection of the natural rights of individuals. Paine's conception of natural rights was uncompromisingly individualist and universalist: the Rights of Man were the rights of everyone, everywhere, at all times (Paine 1988: 171; Roshwald 1959: 347, 375–8). Paine also believed that a free, commercial society, with its associated inequalities of wealth, could be combined with political democracy in a way that would secure both individual rights and the common good. His emphasis on individual reason as the basis of politics made him a more robust champion of popular sovereignty than Locke had been, although he never considered votes for women (Philp 1989; Dickinson 1977).

Paine argued that historic rights were indefensible because no moment in history had priority over others as the basis of rights. The origin of human rights could only be the divine creation of human beings. Equal rights were necessary to motivate everyone to fulfil his duties to others. A system of rights was necessarily also a system of duties, for, if we all have rights, we all have duties to respect the rights of others. Notwithstanding his reference to the divine origins of rights, Paine's theory of the Rights of Man was grounded in reason, which could support a purely secular conception of human rights (Paine 1988: 65–70, 114; Philp 1989).

Paine saw civil society as naturally co-operative and progressive, and the need for governmental regulation as limited. By contrast, the essence of the state was coercion. As civil society grew more complex and stronger, so it both needed protection from the depredations of the state and had the ability to secure it. Paine thought that the pursuit of self-interest was legitimate in civil society, but that it ought to be subordinated to the common good in the political realm. Paine, like Locke, accepted inequalities of wealth as legitimate if they were products of differential rationality and industry, but he was more concerned with the misery of poverty than Locke was. In *The Rights of Man* and *Agrarian Justice* he made proposals for a system of public welfare financed by progressive taxation. Paine anticipated the social-democratic argument that public guarantees of minimal welfare, far from violating the natural rights of anyone, sustain the rights of all (Philp 1989).

The decline of natural rights

At the end of the eighteenth century the concept of natural rights was opposed by conservatives because it was too egalitarian and subversive, and by some radicals because it endorsed too much inequality of wealth. It suffered philosophically from uncertain foundations once its theological basis had faded. The violence of the French Revolution seemed to confirm the fears of the conservatives. The Revolution discredited the concept of natural rights in England, but did not hold back the movement for reform. Conservatives and reformers, therefore, sought alternatives to natural rights from different motives.

Edmund Burke did not reject the concept of natural rights completely. He recognized the natural rights to life, liberty, freedom of conscience, the fruits of one's labour, property, and equal justice under the law. Nevertheless, he considered the concept generally to be, at best, a useless metaphysical abstraction, and, at worst, subversive of social order. Thus, the 'real rights of men' were social not natural rights. Burke distrusted all abstract theoretical ideas in the making of public policy, as he believed politics to be essentially a practical activity that involved the making of judgements in complex circumstances. The French revolutionary doctrine of the Rights of Man was dangerous because it was simplistic and dogmatic.

Although Burke subscribed to natural-law theory, he opposed the universalism of the natural-rights concept for its failure to take account of national and cultural diversity. This cultural relativism offered little to those who had to endure tyranny. Significantly, Burke appealed to the concept of natural rights when analysing what he regarded as intolerable tyrannies, such as Protestant rule in Ireland (Freeman 1980).

Jeremy Bentham rejected the concept of natural rights more thoroughly than Burke did. Bentham sought to establish law on a rational basis. This required the elimination of all concepts that were vague or fictitious. The concept of natural rights was both. Natural rights were supposed to derive from natural law, but this was fictitious. Once natural rights had been detached from the concept of divine law, Bentham argued, they were based on nothing at all. For Bentham the only rights were legal rights. The facts of pleasure and pain were the basis upon which rational laws could be built, and the object of ethics and politics was the greatest happiness of the greatest number, or the common good. This was the principle of utility, which was an objective standard by which the goodness or badness of laws could be evaluated. Legal rights were valid in so far as they contributed to the common good. Natural rights were not only nonsense; they were also dangerous because they might make society unstable. Claims of natural rights were vague and so disputes over natural rights were likely to be settled by violence. Bentham believed that this explained the co-existence of the Rights of Man and violence in the French Revolution. Moreover, no rights could be absolute, because one rights-claim might conflict with another, but, if the scope of rights was limited, there must be clear criteria for limiting rights and resolving conflicts among rights-claims. The theory of natural rights could not give a clear account of the limits of rights, whereas the principle of utility could by evaluating rights-claims by their relative contribution to the general good. Both the appeal and the danger of natural-rights discourse lay in its simple dogmatism, and its refusal to engage in the hard intellectual work of thinking through the consequences of implementing general principles in the complex circumstances of society. The principle of utility should therefore be adopted, and that of natural rights should be rejected (Waldron 1987: 35–43).

In the nineteenth century Utilitarianism superseded the concept of natural rights as the theoretical basis of reform in both England and France. In France, as in England, the concepts of natural rights and utility had been thought to be mutually compatible. As the Revolution progressed, there was support in France for the view that the concept of natural rights was anarchic. A group of philosophers known as the Idéologues sought to set aside the concept of the Rights of Man, and to show how society could be reconstructed on the basis of a science of the mind with the aim of promoting happiness. They were, however, never able to convert their psychological theories into a convincing political programme (Welch 1984).

In contrast with this psychological approach, French social science moved away from the concern with political power and natural rights to an interest in economics. Economic science would deliver what natural rights had failed to (Welch 1984). Saint-Simon developed a proposal for the organization of industrial society on a scientific basis that assigned priority to the social and economic over the political, the collective over the individual, and the scientific over the philosophical. The intellectual world of liberal political philosophy was left behind. The Lockean theory of *property* rights was transformed into the search for the *laws* of material production. The Saint-Simonians concluded that Utilitarianism under the conditions of industrialism required socialism. The cause of the poor, neglected by the natural-rights ideologists of the French Revolution, was now transformed by the organized working-class movement.

Karl Marx argued that the Rights of Man were the rights of egoistic man, separated from the community. The concept treated society as external to individuals and as a limit on their natural freedom. It purported to be universal, but in fact expressed the interests of the bourgeois class, and, by emphasizing the rights of individuals, concealed the structured inequalities of class-based societies. It assumed, further, that individuals were actual or potential enemies, which might be true under the conditions of capitalism, but was neither natural nor universal. It treated the pre-social, autonomous individual as natural and political life as merely the means to protect the supposedly natural rights. This bourgeois conception of rights ignored the fundamental importance of labour, production and wealth to human well-being. Human emancipation, therefore, would be socio-economic (Waldron 1987: 126–32; Dagger 1989: 302–3). Marx was unclear as to whether the Communist society would need no concept of rights or would eliminate the *bourgeois* concept of rights. This was to prove to be a serious defect in Marx's theory when the twentieth century witnessed the development of strong Communist states with official Marxist ideologies and no commitment to individual rights. A neo-Lockean concern with the protection of individual rights from abuse of power by the state was to play an important role in the politics of actual Communist societies.

In the nineteenth and early twentieth centuries the Founding Fathers of sociology – Marx, Weber and Durkheim – were impressed by the massive social changes introduced by modern industrial capitalism, and sought to understand the larger historical forces that had brought them about. Individuals and their supposed natural rights dropped out of the picture. The first sociologists saw society as a natural entity to be understood scientifically, and not as an artificial creation to be shaped by ethical principles. If the concept of rights appeared in such analyses at all, it did so not as a fundamental philosophical category to guide ethical and political action, but rather as an ideological construct to be explained by social science. Rights survived in the US Constitution, and thinkers such as de Tocqueville, J. S. Mill and Weber worried about individual freedom in the age of large-scale, impersonal organization. However, Utilitarianism generally replaced natural rights as the basis of movements for social reform (Waldron 1987: 17–18, 151–3). The working-class and socialist movements nevertheless played a vital role in the struggle for economic and social rights.

The concept of individual rights survived in the late nineteenth century, but rights were defended, not as natural rights, but as conducive to the common good, either on Utilitarian or neo-Aristotelian grounds transmitted through the philosophy of Hegel (Dagger 1989: 303). Certain practical political questions – such as slavery, minorities and colonial rule – were sometimes discussed in the language of the Rights of Man, and some predecessors of modern human-rights non-governmental organizations, such as the French Ligue des Droits de l'Homme, were set up (Waldron 1987: 154). Other social movements and developments – such as the campaign for the social and political rights of women, workers' and socialist movements and the development of humanitarian laws of war – laid important foundations for the future of human rights in two particular respects. Firstly, they brought to the foreground what are now called economic and social rights, although it is a common mistake to believe that these had been ignored in previous eras. Secondly, the international solidarity of NGOs was pioneered as technological advances made international travel and communication faster and easier.

The First World War was a humanitarian disaster, but it also advanced the causes of economic and social rights, the rights of women and minorities, and the right of national self-determination against imperialism. At the end of the war the League of Nations was established, and addressed questions of justice in the colonies, minorities, workers' rights, slavery, the rights of women and children and the plight of refugees. The Covenant of the League made no mention of the Rights of Man. Japan proposed a clause upholding the principle of racial equality, but this was defeated on the initiative of the USA and the United Kingdom.

The League of Nations turned out to be a practical failure. It took the horrors of Nazism to revive the concept of the Rights of Man as human rights.

Conclusion

The history of human rights is characterized by continuity, diversity and change. The concept has been continuously associated with struggles for freedom, autonomy and resistance to oppression. These struggles have taken place in diverse social contexts, and consequently these concepts have had different meanings. Nevertheless, there is a core to the history of human rights that enables us to see commonalities in struggles for freedom from Antigone to contemporary Syrian democrats. The value of human rights is not 'self-evident' nor can it be derived solely from positive law. The concept of human rights, with its different meanings in different contexts, has always been, and remains, contested. Human-rights lawyers and activists do not generally take the history of human rights seriously; perhaps they sense that this history is one of controversy and conflict, and noticing this may weaken the resolve that the struggle for human rights requires. The history is both inspiring and troubling; this constitutes its relevance to human rights today.

3
After 1945
The New Age of Rights

The UN and the rights revival

Although the concept of the Rights of Man was largely discredited in the nineteenth century, concern with what we now call human-rights issues continued to develop in the campaigns against the slave trade, slavery, racial discrimination and colonialism, and for workers' rights, humanitarian laws of war, the protection of minorities, and the emancipation of women. An international treaty to abolish the slave trade was concluded in 1890, and a treaty to abolish slavery was drafted in 1926. The International Labour Organization concerned itself with workers' rights. The League of Nations set up a number of minority-rights treaties for eastern Europe, which it was, however, unwilling to enforce. After the First World War, a transnational human-rights movement began to develop. Two organizations were founded in Paris: the Fédération Internationale des Droits de l'Homme, established in 1922, campaigned for a global bill of human rights; the Académie Diplomatique Internationale, established in 1926, set up a commission to draft an international declaration of human rights. The report of this commission became a source of the Declaration of the International Rights of Man that was published in 1929 by the Institute of International Law in New York. Various individuals also drafted declarations of human rights, which typically called for human rights to be legally binding and enforceable on states. These efforts, however, remained marginal to the politics of the time.

On 6 January 1941 President Roosevelt, in his annual State of the Union address to Congress, presented his vision of a world based on 'four essential human freedoms': freedom of speech and expression, freedom of worship, freedom from want, and freedom from fear. 'Freedom', he declared, 'means the supremacy of human rights everywhere' (Franklin D. Roosevelt Presidential Library and Museum). In August 1941, President Roosevelt and the British Prime Minister, Winston Churchill, agreed on a document that became known as the Atlantic Charter. It set out as a common aim, among other things, the establishment of a peace which would ensure that all men might live in freedom from want and fear. The Declaration by the United (Allied) Nations on 1 January 1942 asserted that victory was essential 'to preserve human rights and justice'. President Roosevelt, in his State of the Union message of 11 January 1944, announced 'a second Bill of Rights' that included the rights to health, education, work, food, clothing, housing and recreation (Newman and Weissbrodt 1996: 49–50). These texts helped to propel human rights onto the agenda of international law and politics, although they have been criticized for their vagueness and hypocrisy; Britain had no intention of extending human rights to its empire, and in 1942 the USA interned more than 100,000 Japanese-Americans without trial (Normand and Zaidi 2008).

At the Dumbarton Oaks conference of the great powers (USA, USSR, UK and China) in 1944, called to discuss the establishment of the United Nations Organization, China proposed that the UN should be committed to racial equality and human rights, but this was opposed by the UK and USSR, and the final conference statement barely mentioned human rights. This produced a hostile reaction, especially in the USA, India and South America. US public opinion ensured that the Charter included an unprecedented commitment to human rights, but the governments of 'the big three' – USA, USSR and Britain – secured a qualification of this commitment in the form of a strong prohibition of interference by the UN in the internal affairs of member states. The Charter committed the UN to *promoting* human rights, but included neither means of enforcement nor remedies for victims of human-rights violations.

Nazi Germany had discredited the idea of minority rights by using it as a smokescreen for aggression; the League of Nations' minority-rights regime had failed; and the majority of UN states had an interest in rejecting minority rights. The UN therefore declared the League of Nations' minority-rights regime to be dead, and replaced it with a regime of individual human rights. However, as some UN states favoured minority rights, these rights were entrusted to a UN sub-commission.

The immediate cause of this rights revival was the growing knowledge of Nazi atrocities in the Second World War. Neither Utilitarianism nor scientific positivism – the two philosophies that had undermined the concept of natural rights in the nineteenth century – was well suited to explain the evil nature of Nazism. The language of human rights seemed more appropriate. The Nuremberg trials of Nazi leaders created a favourable context for human-rights thinking, even though they were restricted to war crimes.

The UN was set up to establish a new world order in accordance with the principles upon which the war had been fought. Support for a strong human-rights commitment came mainly from smaller countries, in Latin America, the West and the 'third world', and from non-governmental organizations. Opposition came mainly from the great powers. Partly as the result of determined lobbying by NGOs, the UN's San Francisco conference of 1945 included a number of human-rights provisions in the UN Charter (Cassese 1992: 25–7).

The preamble to the Charter declares that one of the chief aims of the organization is 'to reaffirm faith in fundamental human rights, in the dignity and worth of the human person, in the equal rights of men and women and of nations large and small'. Article 1 states that one of the principal purposes of the UN is 'to achieve international co-operation…in promoting and encouraging respect for human rights and fundamental freedoms for all'. Article 55 provides that the UN shall promote 'universal respect for, and observance of, human rights and fundamental freedoms for all without distinction as to race, sex, language or religion'. Article 56 tells us that all members of the UN pledge themselves to take joint and separate action in co-operation with the UN for the achievement of the purposes set forth in Article 55. Article 68 required the Economic and Social Council (ECOSOC) to set up commissions in economic and social fields and for the promotion of human rights, and, on this basis, the Council set up the Commission on Human Rights that was to draft the Universal Declaration of Human Rights (UDHR). Article 62 said that the Council 'may make recommendations for the purpose of promoting respect for, and observance of, human rights', and this was the basis on which it recommended to the General Assembly that it adopt and proclaim the UDHR (Robertson and Merrills 1996: 25–6; Morsink 1999: 2–4).

These provisions were qualified by Article 2, paragraph 7, which says that nothing in the Charter shall authorize the UN to intervene 'in matters which are essentially within the domestic jurisdiction of any state'. The question as to whether violations of human rights are such matters has been one of the most controversial in the law and politics of human rights. The first attempt to challenge sovereignty on the basis of human rights was made by India, which raised the question of South Africa's racist policies. South Africa protested that the UN had no right to interfere in its internal affairs, a position supported by the USA, Britain, Canada and Australia. The UN General Assembly claimed the right to discuss human rights, and Article 2 (7) of the Charter proved to be no barrier to consideration of racial policies in South Africa.

The General Assembly has not been much inhibited by Article 2 (7) in discussing human-rights issues, and 2 (7) has not prevented the establishment of UN procedures to investigate human-rights violations, although it may have been a barrier to their effectiveness (Cassese 1992; Robertson and Merrills 1996: 31).

The great powers successfully opposed attempts to introduce a legally binding human-rights covenant, other potentially effective enforcement measures, and the right to petition the UN about human-rights violations. This achieved, they were willing to accept a non-binding declaration of human rights. Human-rights protection was not extended to Germans: at the end of the war more than ten million Germans were forced from their homes in eastern Europe – the largest 'ethnic cleansing' in Europe's history.

The Universal Declaration of Human Rights

Since the UDHR is sometimes treated as a quasi-sacred text by its supporters and as a clumsy piece of bad philosophy by its critics, it is worth noting how it was made. A Canadian lawyer, John Humphrey, produced a first draft, based on a comparative survey of national constitutions. The Commission on Human Rights then held 81 meetings over almost two years. The Commission approved the final draft almost unanimously. Then the General Assembly Third Committee on Social, Humanitarian and Cultural Affairs held more than 100 meetings between September and December 1948. In this process, 1,233 individual votes were cast. The Third Committee adopted the Declaration by a vote of 29 to 0 with seven abstentions. The General Assembly adopted the Declaration on 10 December 1948, with 48 states voting for, none against, and eight abstaining (six Communist states, Saudi Arabia and South Africa). Thus, most UN members endorsed most of the Declaration, but those states were mainly from Europe, North and Latin America, with a few states from Africa and Asia. Eight states from the Muslim world participated in the drafting of the Declaration. Seven voted for the final draft; Saudi Arabia abstained (Waltz 2004).

Some states that played leading roles in drafting and approving the Declaration had colonial empires, and much of the world's population lived under colonial rule. Since the adoption of the Declaration, UN membership has more than trebled, with new members coming overwhelmingly from Africa and Asia. This has raised the question as to the applicability of the Declaration to these countries. In this connection, it is worth noting that even the 1948 UN included capitalist and socialist states, rich and poor countries such as the USA and Ethiopia, and societies that were predominantly Christian, Muslim, Hindu and Buddhist. The Western states may have been dominant, but 'third-world' states supported the human-rights project as a means to fight colonialism and racism, and to promote social justice. Some of the most innovative features of the Declaration – for example, racial and gender equality, economic and social rights – were promoted by states other than the dominant Western powers, which, in various ways, viewed them with misgivings. The common view that 'the West' imposed human rights on the rest is not only historically inaccurate but also exaggerates the West's commitment to human rights (Morsink 1999; Cassese 1992; Waltz 2001: 65, 70–2).

The UDHR was intended to prevent a repetition of atrocities of the kind that the Nazis had committed. This is expressed particularly in the second paragraph of the preamble, which states that 'disregard and contempt for human rights have resulted in barbarous acts which have outraged the conscience of mankind'. The Commission on Human Rights, aware of the religious, philosophical and ideological diversity of UN members, displayed little interest in the philosophical foundations of human rights. Nevertheless, given that Nazism violated human rights in theory and practice, the adoption of the concept of human rights by the UN in opposition to Nazi ideology clearly implied the commitment to some kind of neo-Lockean political theory. The substitution of the term 'natural rights' by that of 'human rights' was probably to eliminate the controversial philosophical implications of grounding rights in nature (Morsink 1999: 283, 294–6, 300–2). The Declaration rejected the concept of natural rights, but did not replace it with a clear philosophical alternative. It sought agreement on *norms* (rules) without seeking agreement on fundamental values. The concept of human rights is, however, sufficiently similar to the Lockean concept of natural rights that it is located in the Western liberal tradition. This makes it doubly controversial: because it is Western, and because it is liberal. However influential the concept of human rights may be, and however appealing it may be to many people, it is philosophically ungrounded (Waldron 1987: 151, 166–209). The problem of 'grounding' *any* concept philosophically is, however, notoriously difficult, and concepts may be morally and politically useful, even though they are philosophically controversial. The actions of those who heroically resisted the Nazis may have been philosophically ungrounded, but no worse for that.

The Declaration allegedly has a Western bias by emphasizing rights rather than duties, individual rather than collective rights, civil and political rather than economic, social and cultural rights, and in its lack of explicit concern with the problem of imperialism (Cassese 1992: 31). The Declaration did, however, include the economic and social rights – such as the rights to work, health and education – that had been won in several industrial countries in the nineteenth and early twentieth centuries.

The Declaration was not intended to impose legal obligations on states, but, rather, to set out goals for which states were expected to strive (Robertson and Merrills 1996: 28–9). It was, nonetheless, the first declaration of moral and political principles that could make a *prima facie* plausible claim to universality (Morsink 1999: 33). Locke's theory and the French revolutionary Declaration may have been universal in principle, but the UDHR was endorsed by political powers with global reach. Whatever its philosophical limitations, the Declaration has had great legal and political influence. Before the Second World War there was almost no international law of human rights. There are now approximately 200 international legal human-rights instruments, of which 65 acknowledge the UDHR as a source of authority. The Declaration is also the source of an international movement, and of numerous national movements, of political activists who struggle against oppression, injustice and exploitation by reference to this document (Morsink 1999: xi–xii, 20).

Article 1 announces that all human beings are born free and equal in dignity and rights. They are endowed with reason and conscience, and should act towards one another in a spirit of brotherhood. Notwithstanding the echoes of Locke and the French Revolution, this is not unreconstructed natural-rights theory, but a liberal riposte to Fascism (Morsink 1999: 38). Article 2 says that everyone is entitled to all the rights and freedoms set forth in the Declaration 'without distinction of any kind, such as race, colour, sex, language, religion, political or other opinion, national or social origin, property, birth or other status'. This is both an explicit statement of the egalitarian implications of the concept of human rights, about which classical natural-rights thinkers had been so evasive, and a direct rejection of Nazi racist ideology (Morsink 1999: 39). Article 2 is elaborated by Article 7, which states that all are equal before the law, and are entitled to equal protection of the law without any discrimination.

Articles 3–5 deal with what are sometimes called 'personal integrity rights'. Article 3 restates the classic rights to life, liberty and security of person. Article 4 forbids slavery, servitude and the slave trade. Article 5 forbids torture and 'cruel, inhuman or degrading treatment or punishment'. Torture is widely condemned in the contemporary world, and widely practised, but the interpretation of the phrase 'cruel, inhuman or degrading treatment or punishment' has proved to be controversial.

Articles 6–12 deal with legal rights. These provisions are not controversial in general, although their particular applications may be, but the balance between legal rights, on the one hand, and social and economic rights, on the other, has been criticized for being excessively influenced by the Western history of rights as legal protections for private individuals against the state rather than as positive contributions to the life of dignity.

Article 14 says that everyone has the right to seek and to enjoy in other countries asylum from persecution. The right of asylum has become one of the most important and controversial of human rights in recent times, as gross violations of other human rights have generated massive refugee flows, and many countries that claim to be champions of human rights are reluctant to defend the Article 14 human rights of foreigners.

Article 16 states that men and women of full age have the right to marry and to found a family without any limitation due to race, nationality or religion. They are entitled to equal rights as to marriage, during marriage and at its dissolution. Marriage shall be entered into only with the free and full consent of the intending spouses. This is the liberal view of marriage, and was a reaction against Nazi racial marriage laws. However, since the family is often at the centre of religious ethics, considerable tension has developed between this liberal conception of marriage rights and others, especially those that endorse 'arranged' marriages. Article 16 (3) asserts that the family 'is the natural and fundamental group unit of society and is entitled to protection by society and the state'. This unusual example of a collective right in the Declaration was understandable in the light of Nazi family policy. However, families, like all collective bodies, can be violators of human rights, for example through domestic violence against women and the abuse of children, so that 16 (3) is more problematic than it first seemed to be.

Historically, the concept of rights had been closely associated with that of property. The socialist movement that arose in the nineteenth century had made that association problematic. Article 17 of the Declaration states that everyone has the right to own property alone and in association with others, and that no one shall be arbitrarily deprived of his property. This right to property is compatible with various property systems.

Article 18 says that everyone has the right to 'freedom of thought, conscience and religion' and 'to manifest his religion or belief in teaching, practice, worship and observance'. This has been, historically, one of the most fundamental liberal rights, but it carries the potential problem that some religions may not respect some other human rights, and thus there can be a conflict between Article 18 and some other Declaration rights. Similarly, Article 7, which proclaims equality before the law, includes the right to equal protection against incitement to discrimination. This might conflict with Article 19, which says that everyone has the right to freedom of expression. This gives rise to the question as to whether so-called 'hate speech' – speech expressing hatred or contempt for specific groups – can be made illegal without violating the right to freedom of expression.

Article 22 says that everyone is entitled to realization of the economic, social and cultural rights indispensable for his dignity and the free development of his personality, 'through national effort and international co-operation' and 'in accordance with the organization and resources of each state'. Article 25 states that everyone has the right to a standard of living adequate for the health and well-being of himself and of his family, including food, clothing, housing and medical care and necessary social services, and the right to security in the event of unemployment, sickness, disability, widowhood, old age or other lack of livelihood in circumstances beyond his control. Article 22 makes the realization of economic, social and cultural rights dependent on the resources of each state, whereas Article 25 does not.

Article 27 says that everyone has the right 'to participate in the cultural life of the community'. This is ambiguous as to whether 'the community' is the national community or includes minority communities.

The UDHR was drafted and approved by representatives of a wide range of cultural and ideological belief-systems. Agreement was reached by avoiding explicit religious or philosophical commitments; by deliberately vague wording, employing such terms as 'arbitrary', 'just' and 'reasonable'; and by qualifying 'the right to have rights'. Article 29, paragraph 1, states that everyone 'has duties to the community in which alone the free and full development of his personality is possible'. Paragraph 2 allows the limitation of human rights in order to secure the rights of others and to meet 'the just requirements of morality, public order and the general welfare in a democratic society'.

The UDHR omitted the right to self-determination, which was of paramount importance to anti-colonial activists. This omission was rectified when the right was included as Article 1 of both the 1966 human-rights covenants. It omitted the right to rebel against tyranny, which had played an important role in the American and French revolutions, and which was supported both by several 'third-world' leaders and by the USSR; in its place the UDHR presented human rights as the antidote to rebellion. It included no right to petition the UN about human-rights violations, and no means to implement the rights that it proclaimed. It was therefore much weaker than most proposals for international human-rights law that had been made previously throughout the twentieth century. The UDHR was intended to be a manifesto, not enforceable law, nor philosophical treatise, nor social policy for the world. It was written for a popular audience in relatively simple terms, and it is therefore necessarily oversimplified as a guide to policy-making.

From theory to practice

The Cold War

The UDHR is only a declaration. It makes no provision for its implementation. It allocates rights to everyone. It says little about who is obliged to do what to ensure that these rights are respected. In 1948 the UN was committed to state sovereignty and human rights. It could not decide what was to be done if sovereign states violated human rights. At that time virtually all governments said that the Declaration was not legally binding. No human-rights violations, except slavery, genocide and gross abuses of the rights of aliens were illegal under international law. The UN established a Commission on Human Rights, but it was composed of the representatives of governments, and NGOs had limited access to it. The Commission's mandate was largely confined to drafting treaties and other legal texts. In 1947 the Economic and Social Council declared that the Commission had no authority to respond to human-rights violations in any way. A procedure was established to channel the thousands of complaints that the UN received each year, which the head of the organization's human-rights secretariat described as 'the world's most elaborate waste-paper basket' (Alston 1992: 128–9, 140–1; 1994: 375–6). From 1948 until the late 1960s the ability of the UN or the 'international community' to take effective action to protect human rights was extremely limited (Alston 1992: 139).

The Cold War reinforced the reluctance of states after 1948 to submit to the international regulation of human rights, and, consequently, notwithstanding the UDHR, human rights returned to the margins of international politics in the 1950s. The two main Cold War protagonists, the USA and the USSR, used the concept of human rights to score propaganda points off each other, while directly or indirectly participating in the gross violation of human rights. Plans to introduce binding human-rights treaties were delayed until the mid-1960s.

In the 1950s and 1960s the world-wide decolonization movement created many new member states of the UN with new priorities and issues for the human-rights agenda: decolonization, the right to self-determination and anti-racism. The Convention on the Elimination of Racial Discrimination was adopted by the General Assembly in 1965. The arrival of new states at the UN, therefore, injected a new activism, although it was very selective: South Africa, Israel and Chile received particular attention. The new anti-colonialist and anti-racist agenda helped to diminish the apparent 'Western' bias of human rights, while, at the same time, the selectivity of the new human-rights politics threatened the universality of the concept. Leaders of former colonies sometimes appealed to human rights in advancing their cause, but, on attaining independence, they emphasized the principles of state sovereignty and non-interference in the affairs of other states, often to defend themselves against criticisms of their human-rights violations, which included some of the worst in the world, such as the mass killings under Idi Amin in Uganda or Macías Nguema in Equatorial Guinea. In the 1970s, the increasingly assertive human-rights policies of Western governments and NGOs – often targeted at post-colonial governments – produced a reaction in the form of economic and/or cultural relativism: the argument that supposedly 'universal' human rights did not apply to developing countries and/or non-Western cultures.

Even this selective activism, however, advanced the cause of universalism, because it set precedents that were broadened later. For example, in 1965 the Special Committee on Decolonization asked the Commission to respond to the petitions that the Committee had received about the situation in Southern Africa. The Council then asked the Commission to consider violations 'in all countries'. In 1966 the General Assembly asked the Economic and Social Council and the Commission on Human Rights 'to give urgent consideration to ways and means of improving the capacity of the United Nations to put a stop to violations of human rights wherever they might occur'. This led to the adoption of two new procedures. In 1967, Resolution 1235 of the Economic and Social Council authorized the Commission to discuss human-rights violations in particular countries. In 1970 Resolution 1503 of the Council established a procedure by which situations that appeared to reveal 'a consistent pattern of gross and reliably attested violations of human rights' could be pursued with the governments concerned in private.

The work of the Commission under its 1235 powers was very selective in the 1970s. It was, for example, very concerned with South Africa, Israel's occupied territories and Chile, but did not respond to gross human-rights violations in East Pakistan (now Bangladesh), Uganda, the Central African Empire, Cambodia, East Timor, Argentina, Uruguay, Brazil and many other places. In the 1980s the 1235 work of the Commission broadened considerably. The Commission was criticized for lack of political balance, but its scope became much wider than it had been, and much wider than it could have been before the adoption of 1235. Its response time was slow, and potential sanctions were remote. The 1235 procedure was an advance in the implementation of UN human-rights standards, but it worked unevenly, and remained marginal to the world's human-rights problems (Alston 1992; Donnelly 1989: 208; 1998: 9; 1999: 76, 101).

The 1503 procedure enabled individuals to petition the UN about human-rights violations, but offered them no redress. The Commission named countries that it had considered, and might, therefore, put some pressure on governments by publicity. However, the procedure could be brought fully into effect only at least two years after receipt of the complaint. Stalling tactics by governments and the politics of the Commission could delay action much longer. 1503 has had little impact on situations of gross human-rights violations (Alston 1992; Robertson and Merrills 1996: 79–89; Donnelly 1998: 9, 53–4). There is a consensus that 1503 has been slow, complex, secret and vulnerable to political influence. There is a difference of view among experts as to whether it has done more harm than good (Alston 1992: 150–5; Donnelly 1989: 208).

In 1966 two international treaties – the International Covenant on Civil and Political Rights and the International Covenant on Economic, Social and Cultural Rights – were adopted unanimously, and opened for signature and ratification. They entered into force in 1976 when the necessary 35 ratifications had been received. The 1966 Covenants leave out the right to property, but include the right to self-determination. The UDHR and the two Covenants, together known as the International Bill of Rights, constitute the core of international human-rights law. By 10 February 2016 more than 80 per cent of the 193 UN states had ratified the two covenants.

The Human Rights Committee was established in 1976. It is supposed to consist of independent experts whose task is to monitor compliance with the Covenant on Civil and Political Rights. The states that are parties to the Covenant are obliged to submit reports on what they have done to implement the rights in the Covenant. The Committee can also receive complaints from states under the Covenant, and individual complaints under its Optional Protocol. NGOs have played an increasing role as sources of information. Co-operation with the Committee by states is variable, but the Committee has brought about legislative changes in some countries, and can contribute to human-rights improvements through discussion, debate and advice. In a few cases, individual complainants have benefited from a decision of the Committee (Opsahl 1992; Robertson and Merrills 1996: 45–6, 66, 71; Donnelly 1989: 208–10; 1998: 57–9).

There are nine other treaty-monitoring bodies. There are differences of detail in the resourcing, working methods and effectiveness of these committees. The main obstacles to their effectiveness have been the inability or unwillingness of some governments to co-operate with them, and the unwillingness of governments to provide them with adequate resources (Alston and Crawford 2000). These treaty bodies have no power to compel states to submit their reports on time (or at all), no powers of investigation, no enforcement powers, and little or no capacity to follow up their recommendations to states. They have developed a substantial body of human-rights jurisprudence by concluding observations on state reports, by general comments on broader points of law, and by making decisions on petitions. There has been little systematic research on the impact of these treaty bodies on the actual enjoyment of human rights, but the general scholarly judgement is that this impact has been limited.

New initiatives to implement human rights were taken in the 1970s in the foreign policies of certain states. In 1975 US foreign aid policy was required to take account of the human-rights practices of recipient countries. When Jimmy

Carter became President in 1977, he introduced human rights into his foreign policy. This was an innovation, although the policy was implemented unevenly in practice (Donnelly 1998: 10). Human-rights NGOs were making an increasing impact. Amnesty International, for example, was awarded the Nobel Peace Prize in the year in which Carter became President. The UN adopted the Convention on the Elimination of Discrimination Against Women in 1979, the Convention Against Torture in 1984, and the Convention on the Rights of the Child in 1989.

Pursuant to Resolution 1235 the Commission on Human Rights established monitoring mechanisms for Southern Africa, the Arab territories occupied by Israel, and Chile. A Working Group on Enforced or Involuntary Disappearances was established in response to events in Argentina and Chile. Special rapporteurs were appointed on summary or arbitrary executions, torture, religious intolerance, and human-rights violations by mercenaries. A Working Group on Arbitrary Detention was set up. Almost all these early 'thematic procedures' applied only to civil and political rights, but, more recently, special procedures have been introduced for human rights and extreme poverty, structural adjustment and foreign debt, and for the rights to education, food, housing and health. Special rapporteurs were appointed to study the human-rights situations in a growing number and increasingly diverse range of countries. As of 27 March 2015 there were 41 thematic and 14 country mandates for special procedures.

The special procedures' mandate holders are independent; they may draw on any part of international human-rights law; they may act on individual complaints; they connect international human-rights law with local conditions; and thematic procedures may investigate any country. They are the most accessible part of the UN human-rights system for victims of human-rights violations and their representatives. They press governments to prevent or rectify violations, they publicize violations, and contribute to the specification of international human-rights norms. The two main challenges for special procedures are uncooperative governments and meagre resources. Special procedures have no powers of enforcement, but have the power of publicity. They have had success in improving human rights in some countries. There is no systematic evidence of the impact of special procedures, and some observers hold that they remain marginal to the protection of human rights world-wide (Alston 1992: 180–1; Weissbrodt 2011; Piccone 2012).

In the early 1970s the Communist bloc sought agreements with the West on security and economic matters. The West demanded human-rights guarantees in return. In 1973 the Conference on Security and Co-operation in Europe (CSCE) was convened, later to become the Organization for Security and Co-operation in Europe (OSCE). This led to the Helsinki Final Act of 1975, in which the Communist states accepted a range of human-rights commitments. In the following years, Helsinki-based human-rights NGOs were established in the USSR, but were severely persecuted. In 1977 the human-rights group, Charter 77, was set up in Czechoslovakia. The short-term, practical effects of these events appeared slight, but they increased the intensity of international debates about human rights, and such groups played a role in the dismantling of the Communist system in eastern Europe (Donnelly 1998: 78–82; Forsythe 2000: 124–5).

The admission to the UN of a large number of poor, non-Western states introduced a new emphasis on economic rights into international debate. In 1974 a number of texts concerning the so-called New International Economic Order were approved. These texts sought to draw attention away from human-rights violations in individual states to the structural causes of human-rights violations in global economic inequality. This third-world approach to human rights led to a controversial conceptual development: the so-called 'third generation' of human rights. According to this new thinking, civil and political rights were the first generation of 'liberty' rights; economic and social rights were the second generation of 'equality' rights; and there was now a need for a third generation of 'solidarity' rights. These were the rights to development, peace, a healthy environment and self-determination. In 1986 the General Assembly adopted a Declaration on the Right to Development.

'Third-generation' rights have been criticized on several grounds, including the following: (1) the language of 'generations' is inappropriate, because generations succeed each other, but so-called generations of human rights do not; 2) the concept of 'generation' presupposes a questionable history of human rights: the supposed first two generations were both recognized in the UDHR; 3) it is not clear whether the holders of these rights are individuals, peoples, states or some combination of these; 4) it is not clear what the bearers of these rights have a right to; 5) it is not clear who the corresponding duty-bearers are, nor what their duties are; 6) these rights-claims provide cover for authoritarian governments to violate established human rights; 7) what is valid in third-generation rights is already contained in established human rights: for example, the right to development is covered by taking economic and social rights seriously (Donnelly 1993).

In the 1980s and early 1990s the theme of 'cultural relativism' became more salient in UN debates about human rights. In 1984 the Islamic Republic of Iran announced it would not recognize the validity of any international principles that were contrary to Islam. In the run-up to the UN World Conference on Human Rights that was held in Vienna in 1993 there was much talk of a conflict between 'Asian values' and human rights. The final declaration of the Vienna Conference reaffirmed the universality of human rights, but conceded that human rights 'must be considered in the context of a dynamic and evolving process of international norm-setting, bearing in mind the significance of national and regional particularities and various historical, cultural and religious backgrounds'.

Both the universality and the diversity of human rights are demonstrated by the existence of regional human rights organizations such as the Council of Europe, with its European Convention and Court of Human Rights; the Organization of American States, with its American Convention on Human Rights; the African Union, with its African Charter of Human and Peoples' Rights; the League of Arab States, with its Arab Charter on Human Rights; and the Association of South-East Asian Nations, with its Intergovernmental Commission on Human Rights. The effectiveness of these regional organizations varies greatly. Individual states incorporate human-rights protections in their constitutions and/or legislation, implementing in various ways and to various degrees international and regional standards.

After the Cold War

Although the end of the Cold War brought some immediate human-rights improvements, such as the establishment of civil and political rights in former Communist societies, the new world order produced complex human-rights patterns. Both the General Assembly and the Commission on Human Rights became more active. The challenge to Western domination of the human-rights agenda by the poorer states of the so-called South weakened. The UN goals of peace-keeping and human-rights protection became increasingly combined. The Secretary-General's office negotiated a human-rights agreement between government and rebels in El Salvador, which involved intrusive monitoring by UN civil and military personnel. Similarly, in Haiti and Liberia, the UN became involved in monitoring respect for human rights as part of political settlements. In Namibia and Cambodia, the UN had a more comprehensive role in protecting human rights in the context of overall political re-organization. Initiatives by the Secretary-General or mandates from the Security Council provided bases for UN supervision of elections in Nicaragua, Haiti, El Salvador, Namibia, Angola, Cambodia and elsewhere. In 1991 Operation Desert Storm reversed the Iraqi military occupation of Kuwait, and was followed by military interventions in northern Iraq to create a 'safe haven' for the persecuted Kurds, and in southern Iraq in an attempt to defend the Shi'a population. In the following year the UN intervened in the civil war in Somalia to end the fighting and provide humanitarian assistance. It was more successful in the latter operation than in the former, but the intervention was problematic for the UN, the intervening states, especially the USA, and the intended beneficiaries.

The dissolution of the former Yugoslavia left a Serb minority in Croatia, three minority populations in Bosnia-Herzegovina (Serbs, Croats and Muslims), and an oppressed ethnic Albanian minority in Kosovo. Serbia launched a war against Croatia, ostensibly to protect the Serb minority, and intervened in Bosnia on behalf of the Bosnian Serbs. The war in Bosnia involved 'ethnic cleansing' (forcible moving of populations in order to create ethnically homogeneous territories) and other gross human-rights violations, including massacres and mass rapes. The major powers were reluctant to intervene militarily, partly because of their experience in Somalia and partly because of the perceived military and political difficulties. Considerable success was achieved in delivering humanitarian assistance, but the UN's failure to prevent gross human-rights violations was catastrophic. In 1999 NATO intervened militarily in Serbia, when the UN could not because of Russian and Chinese opposition in the Security Council, in order to prevent violations of the human rights of ethnic Albanians in Kosovo. The immediate effects were worse violations against the Albanians, considerable war casualties among Serb civilians, and, after the NATO military victory, reprisals by Albanians against Serbs. The brutal and corrupt regime of the Serbian President, Slobodan Milošević, was overthrown, and Milošević was arrested and charged with crimes against humanity, war crimes and genocide by the International Criminal Tribunal for the Former Yugoslavia. He died before the tribunal could reach a verdict. The legality of the NATO intervention was dubious, and it was controversial, even among human-rights observers. After several years of UN administration, Kosovo declared independence in February 2008.

The establishment of international criminal tribunals for the former Yugoslavia and following the genocide of 1994 in Rwanda were further innovations by the UN. In 1998 120 states adopted the Rome Statute establishing the International Criminal Court (ICC). The Statute entered into force in 2002. As of January 2016 only two persons had been convicted. The Court has been criticized for concentrating almost exclusively on Africa. There have been several responses to the charge of anti-African bias: (1) these cases have been referred to the Court by African states; (2) they seek justice for African victims of gross human-rights violations; (3) Africans hold important posts in the Court, as prosecutors and judges. Nevertheless, the success of the ICC remains uncertain.

The UN has had for a long time a small and poorly funded programme of technical assistance for human rights, for example in legal institution-building. In the early 1990s this was somewhat expanded. Some observers prefer this constructive assistance for human rights to more adversarial pressure, while others believe that such programmes achieve little, and can divert attention from human-rights violations.

The Vienna Conference emphasized the special vulnerability of certain groups such as women, children, minorities, indigenous populations, persons with disabilities, migrant workers and refugees. Among the consequences of these concerns were the appointment of a Special Rapporteur on Violence Against Women, the International Convention on the Rights of Migrant Workers, and the Convention on the Rights of Persons with Disabilities.

The Vienna Conference also recommended the creation of a High Commissioner for Human Rights, and this was approved by the General Assembly. High Commissioners are UN civil servants, human-rights advocates, defenders of victims, and managers of the international human-rights bureaucracy. They have to work with governments that they must also criticize. They raise funds for the UN's human-rights work, and support the treaty bodies and the special procedures. Several high commissioners have been outspoken in condemning human-rights violations in a number of countries, thereby attracting criticism from governments. As of 31 December 2013 the Office of the High Commissioner had 13 country offices and 13 regional offices to provide 'capacity-building' to governments and advice and support for other UN agencies, including peace-keeping operations and special procedures (Gaer and Broeker 2014).

In 1997 Kofi Annan, the UN Secretary-General, called for the integration of human rights into all UN work, especially development and humanitarian action – a programme known as 'mainstreaming'. UN agencies responded to this call with varying degrees of enthusiasm.

The UN Security Council was for many years not much concerned with human rights. Recently, however, it has incorporated human rights in its resolutions on conflict resolution and peace-keeping. In 2011 it condemned human-rights violations by the Libyan government and authorized 'all necessary force' to protect civilians.

Serious concerns have been raised about human-rights violations by the UN and NGOs. These include the sexual abuse of women and children by UN troops; the mistreatment of refugees; the unfair imposition of sanctions; complicity with local human-rights violators; and unfair employment practices. The UN is a large bureaucracy, and, in some post-conflict situations, exercises quasi-governmental powers. It is therefore a potential, and actual, human-rights violator, and, it is argued, not subject to the checks which make states somewhat accountable (Verdirame 2011).

9/11 and after

On 11 September 2001 the militant Islamist group, Al-Qaeda, carried out an attack, using hijacked civilian airliners as missiles, on the World Trade Center in New York and the Pentagon in Washington, DC. Another plane was brought down by its passengers in Pennsylvania. Some 3,000 people were killed.

Al-Qaeda had been formed by Osama bin Laden, son of a wealthy Saudi Arabian businessman, during the resistance to the Soviet invasion of Afghanistan. After the withdrawal of Soviet troops from Afghanistan, bin Laden turned his attention to his own government, and its superpower ally, the USA. He appeared to have been particularly angered by the willingness of Saudi Arabia to allow US troops to use that country, the homeland of Islam, as the base for its invasion of Kuwait to expel the occupying Iraqi forces in the Gulf War of 1991. Al-Qaeda is a loose network rather than a disciplined organization, and its supporters have various ideologies. Bin Laden's ultimate goal, however, was the reversal of Western intrusions into 'Muslim lands' that took place after the dismantling of the Ottoman Empire after the First World War. On 2 May 2011 bin Laden was killed in Pakistan by US special forces.

The USA, and some of its allies, responded to 9/11 by helping the Northern Alliance to overthrow the Taliban regime in Afghanistan, which had been sheltering Al-Qaeda. In March 2003 the USA invaded Iraq on the ground that its President, Saddam Hussein, had 'weapons of mass destruction' in violation of Security Council resolutions, that he was supporting terrorism, and that he was a dictator whose removal from power was justified. The US administration hinted that Saddam Hussein was somehow linked to 9/11. The war was extremely controversial, because no weapons of mass destruction were found and no links with Al-Qaeda were established. Although Iraq acquired a democratically elected government it failed to attract the allegiance of the Sunni minority, and violent conflict ensued, giving rise to the terrorist organization, ISIS (Islamic State of Iraq and Syria), which has committed many atrocities in Iraq and Syria.

In the so-called 'war on terror' several countries passed anti-terrorism laws that were criticized by human-rights groups, and sometimes by courts. The most notorious human-rights issues in the 'war on terror' were the detention without trial of several hundred suspected terrorists at Guantánamo Bay, Cuba, and the use of torture and/or inhumane treatment in Afghanistan, Iraq and Guantánamo, and by 'extraordinary rendition' to countries where torture is common. The USA and its allies supported governments with poor human-rights records in exchange for their collaboration in the 'war on terror'.

On 20 January 2009 Barack Obama was inaugurated as President of the USA. His human-rights record has been mixed. He sought to end the 'war on terror' and close the Guantánamo detention centre; he banned torture and closed the CIA's secret prisons; he promised compliance with the Geneva Conventions. But he would not hold members of the Bush administration accountable for alleged human-rights crimes; on 16 August 2016 there were still 61 prisoners in Guantánamo; military detention of suspected terrorists without trials and military commissions (with somewhat improved procedures) continued; interrogation techniques were improved, but not to the satisfaction of human-rights critics; extraordinary rendition continued though supposedly with better diplomatic assurances of appropriate treatment; government surveillance powers have increased;

'whistleblowers' have been vigorously prosecuted; appeals to state secrets have obstructed judicial oversight. Obama has used far more drone strikes in more countries than Bush did, with reportedly considerable civilian deaths. Obama has been constrained by public opinion, Congress and the reluctance of other states to receive Guantánamo detainees. He also had an ambitious social programme to get through Congress. There is a consensus that Obama's policies were better than those of his predecessor, but fell short of human-rights campaigners' expectations.

The so-called Arab Spring, which began in Tunisia in December 2010, has played out differently in different countries in North Africa and the Middle East, but only in Tunisia itself has the outcome been good for human rights and democracy, and that achievement looked fragile at the beginning of 2016. Libya, after the overthrow of Muammar Gaddafi in October 2011, descended into violent chaos. Egypt passed from dictatorship through a form of democracy to a new, highly authoritarian dictatorship. Relatively peaceful protests against the dictatorship of Bashar al-Assad in Syria developed into a complex and extremely bloody civil war, in which hundreds of thousands were killed and millions displaced from their homes as refugees.

Reform of the UN human-rights regime

In 2006 the UN General Assembly abolished the Commission on Human Rights, replacing it with the Human Rights Council. There had been widespread dissatisfaction with the Commission because some of its members represented governments with very bad human-rights records and it had become too politicized. The Council was designed in various ways to strengthen the impartiality of its commitment to human rights. The two most important features of the Council are the Universal Periodic Review (UPR), by which the Council reviews the human-rights records of *all* states, and the retention of the special procedures.

Some see the Council, especially its UPR, as progress. A study by *UPR Info* on the level of implementation in 165 countries concluded that half of all recommendations were either fully or partially implemented three years after the UPR review (Hegarty and Fridlund 2016). Critics point out that serious human-rights violators are elected to the Council; that it is still too political; it remains remote from the victims it purports to serve; its 'universality' conceals great inequality among nations; it is under-resourced; and it fails to address the most serious violations. The Council suffers from two problems arising from the 'statist' nature of the international human-rights regime: many states are not seriously committed to human rights; and human-rights violations may be caused by forces beyond the control of states, such as the structure of the global economy.

Conclusion

Since 1945 the UN has done a lot of 'standard-setting', institution-building and human-rights promotion. The concept of human rights is one of the most influential of our time, and many poor and oppressed people appeal to it in their quest for justice. The capacity of the UN to implement its own standards is still modest, however. The concept of state sovereignty and the realities of international power politics still make the implementation of human-rights standards uneven, and generally weak. The regime has been unable to prevent such disasters as the genocide in Rwanda and the civil war in Syria. It neglected economic, social and cultural rights until recently, and there remain doubts as to whether it is suited to address problems of global poverty and inequality.

The achievements of human-rights practice have been limited, if judged by the ambition of the UDHR, but astonishing given the controversial history of the idea and its vulnerability to political and economic power. The concept of human rights pervades the world's legal systems at the international, regional and national levels. The legal architecture is impressive, but often it bears little relation to what happens in the streets and the fields.

The concept of human rights is a concept whose time has come. But what is it precisely that has come? How should we evaluate it in the light of (1) the criticisms that were made of its historical predecessors; and (2) its uneven record of success in practice? In the next chapter we shall examine theories of human rights that have attempted to clarify and justify the concept, and that have offered relatively precise answers to these questions.

4
Theories of Human Rights

Why theory?

The member states of the UN have been able to agree on a set of human-rights norms in part because they have avoided questions about the philosophical justifications of human rights and ignored the criticisms that had been made of the earlier concept of natural rights. The UN practice of human-rights declarations, promotion, standard-setting and institution-building has been carried out by diplomats and lawyers, prompted and assisted by activists. Human-rights practice is addressed mainly to obvious human wrongs – such as racism, colonialism and political oppression – and it might be tempting to follow the American Declaration of Independence and to consider the truth of human rights to be 'self-evident'. This is unsatisfactory, however, because what some commentators have called 'the overlapping consensus' of the international community conceals fundamental disagreements. The concept of human rights is not self-justifying; it therefore needs justification.

Since the concept of natural rights had been based on Christian natural-law theory, the secularization of the concept called its foundations into question. When the validity of the concept could no longer be guaranteed by the will of God, the Rights of Man were said to be derived from reason and/or nature. However, this derivation was very controversial.

The critics of the Rights of Man – such as Burke, Bentham and Marx – could appeal to reason and nature in different ways in order to reject the concept. In the nineteenth century 'reason' came to mean 'scientific reason' and science was hostile to the concept of natural rights. There was also a reaction against the individualism of natural-rights theory, and a revival of the Aristotelian idea that society was the primary concept of political philosophy. Thus, *social science* was hostile to natural rights on two grounds: the concept was unscientific and it was anti-social. From the perspective of modern philosophy and social science, the UN adoption of the concept of human rights was problematic.

Scepticism about human-rights theory can be defended theoretically. Rorty argued that there is *no* theoretical foundation for human rights, because there is no theoretical *foundation* for any belief. This is not, however, something we should regret, both because it is a necessary philosophical truth, and because the cause of human rights does not require theory for its success, but, rather, sympathy (Rorty 1993). Rorty's argument, however, confused *motivation* and *justification*. Sympathy is an emotion. Whether the action we take on the basis of our emotions is justified depends on the reasons for the action. Rorty wished to eliminate unprovable metaphysical theories from philosophy, but in his critique of human-rights theory he went too far, and eliminated reasoning. We need reasons to support our human-rights actions, both because it is often not clear which actions human-rights principles require and because opponents of human rights can support their opposition with reasons, and we must understand whether our reasons are superior, and, if so, why. A different kind of objection to human-rights theory has been put forward by the political scientist David Forsythe. He argues that philosophical theories are inherently controversial, and that concern with theory will undermine human-rights practice (Forsythe 1989). Forsythe is interested primarily in the politics of human-rights law. However, human-rights politics is influenced by its implicit theory, and the neglect of theory will lead to an inadequate understanding of the politics as well as an insufficient justification of the practice. Forsythe implicitly admits this when he says that for many actors in world politics, the philosophy of human rights matters (Forsythe 1989: 60).

Burke, Bentham and Marx all believed, for different reasons, that declarations of rights such as that of the French Revolution should be severely criticized. Their arguments could be applied to the Universal Declaration of Human Rights (UDHR). It would be irresponsible to assume dogmatically that such arguments are mistaken. Theoretical criticisms of rights declarations require a theoretical response. Practical agreement among those with different theories is certainly desirable in international politics. However, if we wish to understand why such agreements are desirable, how they are possible, and why they are difficult to implement, we should examine the different theories that support or challenge the concept of human rights. Forsythe suggests that human-rights law and practice should be evaluated, not by ideal standards, but by 'real possibilities' (Forsythe 1989: x). Political theorists now sometimes distinguish between 'ideal theory' and 'non-ideal theory'. Ideal theory does not describe reality, but puts forward reasoned argument for certain standards with which to evaluate reality. Non-ideal theory introduces reality, and thereby analyses 'real possibilities'. Ideal theory directs us to the 'real possibilities' that are *worth realizing*. Ideal theory is very practical, therefore. It endorses standards for evaluating practical reality and for guiding our actions. Reality may well limit the pursuit of the ideal quite strictly, but we cannot understand how it does so if we have no conception of the ideal. Forsythe rightly says that the concept of human rights is contested, and that its meaning is established by a never-ceasing process of moral, political and legal debate and review (Forsythe 2006: 253), but the task of human-rights theory is to make available the best arguments for evaluating that process.

Gewirth has given the following arguments for human-rights theory. All claims of human rights assume that they are justified. However, the reasons for this belief are often not clear, and, if they are not clear, we cannot know whether or not they are good reasons. Also, different persons may make conflicting human-rights claims, and, without a theory of human rights, we cannot rationally choose between them. Human-rights theory seeks to answer questions such as the following. Are there any human rights? What is their content and scope? How are they related to each other? Are any of them absolute, or may they all be overridden in certain circumstances (Gewirth 1981)? Donnelly proposes that the theory of human rights must explain the meaning of the concept, its justificatory basis, to which obligations they give rise, and the relation between human rights and other values (Donnelly 1985a: 1). We can give *legal* answers to these questions, but such answers only give rise to the further question as to whether the law is what it ought to be (Griffin 2008: 204). Human-rights law presents the conclusions of certain arguments. Human-rights theory provides the arguments.

While the UDHR was being drafted, UNESCO, the UN cultural organization, undertook an inquiry into the theoretical problems of such a declaration. In his introduction to the published results of this inquiry, Maritain suggested that the diversity of philosophies in the world made a consensus on the justification of human rights impossible. There could be agreement on what human rights there were, but not on why there were these rights. There must, therefore, be different ways to justify human rights philosophically. The different underlying philosophies might well generate disagreement about the proper limits to human rights and the best way to relate human rights to each other. We should, therefore, not expect theoretical agreement, but we could hope for practical agreement (Maritain 1949). Maritain failed to distinguish actual from rational disagreement: actual disagreement is irrational if it arises from errors of fact or logic.

Several UNESCO contributors were concerned with the relation between rights and duties. Mahatma Gandhi suggested that all rights had to be deserved by the performance of corresponding duties (Gandhi 1949). E. H. Carr argued that rights implied duties, because governments could not protect the rights of citizens if citizens failed to support their governments and to provide them with the necessary resources (Carr 1949: 21–2). We shall see that most human-rights theorists now say that the performance of duties is not a *precondition* of human rights, but that human rights entail duties both to respect the human rights of others and to fulfil other moral and social obligations.

Macdonald, in an essay written originally at the time at which the UDHR was being drafted, questioned the concept of natural rights from a positivist point of view. How, she asked, could propositions about natural rights be validated? They could not be verified by empirical observation. Natural-rights theorists claimed that human beings had natural rights because they were rational. Against this Macdonald argued that the supposed fact that human beings were rational did not entail the conclusion that they had natural rights. Nature provided no standards of evaluation; such standards were the product of human choices (Macdonald 1963). Macdonald's argument that natural rights are neither empirically verifiable facts nor deductions from self-evidently true premises clarifies the challenge that a justificatory theory of human rights has to meet. Her conclusion that human rights are the products of human choice, however, leaves them with no justification at all. As a response to Nazism, this is not satisfactory.

The UN introduced the concept of human rights into international law and politics, therefore, at a time when its philosophical justification was very uncertain. This uncertainty was produced both by the historical critique of the concept of natural rights and by the lack of any philosophical consensus on the basis of human rights. Worse, the concept of human rights was called into question by the following arguments, among others.

1. Human rights do not exist in nature: they are human constructions. They are, therefore, neither 'natural' nor 'self-evident', but are morally compelling only if they follow from a morally compelling justificatory argument.
2. Aristotle was right to say that human beings are social animals. A theory of human rights must, therefore, *follow from* and not *precede* a theory of the good society.
3. Since the good of society is prior to the rights of individuals, the duties of individuals to society are prior to the rights of individuals.
4. There are different conceptions of the good society, and there are different conceptions of rights that can be derived from them.
5. International human-rights law is the product of political power, pragmatic agreement and a limited moral

consensus. It has no deeper theoretical justification. Verbal agreement on general principles may conceal disagreement on the meaning and policy implications of those principles.

The justification of human rights has to confront these arguments. This is the task of human-rights theory.

Human-rights theory

Rights

Human rights must be a special kind of rights. They are often contrasted with *legal* rights or *civil* rights that derive from the laws or customs of particular societies. It is commonly said that human rights are the rights one has simply because one is a human being. This is, however, not a satisfactory formulation. It is not clear why one has *any* rights simply because one is a human being. It is particularly unclear why one has the rights listed in the UDHR. Article 21, for example, says that everyone has the right to take part in the government of his country, but one does not have that right because one is a human being, since children do not have this right. Article 22 says that everyone, '*as a member of society*', has the right to social security.

The point of rights discourse, which distinguishes it from other moral discourses, such as those that emphasize duties and/or benevolence, is that, if you have a right to x, and you do not get x, then this is not only wrong, but it is a wrong to *you*. The distinctive value of a right is that it gives the right-holder a special entitlement to press the relevant claims if enjoyment of the right is threatened or denied (Donnelly 1989). Some theorists say that rights must be *enforceable*. One can, however, have a moral right even if it is unenforceable. The Jews in Nazi Germany had moral rights that were unenforceable. The recognition of moral rights that are unenforceable now may help to get them enforced in the future.

Human rights are rights designed to protect morally valid and fundamental human interests. They carry special weight against other claims. Dworkin has famously suggested that rights are 'trumps'. This does not mean that rights always defeat other moral and political considerations; Dworkin's view was that rights 'trump' only 'the routine goals of political administration' (Dworkin 1978: xi, 92). Human rights may be 'trumps' in a stronger sense, in that they override more than routine political policies, but they should not override all other considerations. Article 29 of the UDHR provides for the limitation of human rights to meet 'the just requirements of morality, public order and the general welfare in a democratic society'. This provision is very vague, and seems to provide a worryingly broad permission to limit human rights.

There is a consensus that human rights have three distinctive characteristics: (1) they are universal: everyone has human rights; (2) everyone has them equally; (3) they are the rights of individuals. Each of these characteristics presents challenges to the justificatory theory of human rights. To show that there are universal rights, we must offer plausible, cross-cultural reasons for such rights. To show that everyone is equal in rights, we have to clarify, and to justify, the sense in which everyone is equal. The view that human rights are always the rights of individuals is widely held, but the idea that groups have human rights has recently become influential.

Justifications

Human rights are sometimes justified on the ground that there is an international consensus on such rights in international law (Donnelly 2003: 40–1, 51–3). The apparent consensus on international human-rights law is, however, neither complete nor sincere. There is a consensus neither on such fundamental values as 'autonomy' nor on such specific rights as those of women to gender equality. There is no consensus on human rights even among Western philosophers. Most fundamentally, consensus is a matter of fact, and justifies nothing in the absence of independent reasons showing why the consensus is good. Abizadeh suggests that consensus does not *justify* human rights; it is a means for realizing and sustaining rights (Abizadeh 2007).

Some say that human rights are grounded in human dignity. The concept of human dignity is vague, however, and could provide the basis for moral theories that ignored human rights: in some cultures, affirming the dignity of women challenges the dignity of men. Human rights may be grounded in human dignity, but the justification of human rights must provide arguments that lead us from human dignity to human rights. Some philosophers believe that human rights can be defended by appeal to natural law while avoiding controversial metaphysical claims. Modern natural-law theorists argue that there are objective goods that cannot rationally be rejected, such as life, society and knowledge. These things are good, whether or not this is endorsed by consensus or positive law. These goods are said to be objectively necessary conditions for human flourishing, and consequently the basis of moral obligations. Natural-law theorists claim to reconcile the common good with individual rights, arguing that the common good enhances individual freedom by providing it with stable social conditions, while individual freedom enhances the common good by promoting the flourishing of all (Finnis 1980).

This theory is vulnerable to a number of objections. Claims about objective goods are either too vague to be useful or too controversial to be objective. Even those who agree that there are objective goods do not agree on what those goods are. The claim that the common good has been reconciled with individual rights is asserted, but not demonstrated, and begs many questions about conflicts between individuals and society.

The theory of 'capabilities' has attracted some as a justification of human rights, although it was first introduced to replace the conception of 'development' as the increase of national wealth by a focus on the quality of life (Nussbaum and Sen 1993). A person's capabilities are their abilities to do and be certain things that are fundamentally important to any human life, whatever else the person wants. Each capability is valuable, and there are therefore limits to the extent to which they may be traded against each other. The theory can set some priorities when capabilities conflict by requiring that basic capabilities 'trump' non-basic capabilities (food is more important than play, for example), but it can do this only to a limited extent. In this, however, it is like many accounts of human rights. Like the concept of human rights, that of capabilities is said to be valid cross-culturally. The emphasis on cross-cultural validity means that the list of capabilities is always open to challenge through cross-cultural dialogue. Capabilities theorists argue, however, that liberal freedoms, democratic rights and basic welfare are all required by a plausible account of human flourishing.

The concept of capabilities can be associated with that of human rights in so far as everyone has the right to have their capabilities protected. Both capabilities and human-rights theories hold that governments are the primary bearers of the relevant obligations, although capabilities theory is somewhat less tied than the concept of human rights to the doctrine of international law that such obligations are borne solely, or mainly, by states. Both capabilities and modern human-rights theories are secular, and seek to avoid controversial metaphysical or religious commitments. Capabilities theory is well suited to integrate civil, political, economic, social and cultural rights.

Capabilities theory has been very influential in recent thinking about development, especially at the UN. Its relation to human rights has, however, not been fully elaborated. The theory raises several problems. The most fundamental is that capabilities are (actual or potential) facts about human beings, and their moral status is therefore questionable. It may be, for example, that practical reason is a capability that is necessary for human flourishing, but this capability can be used for good or bad purposes, and we need a different moral theory to distinguish between good and bad capabilities. Since capabilities theory is universalistic and egalitarian (all human beings have and need capabilities, equally), good capabilities are those that do not diminish those of others, and may enhance them. Imagination, for example, is a capability that can be used for art and for torture, but art is friendlier than torture to the capabilities of others. However, even if we can define the good capabilities, the theory of corresponding obligations is undeveloped. Capabilities theory, like the concept of human rights, is a theory of *minimal entitlements* and not of distributive justice in that it cannot tell us what is a *fair* distribution of capabilities (Pogge 2002b; Sen 2005). There are problems of identifying, weighting and prioritizing capabilities. The best way to solve these problems may be context-dependent. This raises the further problem as to whether capabilities provide a basis for criticizing cultures or whether cultures provide the basis for identifying capabilities (Clark 2005: 7).

Gewirth placed the concept of agency at the centre of his theory of human rights. He argued that, although there are diverse moralities in the world, morality itself presupposes agency (purposive action), and all agents must regard the proximate necessary conditions of their actions as necessary goods. These necessary goods are freedom and well-being. Freedom consists of choosing one's actions without external coercion on the basis of adequate information. Well-being consists in having the other general abilities required for agency. All agents must, logically, claim, at least implicitly, rights to freedom and well-being grounded in their needs as agents who want to pursue their purposes.

The necessary goods of action are equally necessary goods for all agents, and so all agents must logically admit that others have as much right to these goods as they do. The rights to freedom and well-being are therefore moral rights, since they require of all agents that they take favourable account of the most important interests of all other agents. It follows that everyone ought to refrain from interfering with the freedom and well-being of everyone else, and that everyone ought to assist others to have freedom and well-being, when they cannot have them by their own efforts, and others can assist them without comparable cost to themselves. Such assistance typically operates best through appropriate institutions.

The rights to freedom and well-being are human rights, since every human being is an actual, prospective or potential agent. The human rights of one person may, however, conflict with those of another person, and one human right of one person may conflict with another human right of the same person. Human rights are, therefore, only *prima facie*, not absolute rights (Gewirth 1981).

Gewirth's argument has been criticized on several grounds: he derives rights invalidly from needs; he does not make clear what necessary goods are necessary for; rights are not *logically*, but *empirically* necessary for action; the assumption of moral equality is Western and liberal, and not inherent in morality; since each agent's 'rights' are prudential not moral, they have no moral obligation to respect the 'rights' of others. Gewirth offers a systematic defence of human rights, but it is not as logically compelling as he claims.

Griffin maintains that we lack adequate criteria for distinguishing valid human rights from bogus rights-claims and other claims. Every human being has a fundamental interest in 'personhood' or 'normative agency': the capacity to choose and pursue their conception of a worthwhile life. This consists of autonomy, minimal welfare and liberty. These are fundamental human interests, and this is an objective fact. Persecuted persons do not lack autonomy (the capacity to choose) but they do lack liberty to pursue their chosen way of life. Poor persons who lack education and leisure lack agency. Personhood generates rights to the minimum necessary to support life as a normative agent. This is a *minimalist* account of human rights in order to leave space for other important moral concepts and not to impose unreasonable burdens on the corresponding duty-bearers. Some supposed 'human rights' in international legal texts may be either too burdensome or too indeterminate. There is not a human right to everything that is desirable (e.g., peace), for human rights must have some possible duty-bearer. Disagreement about human rights may reflect not disagreement about values, but differences in empirical conditions. Human rights are 'universal' in so far as they take account of different conditions and find support in different cultures (Griffin 2008).

Griffin's theory has been criticized on the basis that the value of autonomy lacks the universality necessary to ground human rights: it may reasonably be rejected by someone who believes that a good life is one that is lived in subjection to God or one's community. Griffin accepts that the human-rights tradition is Western, but holds that its values are widely shared outside the West. Raz argues that the concept of 'personhood' is either insufficient to justify human rights – slaves may have minimal 'personhood' – or too indeterminate and thus fails to provide an adequate criterion for human rights (Raz 2010). Griffin rejects this criticism. He admits that his criterion is vague, but maintains that there are levels of deprivation that would clearly amount to denial of human rights. All moral, political and legal principles are somewhat vague: it is the task, not of philosophy, but of legislators, courts and civil society to make them more determinate (Griffin 2010). Buchanan argues that it is precisely the legal specification of human rights that counters the charge of indeterminacy (Buchanan 2014: 19–20). Tasioulas criticizes Griffin's theory on the ground that human rights require a more 'pluralistic' foundation (Tasioulas 2010: 663). Griffin finds this proposal too indeterminate (Griffin 2010: 750–1).

One problem with the agency approach to human rights is that human beings who lack full agency – such as children and mentally disabled people – would be less than equal in rights. Some philosophers accept this conclusion, but insist that others may have strong obligations towards such persons. Others hold that human rights are proportional to the capacity to exercise them. Thus, children have the right not to be tortured, but not to vote. The main rival to agency as the ground of rights is sentience (feeling rather than thinking). This view would condemn torture because it was (unjustifiably) painful rather than because it violated agency. However, sentience does not ground a distinction between human and animal rights (an advantage, some may think), and does not ground the special importance normally given to such rights as freedom of expression and association.

Agency has a complex relation to needs. Some human rights – such as the right to subsistence – seem to be based on needs, but we do not have a right to everything we need, because some of our needs are trivial or immoral. Some have suggested the idea of basic needs as the ground of human rights. There is not, however, a human right to have all basic needs fulfilled, for this may be impossible or too burdensome, for example, the need to be loved. The concept of basic needs is also better suited to the duty of charity to the needy than to the dignity of rights-holders.

There is disagreement as to whether human rights are justified because they are necessary for agency or for human flourishing. Some philosophers prefer the former on the ground that, if human rights are to be universal and realistic, they must be minimal, and thus be restricted to the conditions of a recognizably human life, but not necessarily of a good life. The latter, implied by capabilities theory and perhaps the UDHR, has more ambitious aspirations for human well-being. Nickel argues that human rights set minimal standards for the conduct of governments, and thus leave most policy matters to democratic decision-making, and can accommodate considerable cultural and institutional variation (Nickel 2007: 36–7). Buchanan holds that neither the 'personhood' nor the 'minimal standards' accounts of human rights can explain the prohibitions of discrimination on grounds, for example, of race and gender; 'equal status' must therefore be added to the grounds of human rights (Buchanan 2010).

Attempts to derive human rights from 'human nature' have been subjected to two, quite different, objections. The first is that there are many conceptions of human nature, and there is no agreed method for deciding which is the best. The second is that 'human nature' is a biological concept that cannot generate rights. Yet even the minimalist account of human rights assumes that moral agency is a feature of human nature. There is no account of human nature that is both generally accepted and justifies human rights, but any justification of human rights requires some conception of human nature. Some say that human nature is 'socially constructed', but this presupposes a particular conception of human nature: human beings socially create their nature. This is consistent with the usual theoretical presuppositions of human rights.

There is no consensus on the best justification for human rights, and there is no reason to expect that such a consensus can be achieved. However, the fact that there are several strong justifications for human rights strengthens the moral force of the idea (Nickel 2007: 53–4).

Specification

Human-rights theory should justify the concept of human rights, and provide some guidance as to which claims and rights are human rights. The UDHR is often taken to be an approximately correct list of human rights. Some philosophers who support the concept of human rights do not support the whole of this list. Rawls, for example, held that only Articles 3–18 represent genuine human rights because the other rights are either liberal, and therefore not universalizable, or presuppose particular institutions. Rawls located the concept of human rights in the context of his proposal for a 'law of peoples', which, he argued, should not be based on any particular philosophy of human nature, such as that human beings are moral persons. He did not, however, show that there are cultures which deny that human beings are moral persons nor, if there were such cultures, that they could respect human rights. Rawls offered no theory that would justify his limited set of human rights (Rawls 1999).

The concept of 'basic rights' has been proposed by some theorists who believe that the concept of universal rights might be 'imperialistic', but who do not wish to abandon the idea that governments should observe minimal standards of decent behaviour (Miller, D. 1995). Shue has suggested that basic rights are those that are necessary to other rights, but it is difficult to establish, conceptually or empirically, the necessity of one right to another. For example, although eating is necessary to the enjoyment of the right to free speech, the *right* to eat is not necessary. Also, we might think that the right to eat is more basic than the right to freedom of movement, but, in some circumstances, freedom of movement may be necessary in order to eat (Shue 1996; Nickel 2007: 131–2). The *enjoyment* of the right to subsistence is not necessary to the enjoyment of the right to security, nor is the enjoyment of the right to security necessary to the enjoyment of the right to subsistence (Pogge 2009: 118–19). Donnelly worries that the identification of 'basic rights' may lead to the neglect of other human rights, which are, according to his theory, necessary to a life of dignity (Donnelly 1989: 38–41). Many theorists, therefore, hold that some rights are more basic than others, but there is consensus on neither the justification nor the specification of basic rights.

Philosophers sometimes seek to derive specific rights from more general rights. Griffin, for example, suggests that the general right to autonomy entails several specific human rights, such as the rights to subsistence and education; the general right to freedom entails the rights to freedom of expression and association (Griffin 2008).

Some say that only civil and political rights are genuine human rights because they require only inaction by governments (refraining from torture, for example), and therefore can be fulfilled universally, whereas economic and social rights depend on specific, not universal institutions (such as a welfare state), and are too expensive for some governments to afford. There is no duty to do the impossible, and, if it is impossible to meet some economic and social needs, there can be no *right* to have them met (Cranston 1973). Shue and Donnelly have answered these arguments effectively. Donnelly has pointed out that the distinction between the two types of rights is confused: the right to property is considered a civil right, for example, whereas it could as reasonably be considered an economic right (Donnelly 1989: 30). Shue argues that failure to respect certain basic economic rights, such as the right to subsistence, would render civil and political rights worthless. Both authors also argue that protecting civil and political rights can be expensive (providing fair trials, for example) and that both types may require positive action or inaction by governments. There is thus no basis for treating only civil and political rights as genuine human rights (Shue 1996; Donnelly 1989). Mobilizing resources to implement human rights is a common problem, but it affects civil and political rights as well as social and economic rights.

There is consensus neither on which general rights there are nor on how to derive specific from general rights. Consequently, it is difficult to specify human rights in a very determinate way. This is not necessarily regrettable, for, although it opens a space for the violation of rights, it leaves the determination of human rights to democratic debate and permits flexibility under changing circumstances.

Democracy

The Vienna Declaration of 1993 asserted that democracy and human rights were 'interdependent and mutually reinforcing'. The relations between the two are, however, quite complex. Similar values, such as respect for the dignity of the individual, may form the basis of both human rights and democracy. Where the interpretation of human rights is reasonably contested, democratic resolution of disagreements may be appropriate. Democracies, empirically, generally respect human rights better than other political systems, but they do so imperfectly, and authoritarian regimes may protect economic and social rights quite well. Human rights and democracy, however, have different and potentially competing theoretical foundations. Democratic theory asks who ought to rule, and answers 'the people'. Human-rights theory asks how rulers ought to behave, and answers that they ought to respect the human rights of every individual. Human rights limit the power of all governments, including democratic governments. Human rights are consequently often protected by entrenching them in constitutions. This transfers power from democratically elected political decision-makers to judges, who are usually not democratically elected.

Waldron has made a rights-based critique of the constitutional entrenchment of rights. He argues that, if the value of human rights derives from the dignity of individuals, the outcome of democratic participation by such individuals should have priority over the judgements of courts (Waldron 1993). Dahl argued, similarly, that the people are the best judges of what is good for them, and are, therefore, the safest guardians of their rights. Democracy is, in this sense, prior to rights (Dahl 1989). Dworkin, however, makes a distinction between majoritarian and egalitarian democracy. Majoritarian democracy permits the 'tyranny of the majority', and is a defective form of democracy, since it denies the equality of all citizens. Egalitarian democracy recognizes the equality of all citizens, and therefore entrenches their rights in a constitution to protect them from violation by majorities. The constitutional protection of democratic rights is, according to Dworkin, not undemocratic, because it is intended to protect democratic equality (Dworkin 1978; 1996). This dispute is difficult to resolve, partly because it involves complex empirical questions about the outcomes of court decisions. Most actual democracies entrust the protection of basic rights to independent courts. Courts always have to interpret laws, and, if they defend only the most basic rights, their limitation of democracy is minimal. However, neither courts nor elected legislatures guarantee the defence of human rights or democracy. Some theorists argue that a strongly supportive political culture is a better safeguard for human rights and democracy than specific institutions.

Some human rights, such as the right to vote, are *constitutive of* democracy. Others, such as freedom of speech, are necessary to democracy. Yet others, such as the right to education, are necessary to an adequate democracy. Some human rights, such as freedom of religion, seem more remotely connected to democracy, and perhaps sometimes unfriendly towards democracy. In so far as human rights are necessary to democracy, democratic government must be limited to preserve democracy.

Some believe that *international* or *regional* human-rights law is incompatible with constitutional democracy, because it transfers ultimate authority from elected national legislatures and national judiciaries to unelected and unaccountable international judiciaries and other supposed human-rights experts (Buchanan 2014). Whether this is a valid criticism may depend on the contingent outcomes of an international legal regime.

Other values

Critics of rights discourse sometimes say that there are more important moral values than rights, and that appeal to rights may undermine these values. Parents, for example, should love their children, and children should respect their parents. If parents or children appealed to their rights, this mutual relation of love and respect would be damaged. However, if parents seriously harm their children, then children, or adults acting on their behalf, may appeal to their rights. Rights kick in when other values, which may be ideally superior, fail. A principal justification of rights discourse is that it legitimates challenges to social order, when that order is unjust. Where justice prevails, appeals to rights are unnecessary. This answers the objection that the concept of rights undermines social harmony.

Philosophers sometimes talk of 'rights-based' moralities, and human rights may seem to be an example of such a morality. There are good reasons, however, for rejecting this view. Firstly, if rights form the *basis* of morality, it may not be possible to defend rights against their critics by appeal to more fundamental values. Secondly, rights ought to be balanced with other values, and it would be dogmatic to assume that rights are always more fundamental than other values. We must take account of other values if we are to give a plausible account of the *limits* of rights. The question of whether I have the right to insult another person's religion, for example, cannot reasonably be answered simply by assuming that rights always trump other values, for I should identify and evaluate the moral weight of the other values at issue. Rights are important, but they are not the whole of morality. We can have the right to do something that it is not right to do: to criticize our government unfairly, for example. The relations among rights and other moral values are complex, therefore, even if it is true that human rights are especially important values.

The UDHR says that human rights are the foundations of justice, but it may be that justice is the foundation of human rights. Many theorists now consider respect for human rights to be a requirement of justice, but, in so far as human rights set only minimal standards for society, they cannot fully specify the requirements of justice. A society could respect human rights, yet distribute benefits and burdens unjustly. A theory of justice, therefore, says more than a theory of human rights, but the concept of human rights makes a distinctive contribution to the theory of justice by emphasizing the entitlements of rights-holders rather than, say, the duties of rulers.

Some theories of justice require that rewards be allocated according to desert. Such criteria play no role in the theory of human rights. It may be justifiable to restrict the human rights of wrongdoers, as in the imprisonment of certain criminals, but, although such persons may deserve to be justly punished, they do not deserve to lose their human rights. Human rights do not depend on desert, but it has always been accepted that they do not prohibit just punishment.

Two kinds of theory of justice relevant to human rights have been much discussed recently. The first is transitional justice. This raises questions as to how the 'normal' requirements of social justice should be combined with those of justice for the victims of past injustice or gross human-rights violations. These can conflict, and in practice 'forward-looking' justice is often given priority, controversially, over justice for the victims of human-rights violations (Waldron 1992; Méndez 1997; Thompson 2002). The question first arose in connection with the transitions between various forms of authoritarian regimes and democracy at the end of the twentieth century, but has been extended to such questions as the demand for reparations and/or apologies for such past evils as colonialism and slavery. The second kind of theory of justice that has aroused much controversy recently is the theory of global justice. Most theories of global justice endorse human rights to some extent, but the extent varies from those who favour a narrow conception to those who support something like the UN conception (Rawls 1999; Pogge 2002a). Theories of global justice are controversial, but they are a means to specify human rights.

Obligations and costs

Rights generally entail obligations. These obligations include the obligation to respect (not to violate) rights, the obligation to protect others from violations of their rights, and the obligation to fulfil rights and aid the victims of violations. Shue has argued that the common distinction between negative rights, such as the right not to be tortured, and positive rights, such as the right to food, is mistaken. The right not to be tortured may entail a positive obligation on the government to prevent torture, while the right to food may entail a negative obligation not to interfere with a person's ability to produce their own food. All human rights – civil, political, economic, social and cultural – may entail negative and positive obligations. Contrary to what has commonly been asserted, the obligations entailed by social rights, such as the right to health, do not necessarily cost more than civil and political rights: the right to a fair trial may cost more than some public health measures. It is sometimes said that the right not to be tortured is universal because the duty not to torture is universal. Because the duty to feed the hungry is not universal, the right to food is not universal, and is therefore not a human right. However, the duty not to deprive anyone of necessary food is as universal as the duty not to harm them physically. O'Neill criticizes human rights declarations for failing to specify the corresponding obligations, but Shue, while agreeing that identifying these obligations is essential, argues that they may be quite complex and are partly dependent on empirical information about what best secures human rights (O'Neill 2005; Shue 1996). Thus the philosophical analysis of the duties that follow from human rights shows the need for an interdisciplinary approach by which law is supplemented by the social sciences.

Human rights do not depend on the performance of one's obligations. However, respecting human rights entails the performance of obligations, so that anyone enjoying rights without performing obligations would act unfairly. Obligations involve costs, so that the justification of rights requires the justification of imposing the corresponding costs. Nickel believes that human-rights theorists and activists have paid insufficient attention to the costs of respecting rights because this may require an analysis of priorities competing for scarce resources, which belongs to the discipline of economics, not that of human-rights law. The International Covenant on Economic, Social and Cultural Rights obliges states parties to fulfil the listed rights 'progressively'; these obligations would seem to entail the obligation to develop and implement sound economic policies (Nickel 1993).

There is a controversy as to who has human-rights obligations. The orthodox view (especially of international law) is that only, or mainly, states and their governments have. Classical natural-rights theory, however, held that everyone had such obligations. Article 30 of the Universal Declaration envisages human-rights violations by non-state actors. Concern with powerful non-state actors, such as transnational corporations, and feminist analysis of the private sphere as one in which the rights of women are violated, has led to a new view that human-rights obligations should be extended to various non-state actors. It may be countered that the state has the primary obligation to prevent human-rights violations by private corporations and to protect women. There is also a question as to whether, if the concept of human rights is extended to private harms, it would cover a wide range of crimes, and lose its distinctiveness. States are usually thought to have human-rights obligations mainly to their own citizens, but states do have obligations to non-citizens, although the extent of these obligations remains controversial. If the primary obligation-bearers are unable or unwilling to fulfil their obligations, others may have an obligation to assist or to take over the responsibility, but these actors will have other obligations, and it is difficult to say how these different obligations should be prioritized. Most philosophers require us to make only limited sacrifices for the sake of others, but they generally agree that the sacrifices we actually make are less than those that we ought to make.

O'Neill believes that human-rights discourse fails the neediest because it fails to identify who is obliged to do what for whom (O'Neill 2005: 40). Rights must specify corresponding duties. Human welfare rights fail to do this. Welfare duties are borne by *institutions*. Because these institutions are not universal, the rights they fulfil are not human rights. Ashford argues, to the contrary, that *all* rights may need institutions to be effective: the right not to be tortured requires not only that individuals refrain from torture, but also that institutions ensure that they do so. The case for welfare rights derives from their contribution to human dignity. Institutions are necessary for their realization but not for their existence. The causes of both torture and starvation may be complex, and may involve a complex set of duties. If the causes of human-rights violations are complex, those who are involved in the causation share responsibility if they either knew about the violations or were culpably ignorant of them, and could have avoided them (Ashford 2006). Pogge argues that the rich and powerful are primarily responsible for the international order, which is the 'decisive' cause of human-rights violations, and therefore they bear the primary responsibility for reforming that order for the sake of human rights (Pogge 2005a: 31; 2007).

The provision of international law that states may derogate from some of their human-rights obligations in national emergencies recognizes that the cost of protecting human rights can be excessive. This provision is nevertheless controversial both because the concept of 'national emergency' is vague and because the distinction between derogable and non-derogable rights conflicts with the principle that human rights are indivisible. International law allows no restrictions of human rights in dangerous situations that fall short of national emergencies.

Conflicts of rights

Because human rights derive from interests, require resources and are indeterminate, they can conflict. Steiner argues that conflicts of rights lead to intolerable arbitrariness, and that rights therefore should be 'compossible', that is, only a theory of rights that avoids conflicts is rational. His theory of rights, however, recognizes only rights to private property that exclude most of the economic and social rights recognized by the UN (Steiner 1994). His critics complain that his theory would allow an intolerable 'trumping' of basic human rights by property rights. Most theorists of human rights acknowledge that conflicts between human rights are possible, and Article 29 of the UDHR does so.

Such conflicts are of two main kinds. The human rights of some may conflict with those of others and/or one right may conflict with another right of the same person. My right to security may conflict with others' right to a fair trial and/ or my right to freedom of movement. Apparent conflicts of rights may sometimes be resolved by carefully specifying the scope of rights. The right to freedom of speech, for example, would not conflict with the right not to be subject to racial abuse, if the former were specified to exclude the right to express some forms of abuse (Jones 1994: 199–201).

Conflicts of rights may be resolved by assigning them differential importance and determining priorities. It is difficult, however, to do this systematically without transforming human rights into a calculus of interests. One objection to this is that the required calculation simply cannot be made. Another approach is 'the utilitarianism of rights', which requires conflicts of rights to be resolved in whichever way maximizes the protection of rights. This is subject to a criticism commonly made of ordinary Utilitarianism: that it sacrifices some for the good of others. A better approach may be to respect all rights, but, when some sacrifice is unavoidable, to distribute the sacrifice fairly. This may be indeterminate, but it refuses to treat the human rights of some merely as means to the good of others. Those who ground human rights in agency give priority to those rights that are most important to agency: the right not to starve would, for example, have priority over the right to holidays with pay (Gewirth 1982). This is theoretically coherent, but it offers no resolution of conflicts between equally important rights. Those who believe that they can identify 'basic rights' would hold that, to secure basic rights, other rights may be violated, if necessary, but basic rights may not be violated to secure other rights. We have seen, however, that the concept of 'basic rights' is controversial. It may be that no theory of human rights can resolve all conflicts of rights. Life presents us with dilemmas, and human-rights theory cannot change this.

Although the concept of human rights is usually thought to be incompatible with the philosophy of Utilitarianism, because the latter would sacrifice human rights for the sake of maximizing utility, Jones has suggested that rule-Utilitarianism might rescue human-rights theory from the dilemmas of rights conflicts. Rule-Utilitarianism says that we ought to live by those rules that best promote the common good. Rule-Utilitarianism would tell us not to violate the human rights of one person to protect the human rights of others because this would violate a justified rule, and rule-Utilitarianism says that this should not be done even if, in the short run, it did more good than harm (Jones 1994: 203–4). This is a plausible solution for those who believe that the human rights of some should never be violated to protect the human rights of a larger number of others, but it is not certain that we should always take this position.

Objections to human rights

The move from 'natural' to 'human' rights eliminated some of the objections to the former in so far as the objections were to arguments from 'nature'. Nevertheless some of the objections to natural rights have been made to the concept of human rights: it is too dogmatic; too absolutist; too individualistic; it lacks philosophical foundations; it stimulates expectations unrealistically and thereby promotes social conflict and disorder; it ignores the importance of responsibilities and marginalizes the value of community; it cannot resolve conflicting values; it is too legalistic and formalistic, thereby failing to address real suffering and injustice. Those who do not necessarily reject the concept complain of 'rights inflation', which trivializes rights, imposes unreasonable burdens on duty-bearers and excessive constraints on freedom, restricts the scope of democratic politics, limits the role of toleration and pluralism, and undermines valuable social relations such as those of the family.

In the 1990s human rights were challenged by 'communitarian' philosophers (Caney 1992; Mulhall and Swift 1996). These philosophers criticized liberalism for overvaluing individual autonomy and undervaluing community. It is mistaken, however, to see human rights and community as mutually exclusive. Some communities violate human rights, but others protect them. Some human rights refer explicitly to the value of community, while others, such as the right to freedom of expression, are best interpreted as requiring communities of an appropriate kind (Gewirth 1996). Communitarians raised complex issues, and not all their ideas are compatible with human rights, but the supposed incompatibility between human rights and community is often overstated. For example, persecution and poverty undermine communities and family life, and better protection of human rights could strengthen the solidaristic values that 'communitarians' like to defend. We should also remember that the value of 'community' often hides cruelty and injustice (especially towards women and children) that should not be defended.

Conclusion

The concept of human rights is often criticized because it is 'individualistic', emphasizes rights *rather than* responsibilities, and encourages selfishness. Locke's classical theory of natural rights, however, was based on natural law that imposed an obligation on everyone to respect the rights of others. The concept of rights can be used selfishly, but all concepts can be abused: the concept of duty, for example, can be used by the powerful to control the weak. Rights advocates often fight for the rights of others, and are, in doing that, not acting selfishly. Article 29 of the UDHR assumes that everyone has social duties, and Gewirth argues that the concept of human rights entails duties to communities that sustain human rights (Gewirth 1996). It is sometimes said that the concept of human rights presupposes the concept of the non-social individual. However, the concept of human rights is primarily the basis of a theory of legitimate government. Thus, the concept is so far from being non-social that it is primarily a *political* concept.

The UDHR states that recognition of human rights is the foundation of justice in the world. The relation between human rights and justice has proved to be controversial, however. Liberal theorists of justice have argued that the concept of justice is more fundamental than that of human rights, and theories of justice can say more about how rights should be allocated than the concept of human rights can. The theory of justice can, nevertheless, find an important place for human rights. Some theorists believe that whether a human-rights claim is valid or not depends on whether it is endorsed by justice. In contrast, Donnelly has argued that the concept of human rights is clearer and less controversial than that of justice (Donnelly 1982). In practice, the concept of human rights may be less controversial than any *particular* theory of international justice, and therefore politically more useful. However, we have seen that many aspects of human rights are very controversial. Liberal theories of justice usually endorse human rights. In so far as the justification of human rights is based on the claim that they are required by justice, we need a theory of justice to justify human rights. It is a matter of practical judgement rather than theory whether a rights-based or justice-based approach to international politics is more effective.

A common objection to the concept of human rights is that rights cannot be derived from nature, but only from the culture and institutions of particular societies. This objection has been made to at least some of the rights in the UDHR. Jones points out that Article 22 says that 'everyone' has the right to social security and to realization, *in accordance with the organization and resources of each state*, of the economic, social and cultural rights indispensable for their dignity. He suggests that Article 22 sets out citizens' rights rather than human rights (Jones 1994: 160–3). This should be read, however, as a statement of universal rights that allows the implementation of the rights to vary according to the organization and resources of different states. In so far as human rights have limits, society sets those limits, and in this sense human rights must be socially and therefore variably specified (Jones 1994: 192–4). Article 29 of the UDHR allows that human rights may be limited by law for certain purposes, though, unfortunately, the wording of this provision is exceptionally vague.

Rights derive from rules governing the relations among human beings. In this sense, rights are essentially social. This is consistent with the idea that rights empower rights-holders. Power is a social relation, and legitimate power is restrained by rules that protect rights. The empowerment of rights-holders is, however, the distinctive feature of rights as a concept. To emphasize human rights rather than human duties is to emphasize the moral worth of the rights-holder without denying that the moral status of human individuals also entails duties to others. The concept of human rights demands respect for human individuals as moral agents and concern for them as vulnerable creatures. It is neither egoistic nor anti-social. It denies neither individual responsibility nor the value of community. It is a concept that affirms human solidarity while respecting individual autonomy. Maritain and Forsythe may be right to say, that, given the religious and philosophical diversity of the world, and the 'essentially contested' nature of philosophy itself, consensus on the 'philosophical foundations' of human rights may be impossible to achieve. There is probably no single philosophical foundation of human rights, but, rather, different human rights may have different justifications, and the very concept of human rights may have various justifications. This is not a serious blow to the concept of human rights, however, because the very idea of philosophical foundations is problematic. There are various strong reasons for supporting human rights, based on respect for human dignity (Donnelly), the bases of moral action (Gewirth), the protection of normative agency (Griffin), the demands of human sympathy (Rorty), or the conditions of human flourishing (Nussbaum). It has been doubted whether a consensus on human rights can be based on a consensus on liberalism in the foreseeable future, but it may be that a 'consensus' may be based on diverse grounds, while the best arguments for human rights are liberal arguments. Human rights do not constitute the whole of morality or politics: they have to be balanced with other values, such as social order. They are not absolute, for human rights can conflict with each other. The moral and humanitarian case for assigning the concept of human rights to a leading role in political theory is, however, very powerful.

Human rights are therefore not 'natural', although they must rest on a conception of human nature and well-being. Nevertheless, they are 'social constructions', and they are as 'valid' as the reasons for supporting them are strong. Talbott has questioned what he calls 'the proof paradigm', which requires that all justified beliefs be rationally beyond question. The fact that human rights are not beyond question does not make them morally invalid, or more doubtful than many other beliefs that it is reasonable to hold (Talbott 2005: 23). The distinction that is commonly made between the individualism of rights and the good of society is misleading in that the concept of human rights entails a conception of how the good of individuals is best reconciled with the good of society. The distinction between rights-based and duty-based theories is also misleading in that a theory of human rights must also be a theory of duties. The *justification* of human rights should be distinguished from *consensus* about human rights, because the consensus is worth supporting only if the justification is compelling. The concept of human rights is a basis for articulating the wrongs done to individuals by unjust and oppressive abuses of power. It gives rise to a number of moral dilemmas and philosophical puzzles, but the moral force of its core meaning remains extremely powerful and deservedly influential.

5
Putting Law in its Place
The Role of the Social Sciences

Introduction: human rights and social science

The concept of human rights originated in theology, philosophy and law. The concept of natural rights was first developed from Roman law in the late Middle Ages to provide a theological defence of property, then both to defend and condemn European imperialism, and, in the seventeenth century, to defend property and what we now call civil and political rights against absolute, monarchical government. This concept was *normative*: it prescribed how people were permitted and obliged to behave. The contemporary concept of human rights has inherited this normative character: it is designed primarily to prescribe to governments what they ought and ought not to do. Between the French Revolution and the establishment of the United Nations, the concept of natural rights was challenged by the philosophy of scientific positivism that strongly influenced the emerging social sciences. According to this philosophy, science is not normative: it does not tell people how they ought to live. The tension between the concept of human rights and social science became apparent in 1947, when the Executive Board of the American Anthropological Association submitted a statement to the UN Commission on Human Rights expressing concern that a universal declaration of human rights might show insufficient respect to the different cultures of the world

(American Anthropological Association Executive Board 1947). The statement was criticized within anthropology on the ground that the Association, as a scientific organization, should not speak about human rights, for there was no scientific approach to human rights (Barnett 1948).

Human rights law bridges the gap between the normative concept of human rights and social science. Law is normative in that it prescribes rights and duties. Social science can, however, study why and how human-rights law is made, and why and how it is or is not implemented. The interpretive social sciences can supplement the legal discourse of human rights by explaining how human-rights problems are understood in different cultural contexts. Interpretive social science bridges the gap between legal abstractions and the everyday lives of the ordinary people they claim to defend.

The legalization of human rights is often the best way to implement them, but it is neither necessary nor sufficient. Sometimes law can achieve what morality cannot. To benefit from human rights, however, people need secure access to what they offer, not legal rights as such. The legalization of human rights may even hinder their implementation if it provides formal institutionalization without effective protection (Nickel 2007: 50–1, 92–3; Pogge 2005a: 13–14).

Some social scientists have studied empirically the actions and impact of those involved with human-rights law, such as governments, inter-governmental organizations and non-governmental organizations. A problem with this approach is that the meaning of human-rights law is problematic: when lawyers, philosophers and social scientists speak about 'human rights', they may not always be speaking about the same thing. A social science of human-rights law that is not informed by philosophy could therefore be misleading.

The dominance and critique of law

Before the 1970s almost all academic work on human rights was done by lawyers, and most articles were published in law journals. A survey of journals published between the early 1970s and the mid-1980s conducted by the UN

Economic, Social and Cultural Organization (UNESCO) found that almost all human-rights journals were predominantly legal, and that the social sciences contributed little to other journals that carried articles on human rights. Several surveys on the teaching of human rights in universities have shown that the legal perspective is overwhelmingly dominant. The legal approach to human rights cannot, however, adequately analyse the ethical, political, sociological, economic and anthropological dimensions of human rights. Human-rights law has social and political origins, and social and political consequences, and legal analysis cannot help us to understand these. Social science has substantive interests and research methods that are quite different from those of legal studies, and that can illuminate the practice of human rights (Pritchard 1989). The social sciences have, however, until recently largely neglected human rights.

Lawyers make *judgements* as to whether human rights have been respected or violated. Social scientists seek to *explain* why human rights have been respected or violated. Judgemental disciplines sometimes make assumptions about the measures that will improve respect for human rights. Social scientists test causal hypotheses empirically, and can thereby contribute to effective policy-making.

Political philosophers have long argued that politics should be subject to the rule of law, and that law stands above the politics of interests and power. However, in so far as law places limits on government, it is political. Law cannot abolish power, but it can conceal or legitimate it. International human-rights law has been criticized because it rests on the fiction of universal equality, and, by masking structural inequalities, conceals the causes of many human-rights violations. It can have a partial autonomy, and thereby provide justice to those subject to power, but this autonomy is never complete. Law appears to be impartial and objective, but this may be illusory. This illusion is appealing, because it seems to provide certainty in an uncertain world. The certainty is also illusory, however, because the interpretation and application of law is contested both legally and politically. The existence, nature, interpretation and implementation of human-rights law unavoidably raise contentious political questions.

The empirical evidence as to whether law protects human rights is mixed. Keith, in a study of the period 1977–96, found that constitutional provisions for freedom of speech, assembly, association, religion and the press generally produced no observable improvement in human-rights behaviour. However, provisions for fair trials did lead to an improvement in personal integrity rights. The evidence suggested that constitutional protection of human rights had less effect than lawyers and activists assumed, but more than sceptics believed (Keith 2002). Blasi and Cingranelli, however, found that constitutions did have a positive effect on human rights if they provided for appropriate institutions, such as an independent judiciary (Blasi and Cingranelli 1996).

Moravcsik found that the success of the European human-rights regime resulted from a combination of a free civil society and an independent judiciary. The regime did not liberalize illiberal regimes; it improved the human-rights records of democratic regimes that already had good records. The most effective institutions for international human-rights implementation rely on prior ideological and institutional support. Human-rights implementation is most difficult when it is most needed. Comparison between the European and the American human-rights regimes shows that consensus on human-rights values is more important than institutions in protecting human rights (Moravcsik 1995: 158–9, 178–82).

Hathaway claims that international lawyers are reluctant to assess systematically whether human-rights law is effective. She found that the human-rights practices of countries that have ratified human-rights treaties are generally better than those of countries that have not. However, non-compliance with treaty obligations is common, and countries with the worst human-rights records often have high rates of ratification. Treaty ratification is often associated with *worse* human-rights practices. Since enforcement of human-rights treaties is extremely weak, and states can gain some prestige from ratifying them, treaty ratification may be a *substitute for* improving human rights. Some claim that human-rights treaties have diffuse, positive effects that cannot easily be measured, but the long-term effects of ratification are unknown. Hathaway concludes that declarations of rights that are not easily defined and measured, and are not accompanied by an effective means for securing remedies for violations, may be counter-productive. Efforts to secure universal ratification of human-rights treaties are therefore problematic (Hathaway 2002). Goodman and Jinks have challenged Hathaway's findings on methodological grounds (Goodman and Jinks 2003). Keith found that, although states that ratified the International Covenant on Civil and Political Rights (ICCPR) had better records than non-ratifiers, economic and political factors, not ratification itself, explained this difference (Keith 1999).

Neumayer found that ratification of human-rights treaties had a beneficial effect in conditions of democracy and a strong civil society. In the absence of these conditions, treaty ratification had no effect, and might be associated with more human-rights violations (Neumayer 2005). Hafner-Burton and Tsutsui found that states which ratify more human-rights treaties are not more likely to protect human rights than states which ratify a small number of treaties. Ratifiers are, indeed, more likely to violate human rights than non-ratifiers. States that ratified the ICCPR and the Convention Against Torture were not more likely to implement the rights set out in these treaties. Neither treaty had a systematic effect on the human-rights behaviour of repressive states even 15 years after ratification. Thus the argument that ratification takes time to have an effect is not supported (Hafner-Burton and Tsutsui 2007). They also found that ratification had either no effect or an adverse effect on human-rights performance, although states with more international NGOs (INGOs) were more likely to respect the human rights of their citizens than states with fewer INGOs (Hafner-Burton and Tsutsui 2005). Landman concluded that there was strong empirical support for a limited effect of international human-rights law on state behaviour (Landman 2005a: 6, 137, 146–7). Simmons found that ratification of human-rights treaties sometimes had positive effects on the executive branch of government, legislatures, judiciaries and civil society, especially in countries that are neither autocratic nor fully democratic, but where there is space for public debate about human-rights reforms. She found also that some human rights are harder to implement than others for various reasons, not only because of scarce resources (Simmons 2009).

Cole found that states which agreed that complaints about human-rights violations could be submitted to treaty-monitoring committees generally improved their records after ratifying treaties. He concluded that ratification combined with monitoring can improve the effectiveness of a human-rights treaty. His investigation was confined to civil and political rights (Cole 2012). Hill found that states that ratified the Convention Against Torture were *more* likely to practise torture than non-ratifiers, and engaged in worse torture practices. By contrast, the Convention on the Elimination of Discrimination Against Women had a positive effect on women's political rights, but no effect on their economic rights (Hill 2010). The Convention can facilitate international solidarity for women's rights and can be useful for courts minded to advance these rights (Nussbaum 2016).

International human-rights law may conflict with politics. Human-rights advocates support prosecutions to end impunity for human-rights crimes and deter further violations. Rodman argues, however, that international criminal tribunals cannot deter human-rights crimes in the midst of conflict. The experience of the former Yugoslavia and the recent indictment of Sudan's President, Omar al-Bashir, by the International Criminal Court (ICC) for war crimes and crimes against humanity in Darfur show that prosecution cannot deter violations if the co-operation of the perpetrator is necessary for peace. In Bosnia, Kosovo, Rwanda and Sierra Leone force not law stopped the violence. Flint and de Waal argue that the arrest and prosecution of Bashir is unlikely because domestic opposition to his regime is weak and the international community is unwilling to use force. China, Russia, Arab and many African states have economic and political interests in supporting Bashir, and against these the ICC has little power. Flint and de Waal believe that the only solution to Sudan's political conflicts is a compromise power-sharing deal. In conflicts such as that in Darfur, politics overwhelms law. International criminal tribunals can contribute to improved respect for human rights, but only if combined with politics (Rodman 2008; Flint and de Waal 2008).

The recent development of international criminal tribunals for the former Yugoslavia and Rwanda, and the establishment of the ICC, have precedents in the trials after the Second World War in Nuremberg and Tokyo. International tribunals have both advantages and disadvantages compared with national tribunals. International tribunals may conform better with international standards for fair trials. National courts may have both more legitimacy and more impact with the people concerned. Human-rights advocates support criminal tribunals for human-rights crimes in principle, but states may sometimes favour them as cheap concessions by realism to idealism, a middle way between high-risk interventions and doing nothing (Rudolph 2001; Barria and Roper 2005: 358). The ICC was established in 1998. The USA has opposed the court and taken measures to prevent it from trying any US citizen. The court became fully operational in June 2003 and began its first trial – of Congolese militia leader, Thomas Lubanga – in January 2009. The court has no police force, and generally must rely on the co-operation of the governments in whose countries it is operating. It is also dependent on international support for funding, intelligence and evidence, the arrest of suspects and pressure on recalcitrant governments. Often that support is not forthcoming. The ICC has been criticized on the grounds that (1) it gives dictators an incentive to cling to power; (2) it obstructs peace negotiations; (3) it has concentrated excessively on Africa. It is defended on the grounds that (1) it provides justice to victims and the international community; (2) it deters would-be human-rights violators; (3) African states have brought cases to the court, and Africans are well represented in key court posts. It has been said that the court makes more impact in international legal and political circles than in the countries in which human-rights violations have occurred (Arnould 2016). On the value of the court the jury is still out.

Because international and national tribunals have different advantages and disadvantages, hybrid tribunals, with national and international components, have been tried in Sierra Leone, Kosovo, East Timor and Cambodia. Finding a satisfactory combination of the merits of international and national courts can, however, be difficult. Some national courts assert 'universal jurisdiction' over the most serious violators. The 1999 case concerning the extradition of the former Chilean President, Augusto Pinochet, in London set an important precedent for this approach. However, while universal jurisdiction exists in limited form in some treaties and national laws, it has gone into relative decline.

Some worry that human-rights trials are political 'show trials'. Wilson has argued, however, that the charge of genocide enabled the tribunal for the former Yugoslavia to combine a fair trial with a broad, historical narrative (Wilson 2011). In contrast, Futamura doubts whether the Tokyo trial gave an adequate account of the Second World War in Asia, and also whether its mixture of collective political aims and individual legal responsibility has helped the Japanese people to come to terms with their past (Futamura 2008). In Cambodia, although the trials took many years to establish, and some of the worst perpetrators had died, there is evidence that surviving victims felt that justice too little and too late was much better than no justice at all.

Some argue that, although law can protect the human rights of the poor, their problems may not require legal solutions, law may oppress rather than liberate them, legal reforms intended to benefit them may not be implemented and/or they may find it difficult to access the courts. The UN Development Programme estimates that more than four billion people, or as much as two-thirds of the world's population, live outside the rule of law. There is, therefore, a need for legal empowerment of the poor. The legal-empowerment approach may have limits: for example, women's rights in areas dominated by Afghan warlords. Legal procedures may obscure the structural causes of violations and the best remedies. Nevertheless, a combination of human-rights education, popular social movements and legal action may offer the best hope for the powerless. External assistance can facilitate local initiatives.

Human-rights tribunals, international and national, have been part of 'transitional justice'. In transitions from repressive to democratic regimes policies on the prosecution of violators have varied. In some countries nothing has been done about past violations; in others violators have been given amnesties. Where there have been trials, sentences have sometimes been light. Truth commissions have sometimes been set up as alternatives to trials, but sometimes they have been combined with trials. One problem with combining truth commissions with trials is that truth commissions may need the co-operation of violators, and violators are not likely to co-operate if they face trial.

The nature of the transition is likely to influence the adoption and nature of transitional justice: negotiated transitions are likely to lead to weak or no transitional justice, whereas the take-over of collapsed regimes is likely to encourage more severe measures. The balance of forces determining whether trials and/or truth commissions are held may change over time, so that transitional justice is sometimes delayed for years. The UN has had no consistent policy on the punishment of human-rights violators. It set up criminal tribunals for Yugoslavia and Rwanda, but required none for South Africa, even though it had often condemned apartheid. Transitional justice began with the end of the military regimes of the late twentieth century in Latin America, spread to Africa, most notably with the Truth and Reconciliation Commission in South Africa, and to Asia. It has played little role in Europe, although, in some former Communist countries, 'lustration', the barring from office of former Communist officials, has been introduced, often controversially.

Between 1974 and 2009 approximately 40 truth commissions were established in all regions of the world and in various political contexts; 21 of these were established in the decade 1999–2009. The 'truth' of truth commissions is not the same as that of criminal trials: the looser rules of evidence at truth commissions mean that more truth can be told but more of what is told may not be true. This is particularly problematic if alleged perpetrators are named without a fair trial. Truth commissions can go beyond questions of individual guilt to the structural causes of violations and recommendations for institutional reform. Truth commissions can give a voice to the victims, and, it is claimed, treat them with more sympathy and dignity than criminal courts, where they may be subject to hostile cross-examination. They may also award reparations, although their record in this is not generous. Truth commissions vary considerably in their mandates and their resources, but most have limited resources, especially of time. Truth commissions have been favoured because they counter denials, acknowledge the wrongs done to victims, and are thought to be less divisive than criminal trials. They have been criticized for failing to deliver justice, while their supposed contribution to reconciliation and stability has been doubted (Hayner 2011). Wiebelhaus-Brahm found that, statistically, truth commissions had negative consequences for physical integrity rights, although further analysis showed complex positive and negative consequences (Wiebelhaus-Brahm 2010).

Snyder and Vinjamuri investigated empirically whether prosecutions deter further human-rights violations. They doubt whether they do. The tribunals for the former Yugoslavia and Rwanda did not deter subsequent gross human-rights violations in the former Yugoslavia and central Africa, while formal or tacit amnesties curbed violations in El Salvador, Mozambique, Namibia, South Africa and Afghanistan. They argue that, if democrats do not dominate anti-democrats, prosecution of human-rights violators increases the risk of violent conflict and further human-rights violations, and hinders the institutionalization of the rule of law. Trials are most effective in stable democracies with a well-institutionalized rule of law, that is, when they are least needed to prevent human-rights violations. Human-rights campaigns against 'impunity' may, therefore, often be bad for human rights (Snyder and Vinjamuri 2003–4).

This argument has been challenged empirically by Sikkink and Walling. They point out that Latin America has the longest experience with human-rights trials, and they have neither undermined democracy nor led to an increase in human-rights violations. Trials have been held in countries with the worst human-rights violations: in most cases, human rights *improved* after the trials. The more trials that were held, the more human rights improved. Trials are positively associated with human rights, independently of the level of democracy. There is no evidence that trials exacerbated conflict. Where transitions took place without trials, human rights *worsened*. There is no evidence that amnesties *caused* human-rights improvements, even where, as in El Salvador, both are found together. We do not know whether the Latin American experience could be repeated elsewhere, but the sceptical view of trials has been excessively influenced by a small number of cases and a short time-frame (Sikkink and Walling 2007).

Another recent development in efforts to implement human rights has been the establishment of national human-rights institutions (NHRIs). These are governmental, administrative bodies whose purpose is to promote and protect human rights. NHRIs vary considerably, but, among their activities, they advise governments; encourage treaty ratifications; review proposed legislation; assist governments in preparing state reports for treaty bodies; work with governments in devising national human-rights action plans; investigate and document complaints; monitor violations; make recommendations for the resolution of particular cases (including remedies for wrongs) or for legislative reform; raise neglected issues; criticize governments; engage in human-rights education; help victims of human-rights violations to seek legal redress; refer human-rights cases to national tribunals; intervene in litigation; and contribute to the development of human-rights jurisprudence. They do not usually have the power to make binding decisions, but they may be useful where the judiciary is ineffective.

By mid-2012 115 states had created an NHRI, a fourfold increase since the early 1990s; over 60 more had agreed to establish one or had taken steps to do so; only 15 states had resisted this trend. NHRIs work under guidelines adopted by the UN General Assembly in 1993, known as the 'Paris Principles'. In 1993 an International Co-ordinating Committee of National Human Rights Institutions, endorsed by the UN Commission on Human Rights, was established. The UN Human Rights Council allows participation by NHRIs in its Universal Periodic Review; NHRIs are also active in the work of human-rights treaty bodies and 'special procedures'.

It is difficult to evaluate NHRIs because of their diversity and complexity. NHRIs may play a useful role in areas of the world lacking a regional human-rights regime, such as Asia. They may, however, be weakest where they are most needed, and, at worst, may be public-relations exercises for repressive governments. They are probably most effective in democracies as one component in a complex of governmental and non-governmental institutions designed to protect human rights. Nevertheless, NHRIs may have some success in countries with weak human-rights institutions, especially in transitions to democracy. Under favourable political conditions they can promote human rights in a way that links international human-rights law with national contexts. NHRIs may be more accessible than courts, but accessibility varies: those who most need access to a NHRI – for example the rural poor and indigenous populations – may have the least access. NHRIs have improved respect for human rights in some places and in some respects, but they have generally had little impact on serious human-rights violations (Cardenas 2014).

International human-rights law is inherently political. Decisions to hold or not to hold human-rights trials are always politically motivated. Law plays a role in human-rights promotion, but understanding that role requires political analysis.

Political science

Political science neglected human rights between the adoption of the Universal Declaration in 1948 and the mid-1970s, except for some descriptive studies. This neglect is explained by two main influences on the discipline: Realism and positivism. Realism taught that politics was overwhelmingly the pursuit of power and that ethical considerations, such as human rights, played at most a marginal role. Positivism taught that social scientists should eliminate ethical judgements from their work because they were unscientific. This situation began to change in the 1970s as human rights became more salient in international politics. A recent study of leading political-science journals calculated that only 34 articles on human rights were published before 1980; 36 were published in the 1980s; 60 in the 1990s; and 459 between 2000 and August 2008. Nevertheless, since the end of the Cold War only about 2 per cent of articles in these journals have been about human rights, and most of these have been in only two journals. Thus the study of human rights in political science has increased but remains marginal (Cardenas 2009).

In 1976 Claude argued that human rights could not be understood by the analysis only of legal processes. Social scientists should investigate the social forces underlying human-rights development. This would involve both historical and comparative approaches. Claude described the 'classical' pattern of human-rights development in France, Britain and the USA. He argued that, in the process of the development of a mature human-rights regime, four problems must be solved: the securing of political freedom; the guarantee of legal rights; the establishment of equal rights to political participation; and the recognition and implementation of social and economic rights.

Claude developed several empirical hypotheses from his comparative historical analysis.

1. The more people engaged in private economic activity, the more likely were legal guarantees for freedom of expression.
2. The stronger the demand for citizenship equality, the stronger the state became.
3. The more elites competed for support, the more they would encourage popular participation and civic equality rights.
4. The more poor people participated in politics, the more likely the implementation of economic and social rights.

The 'classical' model, therefore, proposed that the emergence of private, capitalist economies provided an economic basis for the institutionalization of human-rights law. The development of a mature human-rights regime involved the sequential introduction of three forms of decision-making: market exchange that required legal security; bargaining that extended rights to new social forces; and central decisions to regulate and administer an increasingly complex set of rights. Human rights developed in these countries in a context of relatively gradual social and economic change, and conclusions drawn from the study of these processes might well not apply to those countries that were undergoing or at least attempting rapid change. Claude suggested that this might lead to more centralized decision-making that would prevent the emergence of a human-rights regime according to the classical model (Claude 1976). In the same volume Strouse and Claude found by statistical analysis that rapid economic development had a negative effect on political rights. They concluded that developing countries often faced painful trade-off dilemmas between the protection of civil and political rights, on the one hand, and rapid economic growth, on the other hand (Strouse and Claude 1976).

Donnelly examined the relation between economic development and human rights with a different method. He identified three supposed trade-offs in this relation. The *needs* trade-off sacrificed basic needs to investment. The *equality* trade-off is based on the belief that great inequality is necessary to rapid economic development. The *liberty* trade-off assumes that political rights encourage populist policies that obstruct economic growth. Donnelly tested the proposition that such trade-offs are necessary to economic development by a comparative study of Brazil and South Korea.

South Korea achieved more rapid economic growth than Brazil between 1960 and 1980 with much less inequality and relatively good protection of economic and social rights. This case refutes the hypothesis that the needs and equality trade-offs are necessary for rapid economic development. South Korea's record of civil and political human-rights violations during this period was, however, very bad. This shows that political repression may accompany economic development but not that it is necessary. Donnelly argued that repression may lead to a crisis of legitimacy as, for example, in Indonesia: the liberalization and democratization of developed authoritarian societies may therefore help to stabilize them (Donnelly 1989: 163–202). Liberalization and democratization may, however, sometimes be destabilizing, as the cases of the USSR and Yugoslavia show.

In 1986 Gurr showed how positivism could be used to study problems related to human rights. He by-passed the problem that human rights is a normative concept by studying state violence. He did this by using a model of regimes and their challengers. He treated violence as one of many policy options for states seeking to establish and maintain their authority. He then put forward 14 hypotheses about the state, its challengers, ethnicity and class, and the global environment. Examples of these hypotheses are: the greater the threat posed by challengers, the more likely the state is to use violence; the greater the ethnic diversity and the social inequality, the more likely the state is to use violence; states facing external threats are more likely to use violence internally (Gurr 1986). Gurr left the relations among the hypotheses unclear. For example, threats to the state tend to increase state violence, but democratic institutions tend to reduce state violence. Gurr did not explain what happens if there is a great threat to a democratic state. The hypotheses also do not explain the dynamic of violence. For example, in the former Yugoslavia, ethnic diversity may have been correlated with state violence, but this explains very little about what happened in that society after the fall of the Communist regime.

Foweraker and Landman asked how social movements establish rights regimes. Social movements do not necessarily improve rights: they can provoke increased repression. States may, however, seek to buy legitimacy by granting rights. Rights are guaranteed best by the combination of active non-governmental organizations and an independent, competent and non-corrupt judiciary. Social movements seek to close the gap between law and politics, between 'rights-in-principle' and 'rights-in-practice'. However, as societies move from authoritarianism to democracy, the protection of rights may move to the legal sphere, and social movements may lose their pre-eminent role. Foweraker and Landman claimed that comparative, empirical, quantitative analysis showed that popular social forces could be the makers of democratic rights (Foweraker and Landman 1997).

Landman maintains that the idea of universality in human-rights theory and law implies the need for cross-national, empirical comparison. Comparative studies can help explain the gap between what is claimed in principle and what is observed in practice. He acknowledges that the meaning of the legal standards is uncertain and consequently measuring empirical compliance with normative standards is problematic. However, empirical studies show that democracies and rich countries are less likely to violate personal integrity rights, and that countries involved in international or civil war are more likely to violate them. Thus, wealth, democracy and peace are the best determinants of human-rights protection. Statistical relations that hold globally, however, do not always hold for all regions: for example, the positive relation between economic development and human rights does not hold for Latin America (Landman 2002, 2006).

It has been suggested that the empirical relationship between democracy and human rights is not straightforward, and that more gross human-rights violations are found in the middle between full democracy and full autocracy (Fein 1995). Davenport and Armstrong have challenged this finding, however, and argued that below a certain level, democracy has no discernible impact on human rights, but above this level it improves respect for human rights (Davenport and Armstrong 2004). Old democracies violate civil and political rights less than new democracies (Landman 2005a: 92, 117–18). Davenport points out that, although it is well established that democracy generally reduces repression, we do not know whether all aspects of democracy reduce repression; whether democracy reduces all types of repression; or whether democracy reduces repression in all circumstances, particularly in circumstances of violent conflict. He found that, generally, the mass aspects of democracy were more effective in reducing repression than its elite aspects; democracy was more effective in reducing state violence than in preventing restrictions on civil liberties; and mass democracy was less effective in civil wars (Davenport 2007).

Comparative statistical analysis provides a rigorous means to identify variables that are associated with different levels of respect for human rights, but it does little to illuminate the *causal mechanisms* by which human rights are improved. Risse, Ropp and Sikkink seek to make good this deficiency with a causal model of human-rights change (Risse, Ropp and Sikkink 1999). Risse and Sikkink propose a theory of the stages and mechanisms through which international norms can lead to human-rights improvements. Their five-phase, 'spiral model' seeks to explain variations in the extent to which states have internalized these norms. The five phases are: (1) repression; (2) material and normative pressures met by resistance; (3) tactical concessions, empowerment of domestic opposition, and dialogue; (4) legal reform; (5) internalization of human-rights norms in routine behaviour. The model does not assume evolutionary progress: governments may return to repressive practices.

The diffusion of international human-rights norms depends on the establishment and maintenance of networks among domestic and transnational actors connected to the international regime. Advocacy networks serve three purposes which constitute necessary conditions for sustainable human-rights change: (1) they put repressive states on the international agenda; (2) they assist domestic opposition groups; (3) they apply pressure to repressive governments. These processes may create a 'boomerang effect', whereby domestic NGOs mobilize international actors, who in turn empower domestic NGOs and put pressure on their governments. The process of change through socialization involves the social reconstruction of identities and interests by reference to norms.

Each of the five stages makes the next stage more likely. The third stage is crucial, because instrumental adaptation (by which states make some concessions from practical motives) involves 'talking the talk' of human rights, and this may lead to 'walking the walk', by institutionalizing human-rights norms in the fourth and fifth stages (Risse and Sikkink 1999). This model provides a useful framework for comparing the processes by which international human-rights norms may or may not be institutionalized in national legal systems. However, it has little predictive, and therefore little explanatory, value.

Jetschke and Liese maintain that few states make the transition from stage four to stage five of the spiral model – from legal institutionalization of human rights to actual compliance with human-rights norms – because it is difficult to sustain internal or external pressure on recalcitrant states: China is a good example. The spiral model, they believe, overestimates the power of civil-society actors and underestimates the cultural heterogeneity of civil society, which typically includes forces unfriendly towards human rights. Human-rights advocates assume a *causal link* between governmental action and human-rights protection: if a government does not control its territory and population, this link is broken; if a government can legitimize its human-rights violations, for example by claiming that there are threats to the state and/or the nation, the causal link is maintained but the violations are legitimized (Jetschke and Liese 2013).

Simmons argues that early empirical studies concluding that treaty ratification did not improve human-rights performance ignored the facts that some ratifying states could not improve because they were already almost perfect (e.g., Norway on torture) and that other ratifiers had no intention of honouring their ratification (e.g., North Korea). Ratification was likely to lead to improvement if it was followed by civil-society mobilization: this depended on the value of human rights for the population and the prospects of success. Improvement is most likely 'in the middle', where human rights are highly valued but poorly respected, but where the chances of improvement are good. UN investigations, trials and litigation are all conducive to human-rights improvements. Existing research has, however, paid too little attention to different types of human rights, and has paid excessive attention to states and too little to human-rights violations by non-state actors (Simmons 2013).

Risse and Sikkink conclude that no general theory of human-rights change is possible because the field is much too complex. State capacity-building can improve human rights or strengthen resistance to external pressures for human-rights improvements. Human-rights advocates should be more aware of the conditions of success. The potential for external actors to improve human rights in a state – whether by persuasion, incentives or coercion – is limited (Risse and Sikkink 2013).

Hawkins has sought to produce a stronger explanation of human-rights change by what he calls a 'process tracing' method in a case study of Chile. There was an international campaign against human-rights violations in that country during the rule of the military junta headed by General Pinochet. The success of this campaign depended on a split in the Chilean elite between those prepared to rule by force and those who sought legitimacy through the rule of law. A combination of domestic and international pressures led the regime to move from repression to constitutional reform. Hawkins argues that absence of domestic security or economic crisis, elite divisions, and cultural receptivity to human rights are each necessary and are jointly sufficient to explain variations in the Chilean government's strategies in the face of strong human-rights pressures (Hawkins 2002).

Sociology

Sociology has traditionally been concerned with national societies rather than international relations and consequently taken very little interest in international human rights. Turner has sought to construct a sociological framework for the analysis of human rights by viewing human rights as a global ideology and its institutionalization through the United Nations as part of the social process of globalization. The concept of citizenship has been closely linked with the modern nation-state, but globalization has created problems that are not wholly internal to nation-states, and so the concept of citizenship rights must be extended to that of human rights. Sociologically, the concept of human rights can be explained by the need to protect vulnerable human beings by social institutions, which in their turn pose threats to those human beings. The social and legal institutionalization of human rights is the predominant modern attempt to resolve this dilemma that is inherent in modern societies (Turner 1993).

Waters argues that a sociological theory of human rights must take a social-constructionist approach that treats the universality of human rights as itself a social construction. On this view, the institutionalization of human rights reflects the prevailing balance of political interests (Waters 1996). This approach fails to explain why human rights were chosen to legitimate interests.

Stammers criticizes legalistic and statist approaches to human rights on the ground that human-rights violations occur at the sub-state, social level. The power perspective on human rights that he advocates can show that economic and social rights are often violated by private economic agencies, and that the human rights of women are violated by men. Those who see states as the solutions to human-rights problems may be mistaken, because they locate human-rights obligations where the power to solve human-rights problems may be lacking. Also, in looking to states to solve human-rights problems, statists may have to advocate an increase in the power of states, which is the original source of human-rights problems. The power perspective requires us to consider the impact of institutions and social movements on the distribution of power, and not merely on the legal formalization of rights (Stammers 1999).

Howard argued that there are social-structural causes of human-rights violations and barriers to improvement. In Commonwealth Africa post-colonial rulers inherited authoritarian government from their colonial predecessors. State elites controlled the economy and were consequently intolerant of oppositional actors, who were potential economic and political challengers. This inhibited the rise of bourgeois challengers to the state. The dispersal, low educational levels and economic hardships of the peasants make it difficult for them to mobilize in social movements for human rights.

African states were also authoritarian because they lacked the legitimacy and administrative structures to regulate society, and so resorted to rule by coercion. The legitimacy of the state was weakened by its failure to build nations from diverse ethnic groups, but the ethnic conflict that was common in Africa could not be explained only by ethnicity but had to be understood by reference to state power and social inequality.

Howard's structural approach did not exclude culture. Pre-colonial Africa was generally characterized by communalistic cultures, in which human worth was recognized by reference to social roles and statuses rather than to individual rights. Modernization had, however, substantially disrupted traditional social organization, and thereby much of its traditional culture. Consequently, many Africans had to deal with the modern African state and dominant class as modern individuals without the support of traditional institutions. Modern elites appealed to traditionalism to control modern challengers, but, although traditional culture was incompatible with human rights in some respects, most Africans faced modern problems of structural political and economic inequality. The structural changes of modernization make the development of a human-rights culture possible (Howard 1986).

Woodiwiss rejects Howard's suggestion that modernization tends to create a convergence on similar conceptions of human rights. The economically successful societies of East and South-East Asia have patriarchal cultures that assume the legitimacy of social inequalities. Liberal rights would be unenforceable in such societies. Patriarchalism is compatible with human rights, however, he says, because rights can be expressed in values and institutions that do not endorse autonomy. Human rights, therefore, do not require liberal-democratic states or individualistic values. Patriarchalism is as compatible with human rights as liberalism, except for gender relations. This claim that human rights do not require liberal values derives from a *reconceptualization* of 'human rights' that severs it from equality and autonomy, and the exception of gender relations is considerable. Woodiwiss also assumes that patriarchalist cultures are unchangeable, whereas his own analysis shows that they are not. He maintains that such Asian values as hierarchy and benevolence should be incorporated into international human-rights discourse as additional or alternative sources of virtue so that it can be truly cosmopolitan (Woodiwiss 1998). The concept of human rights does not, however, aspire to be a comprehensive social ethic, but a limited set of norms opposing abuses of power: other social virtues lie outside its scope.

Capitalism, Woodiwiss believes, subverts human rights because it distributes freedoms unequally according to individuals' positions in the relation of capital and labour, whereas human rights require that individuals are treated equally regardless of social position (Woodiwiss 2005). Human rights do not, however, require that all freedoms are distributed equally, only that human rights are. It is questionable whether this can be fully achieved in capitalist societies, but some capitalist societies have relatively good human-rights records, and Woodiwiss proposes no better, feasible alternative.

Sociology has generally neglected human rights. This is partly caused by the different philosophical foundations of sociology and human rights. Nevertheless, sociology covers similar ground to that covered by human rights, e.g., religion, poverty, race, minorities, gender, sexuality, disability. This is reflected in a growing sociological literature (Hynes et al. 2011; Brunsma, Smith and Gran 2015; Nash 2015).

Social psychology

It may be thought that psychology is not a *social* science at all, since it is a science of the (individual) human mind. However, human-rights behaviour is the product of the human mind, and psychology therefore should contribute to our understanding of it.

Governments may violate human rights 'rationally', as an efficient means to achieve certain ends. Some violations, however, are not efficient in this way, and exhibit cruelty that is inefficient or even counter-productive. Cruelty cannot explain human-rights violations by itself, for it is developed, channelled, inhibited or let loose in particular social situations. Human-rights violations are socially structured but the cruelty of individuals may initiate and/or aggravate them.

Some human-rights violations may be partly explained by scapegoat theory, which derives from frustration-aggression theory. This says that a frustrated person tends to become aggressive. The obvious target for this aggression is whoever is responsible for the frustration (the frustrator). The frustrator may, however, be unknown (e.g., world markets), inaccessible (the World Bank), too powerful (the army) and/or morally protected (the Church). If aggression cannot be directed at the frustrator, scapegoat theory says that it is likely to be displaced onto a target that is known, accessible, weak and despised. Ethnic minorities often have these characteristics, which is why they are often the target of irrational aggression.

Experimental psychology has shown that ordinary individuals are likely to conform to the standards of their group or to the orders of a person in authority, even if doing so violates their own moral values (Milgram 1974). These experiments suggest that gross human-rights violations are likely to occur when murderous leaders mobilize the co-operation of ordinary followers, who do not question their social environment or their leaders. However, studies of those who rescued Jews during the Holocaust suggest that actions to defend human rights may be motivated, not by rational and independent moral thinking, but by conformity to groups or authority figures that are themselves humane (Oliner and Oliner 1988).

Anthropology

We have seen that anthropology in the USA after the Second World War was dominated by a mixture of positivism and relativism. In the 1960s relativism was picked up by radical anthropologists to challenge the authority of the discipline's elites and their supposedly 'imperialist' approach to other cultures (Washburn 1987).

In these debates human rights played little role. Some anthropologists, however, began to combine the 'committed' anthropology of the radicals with human rights. In the UK, Survival International, and in the USA, Cultural Survival, were activist organizations that brought together academic anthropology and a concern for indigenous rights. Cultural Survival published a volume entitled *Human Rights and Anthropology* in 1988. The editors acknowledged that the peoples whom anthropologists studied were often victims of serious human-rights violations. Anthropologists had expressed concern for human rights through their professional associations but the discipline of anthropology had neglected human rights. Anthropologists should investigate state policies directed towards eliminating cultural pluralism. Such investigations were both scientifically and ethically justified (Downing and Kushner 1988).

Downing suggested that anthropology could contribute to the understanding of human rights by showing how conceptions of rights functioned in different cultures and how cultures incorporated external ideas (Downing 1988). Barnett argued that anthropologists were sensitive to the value of different cultures to those whose cultures they were, but could also recognize that they might be internally oppressive. The recognition of cultural difference, therefore, did not rule out intervention in other cultures, but it did impose the obligation to respect the context into which that intervention was to be carried out (Barnett 1988). Doughty pointed out that, in Latin America, the concept of 'citizenship' had traditionally been defined so as to exclude indigenous peoples, with the result that these peoples had become victims of gross human-rights violations. Anthropologists had ignored state policies towards cultural difference. This was a scientific and moral error (Doughty 1988).

Messer has argued that anthropologists should no longer study 'cultures' as local, isolated entities, but as part of an interactive and interdependent global system of cultures. International human-rights law must be implemented in a world of diverse cultures, some of which are at least partly incompatible with human rights. Anthropologists can help the cause of human rights by clarifying the relations between international human-rights law and particular cultures (Messer 1993).

Wilson has complained that the legal positivism favoured by the human-rights community misrepresents the subjective experiences of the victims of human-rights violations. Human-rights universalism often ignores local contexts and thereby misunderstands the social and cultural dimensions of conflicts over rights. Human-rights law speaks in a clear and certain voice, while human-rights experience is complex and uncertain. In order to move beyond subjectivity to authoritative objectivity, human-rights discourse paradoxically dehumanizes its subjects. The task of anthropology is to put the human back into human rights (Wilson 1997a, 1997b).

Schirmer and Stoll argue that decontextualized universalism can lead to counter-productive international interventions for human rights, either because of undue emphasis on legal reform with neglect of social consequences, or by oversimplifying what may be complex social and political relations. Anthropology can help to make human-rights interventions more effective by providing them with a deeper understanding of their cultural, social and political contexts (Schirmer 1997; Stoll 1997).

There is a tension between the normative demands of human rights and the ethnographic practices of anthropology, since anthropology encounters cultures that lack the concept of individuals as bearers of rights. Anthropologists can study 'cultures' to examine whether they do or do not conform with human rights and also the 'cultures' of human-rights practitioners. They can study how social movements incorporate human-rights discourse into their legal and political strategies and how transnational actors may modify their practices as they encounter local cultures (Goodale 2006a, 2006b; Merry 2006).

Merry has added that anthropology can tell us where and how human-rights concepts and institutions are produced, how ideas circulate, and how they shape everyday lives. The concept of rights moves from the local to the global, and then back to the local. Yet even the concepts of 'local' and 'global' may be problematic, since global discourses such as that of human rights have their local sites, such as the committee rooms and assembly halls of Manhattan and Geneva. The interaction between 'global' and 'local' discourses is mediated by 'translators' who act as double agents, interpreting the 'global' to the 'local' and the 'local' to the 'global' in a field of unequal power. We may ask whether human rights get lost in translation, as translating one set of cultural categories and meanings into another transforms them. There are limits to the capacity of the producers of discourses to control their meanings. Whether local actors adopt a human-rights approach depends on their perceptions of its success. Human-rights discourse may be rejected by local actors; it may merely decorate local practices; it may combine with local discourses in a hybrid; or it may subvert and displace prior discourses (Merry 2006). A theory of culture, Merry argues, as contested, historically produced and continually defined and redefined in a variety of settings, would enhance our understanding of human-rights processes as promoting gradual cultural change rather than as law without sanctions confronting intractable cultural difference (Merry 2006: 100).

International relations

The academic discipline of International Relations neglected human rights for many years, except for some studies of human rights in US foreign policy. The introduction of human rights into International Relations was pioneered by Forsythe in the USA and Vincent in the UK. Forsythe sought to persuade sceptics that international human-rights law made a difference to international politics, while maintaining that politics set limits to the influence of law (Forsythe 1983). Vincent acknowledged that human rights were marginal to international relations, and states often used the idea to promote their own interests, but noted that the concept of human rights had become part of global law and morality. After the Helsinki Conference on Security and Co-operation in Europe in 1975, at which the USSR accepted human rights in principle, human rights became a salient feature of Cold War international relations. The concept had been incorporated into international relations in such a way that no state could ignore human-rights considerations in its foreign policy. Nevertheless, foreign-policy professionals were typically wary of human rights, preferring standard-setting to implementation, generalities to specificities, and viewing human rights as one of the *problems* of foreign policy rather than as the solution to problems. Against this view, Vincent argued that the cautious incorporation of human rights into foreign policy might promote the interests of states (Vincent 1986).

Human rights can be incorporated into International Relations through regime theory. The international human-rights system is a regulatory regime. Donnelly has classified regimes as declaratory, promotional, implementation and enforcement regimes, each of which can be classified as relatively weak or strong. The international human-rights regime is a relatively strong promotional regime, a relatively weak implementation regime, and at most a minimal enforcement regime. Declaratory regimes with weak enforcement powers are attractive to states because they can appear moral with little risk to their important practical interests. International human-rights regimes can nevertheless help states that wish to improve their human-rights performance by political support and technical assistance. The European regime is relatively strong because the moral commitment of European states is relatively strong, and the risks to states' interests are small. The Inter-American regime has been quite active. Africa has a weak regime, and Asia and the Middle East have no regimes, because moral commitment to human rights among elites is weak, and state interest in not having such a regime is strong. Human-rights regimes are therefore strongest where they are least needed, and weak or non-existent where they are most needed. Regime analysis supports the view that moral concerns play some role in international relations, but generally a marginal one (Donnelly 1989: 206–18, 223, 227–8, 252–8).

Human rights also enter international relations through states' foreign policies. States may be reluctant to include human rights in their foreign policies because they do not perceive it to serve their interests and/or because they generally share an interest in not interfering with each other's internal affairs. These motives are not always decisive, however, because states may have a moral or practical interest in promoting human rights, for example to stabilize a country that may threaten its neighbours or the wider international community. States have a range of means to influence human rights in other societies, from 'quiet diplomacy' through economic sanctions to military intervention. All these methods may fail because the intervenors are self-interested and/or the target states resist intervention (Donnelly 1989: 229–37, 242–9; 1998: 85; 1999: 90–1).

The 'right of humanitarian intervention' has been debated for a long time. Military interventions with a human-rights dimension – such as NATO's bombing of Serbia to protect ethnic Albanians of Kosovo in 1999 and the US-led invasions of Afghanistan and Iraq in 2001 and 2003 – have been very controversial. Such interventions may improve human rights in some respects, but often at great human and material costs, and the difficulty of establishing a stable, rights-respecting society may be formidable. Yet failures to intervene have also been very controversial, as in the cases of the Rwanda genocide of 1994 and the repression of Darfur by the Sudanese government.

The United Nations has accepted the doctrine of 'the responsibility to protect', which suggests that the international community may intervene, even with military force, when governments fail to protect the human rights of their citizens. The legal and political status of this doctrine remain uncertain, however. There is some consensus that, if military intervention for human rights is ever justified, it is only for the most serious violations (Donnelly 2003: 258–60). Weiss points out that the UN Security Council approved military interventions in Haiti (1994) and Sierra Leone (1997) to reverse the overthrow of democratic governments. A survey conducted by the International Committee of the Red Cross in 12 war-torn societies found that two-thirds of civilians wanted more intervention, and only 10 per cent wanted none (Weiss 2004: 139, 142). The problems of 'the responsibility to protect' are well illustrated by the debate between de Waal and Reeves over Darfur. De Waal argues that the application of the doctrine to Darfur is dangerous, as military intervention would cost more lives than it would save. Reeves emphasizes the ongoing humanitarian catastrophe and argues that the UN's failure to intervene more forcefully has enabled what he calls 'genocide by attrition' and damaged the UN's credibility as a human-rights organization. Both agree that Sudan's problems must be solved by a negotiated peace, but disagree on what form of short-term intervention can lead to that solution (de Waal 2008; Reeves 2008).

The United Nations promotes human rights through many agencies, especially since it adopted the policy of 'mainstreaming'. The Security Council, the General Assembly, the Human Rights Council, the Office of the High Commissioner for Human Rights, the treaty-monitoring bodies, special rapporteurs and working groups, the High Commissioner for Refugees, the International Labour Organization, and the specialized agencies and programmes such as the World Health Organization, the UN Development Programme and the World Food Programme, all contribute to the implementation of international human-rights policies. The UN's impact has been limited, however, mainly because powerful states have been reluctant to fund it adequately and have sometimes obstructed its work (Forsythe 2006; Mertus 2005).

However, LeBor has charged the UN with complicity with gross human-rights violations in Bosnia, Rwanda and Darfur, by pretending to intervene, but doing so ineffectively. At least one permanent member of the Security Council has had an interest in its not intervening and has been able to prevent effective action (LeBor 2006). Donnelly has argued that, because the UN has been the source of international human-rights law, its importance in implementing human rights has been exaggerated (Donnelly 1989: 260–9).

The attack on the USA on 11 September 2001 ('9/11') by agents of the Islamist, terrorist group, Al-Qaeda, led to an invasion of Afghanistan by the USA and its allies to overthrow the Taliban government. This led to the replacement of a government responsible for gross human-rights violations by a formally democratic, but corrupt, insufficiently legitimate and unstable government, with mixed results for human rights. The 'global war on terror' waged by the Bush administration involved curtailment of civil liberties for Americans, contempt for the Geneva Conventions for captured terrorist suspects, and serious human-rights violations in many countries in the name of counter-terrorism. The Obama administration modified the counter-terrorism policies of its predecessors, but the rise of international terrorism to the top of the agenda of international relations raised problems for human rights that remain unsolved.

Some have argued that, although the war on terrorism led to human-rights violations and undermined international human-rights norms, it has also led to a reaffirmation of those norms through democratic debate and judicial decisions. Courts and parliaments have resisted some of the human-rights restrictions proposed by executives (Evans 2006: 196). There is a consensus that terrorism should be addressed with respect for human rights, but less consensus on how to do this. Terrorism creates two dilemmas for liberal-democratic states: (1) how to protect their peoples without sacrificing their fundamental values; (2) how to treat an enemy in a conflict that falls between war and crime.

Conclusion

Nietzsche called ethical idealists 'emigrants from reality' (Glover 1999: 29). The task of the social science of human rights is to bring human-rights supporters back to reality. This reality is one both of objective structures and processes and of subjective meanings and values. A social science of human rights demands both sympathy and scientific rigour. The concept of human rights lies in a domain in which normative philosophy, law and social science meet. The field of human rights is still dominated too much by legal texts. Law has an important place in the creation, interpretation and implementation of human rights, but it has more limits than human-rights activists often realize. Social science is necessary to connect law to reality.

Social science is, however, not enough, for it cannot tell us how we ought to live. Philosophy may offer to do so, but it is a weak motivator to action. Understanding human rights requires us to understand both the contribution and the limits of philosophy and science. Social science is itself a social process and its connection with human rights is problematic. Science has been historically connected with the idea of emancipation from authority and ignorance, and therefore with freedom and well-being. But the scientific philosophy of positivism can lead down the path of moral indifference, while the 'interpretive' social sciences, such as anthropology, can lead to moral relativism.

Hirschman has argued that the modern social sciences have been characterized by an 'anti-moralist petulance' that can be traced back to Machiavelli's anti-moralistic political science. Social scientists have a 'trained incapacity' to take morality seriously. Somehow the analytical rigour of science and ethical seriousness have to be brought together (Hirschman 1983: 21–4, 30). Bellah maintains that the division that we make between social science and philosophy arises from an attempt to 'purify' these disciplines. There may be advantages in this differentiation, but the division between science and ethics has costs that can be met only by intellectual activity that crosses the boundaries that we have set up. Positivism in social science sought to reject ethics in order to improve the quality of knowledge that it produced. Ironically, it failed, because it failed to understand itself as a social practice that was inescapably ethical. Like all social practices, social science takes place in a field of power. If it fails to recognize this social fact, it is more likely to serve the powers that be. A social science of human rights must have other purposes, and thus must be self-conscious about its ethical commitments (Bellah 1983). Thus, human-rights law is inadequate without support from the social sciences; the social sciences are inadequate without support from philosophy.

6
Universality, Diversity and Difference
Culture and Human Rights

Universalism

The universality of human rights is a fundamental principle of human-rights philosophy and law. Human-rights theorists commonly say that all human beings have human rights simply because they are human beings (Donnelly 1999: 79). The principal human-rights text is the Universal Declaration of Human Rights (UDHR). Article 1 states that all human beings are born equal in rights. Article 2 says that *everyone* is entitled to all the rights set forth in the Declaration. The Vienna Declaration of 1993 affirmed that the universality of human rights was 'beyond question'.

Yet the universality of human rights *has* been questioned. In 1947 the Executive Board of the American Anthropological Association (AAA) published a 'Statement on Human Rights', in which they asserted that values and standards 'are relative to the culture from which they derive'. This cultural relativism was motivated by a fear that the promotion of human rights as universal values would lead to the hegemony of the dominant global powers (American Anthropological Association Executive Board 1947).

The Cold War was dominated by political and economic differences between Western liberal capitalism, Eastern state socialism and 'third-world' developmentalism. The end of the Cold War briefly promised a 'new world order' in which universal human rights would advance. However, new divisions have arisen over the cultural challenge to universalism. In the run-up to the Vienna Conference certain Asian states and intellectuals argued that there was a distinctively Asian conception of human rights (Bauer and Bell 1999). Similar challenges have been made by some African scholars, and on the basis of Islam (Mutua 2008; Mayer 2007). Philosophically, liberal universalism has been challenged by both communitarianism and the postmodern celebration of 'difference'.

All these challenges are problematic. The anthropologists deployed 'cultural relativism' to defend vulnerable peoples from great-power hegemony, but failed to show that relativism could provide a robust defence. The AAA now supports human rights, but 'extends' them to the collective rights of cultural groups (Engle 2001). The challenge of 'Asian values' to human rights was implausible because (1) Asia is culturally extremely diverse; (2) many Asians support human rights; (3) Asian governments often mistreat the 'subaltern' cultural groups that the anthropologists wished to defend. Communitarians and postmodernists either do not reject human rights or, if they do, fail to offer a persuasive alternative.

The claim that human rights are universal is also problematic, however. It is not, for example, literally supported by the text of the UDHR. Some human rights belong only to special categories of human beings. Article 25 says that motherhood and childhood are entitled to special care and assistance. The Vienna Declaration recognized a number of special categories, such as women, children, minorities, indigenous people, disabled persons, refugees, migrant workers, the extremely poor and the socially excluded. The rights of these persons are now usually considered to be part of the human-rights field, but it is often not clear whether they are thought to have special, and therefore non-universal, rights, or to have only the standard set of human rights, but to be especially vulnerable to human-rights violations.

The universality of some human rights is rather uncontroversial: for example, the right not to be enslaved. Other human rights are universal only *potentially*. There are two kinds of these rights. The first consists of rights that are activated only in certain unusual situations: the right to a fair trial, for instance. The second consists of rights that are activated when human beings meet some criterion – becoming an adult, for example – that most human beings meet: for example, the right to participate in the government of one's country. Some principles of the UDHR have more cross-cultural appeal than others. Article 16, for example, sets forth a liberal right to marry. Saudi Arabia objected to this on the ground that it was incompatible with Islam (Morsink 1999: 24).

The universality of human rights is problematic for two further reasons. Firstly, the philosophical foundations of human rights are problematic (see chapter 4). Secondly, the concept is associated, as the AAA feared, with Western hegemony and imperialism.

Imperialism

The idea of human-rights universalism is sometimes said to be an expression of Western cultural imperialism. It is argued that the concept of human rights is historically Western; it assumes the Western value of individual freedom; the West has dominated the making and implementation of international human-rights law; and the West deploys the concept of human rights to promote its foreign-policy interests.

The concept of human rights certainly has strong Western roots. Some say that it has universal origins in the various cultures of the world. This claim, however, conflates various moral concepts – such as benevolence and justice – with the concept of human rights. It does not follow that the concept of human rights is not universal, in the sense that it is relevant to everyone *now*. Donnelly argues that human rights are universal partly because the conditions that produced them in the West – nation-states and capitalism – have become universal. These social forms have disrupted traditional communities, so that the protection that these communities once provided must now be provided differently. Human rights provide the best defence of human dignity under modern conditions. They address threats to human dignity that are nearly universal; it follows that human rights are (nearly) universal. Modernized, authoritarian elites appeal to cultural traditions, or invent pseudo-traditions, to defend their repressive regimes that have little or no regard for the traditional cultures of their societies. Many human-rights violations are the products of distinctively modern forms of rule, and have no basis in traditional culture (Donnelly 1989: 59–65). The value of human rights as a defence against oppression is now universal, even if the history of the concept is predominantly Western.

The argument that the concept of human rights is Western, not universal, because it assumes the value of individual freedom is greatly oversimplified. The concept certainly entails the value of individual freedom. However, there is no consensus among philosophers or politicians in the West or the rest as to how the balance between individual freedom and communitarian values should be struck; this balance must depend to a significant extent on circumstances. Theoretically human rights, far from entailing a rejection of community, require a rights-respecting community (Gewirth 1996). This idea is reinforced by international human-rights law.

The argument that international human-rights law was produced by, and maintains, Western hegemony is also oversimplified. In the early 1950s, Belgium, Britain and France sought to defend their imperial hegemonies by *denying* the application of human rights to their colonial subjects (Iriye and Goedde 2012). The weakness of the international human-rights regime was the product, not of non-Western cultural relativists, but of the great powers, fearful that the United Nations might use human rights to interfere with their internal affairs (Mazower 2004). The countries that voted for the UDHR represented a great diversity of cultures, political ideologies and economic systems; the two human-rights covenants of 1966 were adopted unanimously; and all UN states participate in the human-rights regime, especially in the Human Rights Council's Universal Periodic Review. The role of the West and the rest in the development of international human-rights law is complex. The West sometimes deploys human rights as an instrument of foreign policy, but non-Western countries use human rights to criticize the West.

The West's commitment to human rights in practice has been uneven. Also, the West has no monopoly on hegemony: local hegemonies – for example, of male religious elites – may be more oppressive for millions of people (Simmons 2009: 369–71).

Criticism of human rights as Western imperialism may express a justified grievance wrongly directed. The West has dominated the rest historically through imperialism, and is still somewhat dominant through post-colonial cultural hegemony. Resistance to the West may be a protest against injustice. Globalization may be experienced as cultural imperialism. Cultural assertiveness may, in these circumstances, be an expression of dignity. This may appear as the defence of conservative against liberal values, but, in historical context, it can also be a claim for equality against domination. Resistance to the concept of human rights, or insistence on 'home-grown' conceptions of human rights, may be part of this self-emancipation from Western domination. This carries the danger that Western injustice will be replaced by home-grown injustice.

The 'Western imperialism' objection to human rights is very implausible in certain particular circumstances. Opposition to the dumping of toxic waste in developing countries by Western multinational corporations on the ground that it violates the right to health of local populations does not express a distinctively Western value or interest. There is also empirical evidence that human rights are widely supported by ordinary people in non-Western countries. A World Bank survey of 60,000 poor people around the world showed substantial support for the principles of the UDHR (Darrow 2003: 90). The human-rights movement is also global and multicultural.

Those who criticize human rights as a form of imperialism often fail to analyse why imperialism is objectionable. Such an analysis might show that imperialism is objectionable because it violates human rights. The concept of human rights, far from defending imperialism, provides powerful grounds for criticizing it.

Since some cultural practices are undoubtedly incompatible with human-rights norms, it may still be thought that there is something 'coercive' about the concept of human rights.

It is important, however, to distinguish between disapproval of a cultural practice in principle and the best strategy for changing the practice. Simple condemnation may be futile or counter-productive: dialogue and support for internal reformers may work better. External reformers should realize that those engaged in such cultural practices may resist pressure to change either because they are committed to those practices or because, even though they would prefer the human-rights alternative, the social cost of defying the prevailing custom is too high.

Some may yet think that human-rights universalism represents cultural imperialism because it claims superiority over cultural alternatives. The most common basis for this claim is cultural relativism. Like imperialism, it is more often asserted than analysed.

Cultural relativism

Cultural relativism holds that there are no, or few, universally valid beliefs, values, norms or practices, because validity can derive only from cultures, and cultures are particular and diverse, not universal. Cultural relativism as a distinct theory in the social sciences was introduced into anthropology by Franz Boas in opposition to the prevailing evolutionary theories, which held that Western cultures were the most evolved and 'primitive' cultures the least. Cultural relativism entailed a respect for all cultures. It became orthodox in anthropology and influenced popular moral relativism (Baghramian 2010).

Cultural relativism appears to express two attractive ideas: (1) everyone is equally entitled to respect; (2) to respect a person entails respect for that person's culture, because culture constitutes, at least in part, a person's identity. However, these principles are inconsistent with cultural relativism, because they are universal principles. The principle that we should respect *all* cultures is self-contradictory, because some cultures do not respect all cultures. The principle of respect for *persons* is inconsistent with the principle that we should respect all cultures; cultures that endorse human-rights violations cannot therefore demand our respect simply because they are cultures. Human-rights supporters are committed to not respecting some cultures, or at least some features of some cultures. Some non-Western critiques of human rights are based not on cultural relativism but on a different universalism. Islam, for example, is a universalist religion, but some interpretations of its principles, for example, on gender relations, are incompatible with some human rights.

A common fallacy is that cultural relativism supports anti-imperialism, but it does not, for cultural relativism provides no basis for criticizing imperialistic cultures. Imperialists have used cultural relativism to deny rights to non-Westerners. Cultural relativism assumes a simplistic conception of 'culture'; it is self-defeating because relativism itself seems to be a *universal* principle; and it seems to endorse practices – such as those of Nazism – that almost no one finds acceptable.

Arguments against human-rights universalism from cultural relativism are often confused with arguments from state sovereignty, because both are used to keep outsiders from interfering with the internal affairs of a society. The appeal to sovereignty is, however, not an appeal to cultural relativism, because the principle of sovereignty is as universal as that of human rights. The principle of sovereignty may have value in discouraging unwarranted interference and in keeping the peace among states, but it may also protect human-rights violators and help to crush cultures.

On culture and rights

Each society has its unique history and culture, and it may seem to follow that each must have a distinctive conception of human rights. This is as true of the West as the rest: the Swedish conception of human rights is different from that of the USA. This variability is hidden by the abstractions of international human-rights law. The European Court of Human Rights has developed the concept of 'the margin of appreciation', which allows some autonomy to member states in interpreting rights. This is, in part, a concession by international human rights to national democracy. The Court has, however, been criticized for failing to develop this idea clearly or coherently. Cultural diversity is much less in Europe than it is world-wide. If the margin of appreciation doctrine is valid (and it is controversial), it provides support for culturally variable interpretations of human rights globally, at least for democratic societies.

Some diversity in the interpretation of human rights may be justified, not by cultural difference, but by differences in practical circumstances. Thus, the right to join a trade union is not a universal right, because it does not make sense in all circumstances, but it may be a right justified by a universal right, such as that to an adequate standard of living, in particular circumstances.

Arguments for diverse interpretations of human rights are, however, problematic in several ways. Firstly, supposed regional or national conceptions often hide, or underestimate, the diversity of conceptions that exist in the region or nation: interpretations of human rights are often *contested*, especially between governments and dissidents and/or minorities. Secondly, claims about regional or national conceptions may overestimate the distinctiveness of the conception. Supposedly non-Western values are often conservative values that many Westerners support. Thirdly, arguments from cultural diversity often underestimate the dynamism of cultures. Those cultures that contain elements incompatible with human rights may have the potential to converge with human rights; whether they do so may depend on political and economic factors. Fourthly, most cultures today are hybrids, mixing home-grown and external elements that may include international standards.

Religion and human rights: the case of Islam

Religion may support or oppose human rights, but where it opposes, it presents a special challenge because it claims an alternative, powerful authority. Human-rights advocates often assume that international human-rights law 'trumps' all rival commitments. But this is far from obvious for the religious, who may believe that, if religion conflicts with human rights, religion must win. Islam is of particular interest in this context, both because of its contemporary political importance, and because it raises questions about religion and human rights in a strong form.

Islam and human rights are not generally comparable: Islam is a religion that governs most aspects of life for its adherents; human rights entail a set of norms for the conduct primarily of governments. The attitude of Islamic governments towards human rights has not been consistent. During the drafting of the UDHR, Muslim countries did not generally find it objectionable on religious grounds. The two 1966 covenants were adopted by the General Assembly by a unanimous vote of more than 100 countries, including 21 Muslim countries. Islamic states have made few reservations to these two covenants, but they have made strong reservations to the Convention on the Elimination of Discrimination Against Women (CEDAW). In 1990 the Organization of the Islamic Conference adopted the Cairo Declaration of Human Rights in Islam, which permits or requires discrimination against women, and offers little protection to freedom of religion (Mayer 2007).

Some believe that religious conservatism and Islamic law (Shari'a) are causes of human-rights violations in Islamic countries. Since Shari'a is based on the Qur'an, deploying international human-rights law against Shari'a may undermine the work of reformist Muslims. The best strategy to promote human rights in these societies is to find resources within Islam. Othman believes that Islam can be interpreted so that it is compatible with human rights. An-Na'im has doubts. For example, Article 5 of the UDHR prohibits cruel, inhuman or degrading punishment. Shari'a provides that theft is punishable by the amputation of the right hand, which surely violates Article 5. An-Na'im believes that neither Islamic reinterpretation nor cross-cultural dialogue is likely to lead to the total abolition of this punishment in Islamic societies. There are, however, resources in the Qur'an for restricting its application, by requiring strict standards of proof or recognizing various extenuating circumstances (Othman 1999; An-Na'im 1992).

The internal-reformist approach has merits and problems. It conceptualizes human-rights progress as self-emancipation rather than external imposition. However, it may fail and lacks a Plan B. This approach has been criticized for being too unorthodox to persuade most Muslims and conceding too much to remain compatible with human rights. It also relies on *internal* Muslim reforms whereas human rights require equality between Muslims and non-Muslims. Shachar argues that internal reform may not help the most vulnerable because they have least power to effect reforms (Shachar 1999: 99). An-Na'im's pessimism may be challenged by the fact that we cannot know whether cross-cultural dialogue and/or social change in Islamic societies will bring the practice of Shari'a into closer conformity with international human-rights law. We do know that beliefs about the will of God and its implication for social policy have changed over time in the West. There are considerable differences between secular Muslims (those who self-identify as Muslims but who do not practise the religion), liberal Muslims who support human rights, moderate reformers and 'fundamentalists'. Which will prevail is a matter more of politics than hermeneutics (Mayer 2007).

In contrast Chase argues that Islam is neither responsible for human-rights violations nor the basis for advancing human rights: political, social and economic factors explain the status of human rights. The question is not whether Islam can be reconciled with human rights, but under what political and economic conditions human rights would be attractive to Muslims (Chase 2006, 2007). Mayer, similarly, argues that it is the failure of secular political regimes and the historical imposition of Western culture in the Muslim world that have for many called into question the legitimacy of human rights. Nevertheless, repression by governments in the Muslim world is similar to repression by governments in other countries, and many Muslims object to it for reasons that are similar to those advanced by non-Muslims. The dominant Islamic conceptions of human rights reflect power struggles between traditionalist elites and liberal modernizers more than the inherent features of Islam (Mayer 2007).

The right to culture

International human-rights law has been more attentive to cultural difference than is sometimes recognized. The UDHR includes a right to culture, although this was somewhat neglected until recently. The International Covenant on Civil and Political Rights (ICCPR) provides that, in the election of members of the Human Rights Committee, consideration be given to the representation of different forms of civilization. UN human-rights agencies often specify that rights be implemented in a way that is culturally appropriate for a particular group (Office of the United Nations High Commissioner for Human Rights 2006). The right to culture entails that there is a right to enjoy all the human rights in a way that is compatible with one's culture.

Universal standards are modified by reservations that states make in ratifying human-rights treaties, which are sometimes made from respect for cultural differences. Regional human-rights regimes take regional cultural differences into account in their interpretation of human rights. The Vienna Declaration affirmed the universality of human rights, but qualified this by insisting that 'the significance of national and regional particularities and various historical, cultural and religious backgrounds must be borne in mind'. In contrast to these concessions to cultural diversity, Article 5 of CEDAW requires states parties to modify cultural patterns to eliminate prejudices and practices based on gender inequality or stereotyped gender roles. Some hold that respect for the dignity of rights-bearers requires that human rights be implemented with respect for cultures. Some believe also that implementation is more likely to be successful if it respects local cultures.

If we are to respect other cultures, we must know what those cultures are. It can be difficult for outsiders to acquire this knowledge. Governments and intellectual elites often act as 'gatekeepers', offering an official version of the culture to the outside world. We have, however, reasons to be sceptical of the claims of elites to speak for the people. We can hear the people only if they have a secure set of rights. If, for example, women are excluded from public life, we cannot know if the culture of the people is being truly represented. Respect for cultural diversity, which is often represented as a threat to the universality of human rights, may require the robust implementation of those rights.

The most difficult case for human-rights universalism is that in which those who are victims of human-rights violations support the culture that legitimates those violations. Women may gain respect in their communities by conforming to traditional values and norms governing gender relations. Asserting women's rights may be punished by ostracism or violence. Efforts by governments or NGOs to change traditional culture for the sake of human rights may produce grass-roots resistance as this change from above lacks legitimacy and is unsettling, replacing hierarchical security with individualist uncertainty. Human rights are said to protect fundamental values from standard threats; however, human-rights advocacy can itself be perceived as a threat to certain fundamental values. Human rights may be perceived as the culture of modern, educated, urban elites seeking to dominate that of rural populations. These populations may deploy the concept of 'human dignity' to defend traditional culture against interventions based on 'alien' conceptions of human rights (Ribohn 2002).

Nussbaum argues that the views of the victims are not morally decisive, because the unjust inequalities that they suffer may deny them education and thus the ability to imagine alternative ways of life (Nussbaum 1993). Both cultural relativism and respect for culture can be biased against the weak. Cultures can and should be evaluated by principles of justice (O'Neill 1993). The widely favoured response of intercultural dialogue may be inadequate because the victims may be excluded. External intervention may be counterproductive. There is no general solution to this problem, but the best strategy requires cultural critique and a contextually sensitive understanding of the likely consequences of intervention. Getting the balance between universal principles and cultural diversity right is helped by having clear reasons for the principles and for the local cultural values.

Conflict between universal principles and local cultures undoubtedly exists, and can result in serious human-rights violations, but the problem of such conflicts is often exaggerated. Universality, for example, is sometimes confused with uniformity; universality, however, promotes diversity by protecting cultural freedom. Conflicts also do not always arise from different, incommensurable values, but may arise from different balancing of shared values, such as individual rights and the common good, which may be balanced differently *within* cultures by different individuals and groups, and at different times.

A neglected problem of universalism is that there is no universal language in which to express the meaning of human rights. International human-rights law is expressed in a limited number of official languages. If human rights are to be understood universally, they must be translated into other languages. Since each language reflects its culture, this translation involves a degree of cultural relativism. Thus linguistic relativism is a necessary condition of human-rights universalism (Garre 1999).

Minority rights

Minority rights are generally assumed to belong to the field of human rights, but the relations between the two kinds of rights are problematic. The UN, in drafting the UDHR, decided to omit minority rights. The League of Nations had had a minority-rights regime, but this was thought to have failed, and the concept of minority rights was believed to have been exploited by Nazi Germany as cover for aggression. The UDHR assumes that individual human rights are sufficient to protect cultural minorities. The UN recognized that there might be a minorities problem by setting up its Sub-Commission on Prevention of Discrimination and Protection of Minorities.

The most important provision of international law governing minorities is Article 27 of the ICCPR, which provides that, in those states in which ethnic, religious or linguistic minorities exist, 'persons belonging to such minorities shall not be denied the right, in community with other members of their group, to enjoy their own culture, to profess and practise their own religion, or to use their own language'.

This goes beyond the UDHR, but contains several problems: (1) it applies only to those states in which minorities exist, thereby encouraging states to deny that minorities exist in their jurisdictions; (2) it recognizes the rights of persons belonging to minorities, not of minorities as such; (3) it imposes on states only duties of non-interference with the rights of such persons, but no duties to assist them.

The reluctance of states to take minority rights seriously has been attributed to the following factors: (1) it would encourage outside interference; (2) minority problems are diverse and it is doubtful that there are universal solutions; (3) minority rights threaten the cohesion of states; (4) minority rights discriminate against majorities (Eide 1992: 221). Nevertheless, in 1992 the UN adopted a Declaration on the Rights of Persons Belonging to National or Ethnic, Religious and Linguistic Minorities. The title of this declaration follows Article 27 in assigning rights to persons, not to minority groups. However, Article 1 of the Declaration provides that states 'shall protect the existence and the national or ethnic, cultural, religious and linguistic identity of minorities within their respective territories, and shall encourage conditions for the promotion of that identity'. Thus, although the Declaration does not recognize minority-group rights, it goes further than Article 27 in imposing on states the obligation to take positive measures to protect minority identities.

The political theory of liberal democracy was not designed historically to solve problems of cultural minorities. The classical conception of democracy entailed the rule of a culturally unified people. In the influential theory of the eighteenth-century French philosopher Rousseau, cultural differences should be subordinated to the 'general will' of the people (Rousseau 1968). Locke's liberal theory was designed to protect the natural rights of individuals. He assumed that, since all citizens were equal, political decisions should be taken by the majority: minorities were simply outvoted citizens. He had no conception of cultural minorities. Government had a duty to respect the natural rights of every individual, but minorities as such had no rights (Locke [1689] 1970). Liberal democracy offers to members of cultural minorities individual rights, including the right to participate in cultural groups. Since all citizens have equal rights, the status of minorities is perfectly just. Actual liberal democracies are, of course, unjust in various ways, but, liberal democrats argue, this is because liberal-democratic principles are often violated in practice. The solution to this problem is the robust implementation of the principles, not their revision.

The persistence of minority claims in even the most developed liberal-democratic societies, the connection between minority problems and gross human-rights violations around the world, and the end of the Cold War ideological conflict have generated practical and theoretical challenges to this liberal-democratic solution. In response, liberal-democratic theorists have reviewed the relations between politics and culture, and between majorities and minorities. The concept of 'multiculturalism' has come to occupy a central place in liberal-democratic theory. Liberal-democratic theorists are far from agreement, however, on how liberal democracies should solve the problems of multiculturalism.

Kymlicka has developed a liberal theory of culture. In a multicultural society, he argues, the state necessarily promotes certain cultures and thereby disadvantages others. In a multilingual society, for example, not all languages can be official languages. This raises the question of justice for minorities. Liberals value individual choice, but individuals make their choices in cultural contexts. Liberals should, therefore, protect the cultures that provide the bases for individuals' choices. Under certain conditions, cultures can be protected only by recognizing group rights (Kymlicka 1995).

Cultural communities are, therefore, necessary to good individual lives, but individuals should have some autonomy from the communities of which they are members to choose the life that seems best for them. Communities are structured by inequalities of power, and are therefore always at least potentially oppressive. Liberals cannot generally approve the restriction by minority groups of the basic rights of their members. Liberals believe that individuals should have the capacity and freedom to question the culture of their community, and decide for themselves which aspects of that culture they will retain. Some restrictions of individual rights may nevertheless be justified to prevent actions that would undermine communities which are necessary for autonomous choices. What makes this justification of community restriction of individual rights liberal is that its purpose is to protect a rights-supporting community (Kymlicka 1995).

Kymlicka believes that the discourse of human rights can be an ideological disguise for the domination of minorities by majorities and that human-rights principles cannot solve some of the most important problems raised by minorities. The right to freedom of speech, for example, does not tell us what language policy a society ought to have. Even in liberal-democratic societies members of cultural minorities may suffer from unfair disadvantages, resulting from the power of majorities, without the violation of human rights (Kymlicka 1995: 4–5, 109). Human rights may even make injustice worse. For example, the rights to freedom of movement and vote may enable members of the majority to move to the traditional homelands of minorities, outvote them, and then undermine their culture. To protect themselves from this form of oppression, minorities may need collective rights to land ownership and language use, and to restrict the rights to freedom of movement and vote of the majority. Such collective rights are not fundamentally inconsistent with human rights, for liberal-democratic states claim the right to regulate immigration, land use and language policies, and such claims are not usually considered to be human-rights violations. In so far as the collective rights of minorities resemble recognized collective rights of nation-states, they should be subject to the same human-rights conditions. Kymlicka claims that minority and indigenous rights are an *extension of*, rather than a *reservation to*, the concept of human rights, but there may be in his theory an unresolved tension between individual and collective rights (Kymlicka 2001, 2007).

Kymlicka has been criticized for being a liberal imperialist, because he supports minority rights only for minorities that are liberal (Chaplin 1993). Kymlicka might reply that liberals are logically committed to disapproving of illiberal groups. His criticisms of human rights are, however, not compelling. The charge that human-rights principles cannot solve all minority problems is not apt, for the concept of human rights is intended to set *minimum standards* and not to provide a comprehensive theory of social justice. The charge that human rights might permit unjust behaviour can be answered by reaffirming that human rights are not unlimited. They may be limited for the sake of protecting human rights or for other reasons, as Article 29 of the UDHR provides.

Tully has put forward an apparently anti-liberal argument about cultural diversity and justice. He argues that cultural diversity is a fundamental feature of the human condition and culture is inherent in human interaction. As citizens interact with each other, so they express their different cultures. Cultural recognition is a basic human need. A uniform political and legal system, to which all citizens are subject in the same way, denies this cultural diversity unjustly. Most liberal constitutions are unjust in this way. Constitutions should consist of a continuing intercultural dialogue. In this dialogue, each speaker should be given their due. This appears to recognize that cultural diversity goes down to the level of the individual, and therefore lays the basis for a conception of (individual) human rights: Tully's 'intercultural' constitutionalism is not as anti-liberal as it appears at first sight. Nevertheless, liberal constitutions, he argues, require cultural minorities to speak in the discourse of the dominant group. They suppress cultural differences and impose a dominant culture, while representing themselves as impartial. By contrast, intercultural dialogue aims for just cultural recognition, while repudiating unjust claims to recognition (Tully 1995). Tully does not make clear his criteria for the justice of claims to recognition, and thereby fails to answer the question to which liberal democracy provides an answer in the form of equal rights for all. Although Tully's theory of intercultural constitutionalism has a liberal core, its reliance on dialogue favours the powerful over the weak, and is therefore in this respect less just than the liberal constitutionalism that he criticizes.

Barry defended a liberal-democratic conception of justice that is 'blind' to cultural difference. Liberalism, he said, accommodates all differences that are just. Liberal democracies are just in that they treat all citizens as equals. They do not tolerate all differences, since some social practices are unacceptably harmful to others and to society. In particular, liberal democracies should not tolerate those who would undermine them. Such toleration betrays justice. Barry opposed the institutionalization of cultural differences, because he believed that this makes minorities more vulnerable to the dominant groups in society. Participation in common institutions creates solidarity, which is the best protection for minorities. Barry's defence of liberal democracy is open to the objection that liberal states cannot be culturally neutral, and that supposedly impartial justice conceals the unjust domination of particular cultures (Barry 2001).

Barry held that liberal democracies should permit voluntary associations to engage in certain illiberal practices (for example, a religious community might refuse to have women priests) provided that their members have a genuine right to leave. However, he supported forceful intervention by liberal states to end unacceptable illiberal practices in minority communities. Few people, he argued, object to state intervention in *families* to prevent child abuse. Kymlicka is cautious about intervention for two reasons. The first is the unsuccessful historical record of liberal states in their attempts to 'improve' minority cultures. The second is that liberal state agents may be insensitive to the value of minority-group cultures to their members (Kymlicka 1989). We may also recall the argument that self-emancipation is better than emancipation by outsiders. These arguments against intervention are not decisive where the group oppression of its members is extreme.

In liberal democracies, Barry maintained, citizens have no obligation to respect each other's cultures, but, rather, they have obligations to respect each other as citizens, irrespective of culture. This missed Tully's point that citizens encounter each other culturally, and they cannot respect each other as citizens if they despise their fellow-citizens' cultures. Barry agreed that cultural differences are unavoidable, but maintained that liberal democracy provides the fairest way of settling disputes among cultures. What all people have in common provides the basis for universal human rights, and their cultural disagreements are best settled by liberal-democratic procedures. Minority rights tend to undermine both human rights and liberal democracy.

Barry's defence of liberal democracy underestimated the problem that actual liberal democracies developed historically through injustices that may not be rectified by equal individual rights. Because the legitimate claims of minorities are typically the product of particular national histories, it is doubtful whether there are *universal* minority rights.

The term 'minority rights' refers to two different kinds of rights: individual rights of minority-group members and collective rights of minority groups. The first may be *required* by human-rights principles, whereas the second may be incompatible with human rights. Collective rights also raise the problem of defining the group that has the rights.

Donnelly argues that, although there are collective rights, there are no collective human rights. Collective rights may be necessary to protect human dignity, and therefore may be compatible with human rights, but, in the event of conflict between collective rights and human rights, the latter should generally prevail. The preservation of cultural groups may be valuable, but, if the group is violating human rights, and its members choose to leave or to abandon its culture, human-rights principles cannot defend the survival of the group. However, since human rights are not absolute, and since rights-violating groups may have some value for their members, there is no general principle governing the right of cultural groups to survival. We should remember, however, that respecting human rights is often the best way of protecting cultural minorities (Donnelly 1989: 149–57). A controversial question is whether cultural minorities have the right to state funding for their culture. It may be good policy for the state to support some minority cultural activities, but it is doubtful whether there is a human right to such support. One problem of recognizing such a right would, again, be that of identifying the right-holders. Critics of such supposed group rights to state support for minority cultures believe that it would encourage competition and division among minority groups and make them more vulnerable to hostility and exploitation by the dominant group.

Indigenous peoples

Minority rights are often confused with the rights of indigenous peoples. Some indigenous peoples' representatives, however, claim that they are not 'minorities', but *colonized peoples*. The confusion is made worse by the fact that there is no agreed definition of either minorities or indigenous peoples in international law or social science. The term 'indigenous people' originates from the American continent, where it refers to those who are descended from the peoples who inhabited the continent before the arrival of Europeans, who retain significant elements of non-European culture, and are economically, socially and politically oppressed. The application of the concept to other parts of the world is problematic, since some groups who have the social characteristics of indigenous peoples are not indigenous, and some indigenous peoples do not have these characteristics. Indigenous peoples can also contain conflicting class, gender and other interests. Most, though not all, indigenous groups are relatively small, but, together, they constitute about 5 per cent of the world's population. Historically, they have been victims of genocide, cultural oppression and labour exploitation. Indigenous peoples do not, however, all have similar cultures nor do they all have similar social problems.

There have been two significant developments in conceptions of the rights of indigenous peoples in recent years. The first has been a move from emphasis on *integration* and *assimilation* to debates about *self-determination*. The second has been a move from the International Labour Organization (ILO) to the Human Rights Commission (now the Human Rights Council) and the General Assembly. Issues concerning indigenous peoples arose in the UN first as questions about the exploitation of indigenous labour. They were taken up by the ILO, and this led to ILO Convention 107 in 1957. This Convention was based on the premise that the problems of indigenous peoples could be solved by extending to them the citizenship rights of the dominant population. It did not recognize their specific cultures. Consequently, it was rejected by indigenous peoples. In 1989 it was amended as ILO Convention 169. Although this Convention called upon states to respect the cultures of indigenous peoples and rejected the policy of assimilation, it failed to meet their demands and was adopted without their participation (Kymlicka 2007).

Indigenous peoples rejected these statist, 'top-down' solutions, and began to mobilize with the demand for self-determination as colonized peoples. National governments and the 'international community' were for a long time reluctant to meet this demand. After many years of campaigning by indigenous peoples and their supporters, the UN General Assembly adopted the Declaration on the Rights of Indigenous Peoples on 13 September 2007 by an overwhelming majority. The Declaration proclaims an extensive set of individual and collective economic, cultural and political rights. In particular, it reflects the indigenous claims to land rights and to be consulted over development projects. As a declaration of the General Assembly it is not legally binding. It is implemented at the international level by the Permanent Forum on Indigenous Issues, the Expert Mechanism on the Rights of Indigenous Peoples, and the Special Rapporteur on the Rights of Indigenous Peoples. It has also been taken up by UN agencies and by some national courts. The 'statism' of international law had not recognized indigenous peoples as subjects of international law; the Declaration affords this recognition, though in terms of the dominant legal discourse; it is thus a compromise between international law and the cultures of indigenous peoples. Critics hold that liberal, human-rights discourse reinforces and conceals the power structures of colonialism (Coulthard 2014).

The Declaration appears to accord indigenous peoples more extensive rights than minorities enjoy under international law, especially the right to self-determination. Kymlicka argues that this is because, unlike minorities, they are not perceived to be security threats by state elites. Nevertheless, the distinction between indigenous peoples and minorities is not clear-cut. Could the Kurds or the Tibetans claim the right to self-determination as indigenous peoples? (Kymlicka 2011).

The indigenous demand for political self-determination is not usually a demand for an independent state, but for self-government within the state in which they live. Equally important for many groups is the demand for *economic* self-determination. Indigenous peoples are not necessarily opposed to economic development, but they wish to control the form that it takes. This often brings them into conflict with states and private corporations that have other plans for these resources.

Indigenous peoples' representatives also claim the right to *cultural* self-determination. This raises the problem of potential conflict between indigenous cultures and human rights. The UN Human Rights Committee has sought to strike a balance between individual rights and the preservation of indigenous cultures. These decisions show that the international-law conception of human rights is not extremely individualistic. The individualistic conception of human rights is, however, not well suited to do justice to collective indigenous land claims (Brysk 2000: 202). Kymlicka maintains that indigenous peoples are more willing to accept adverse judgements from international bodies than from their own states' institutions (Kymlicka 1995: 169). Conflicts between collective indigenous peoples' rights and international, individual human rights may, therefore, not be as intractable in practice as they may appear in theory. The doctrine of cultural relativism may *disempower* indigenous peoples in their struggles against the state by trapping them in politically ineffectual cultures (Brysk 2000: 65).

The tension between indigenous culture and the rights of women has been the site of contestation. Among the issues raised have been the right of indigenous women to leave their community, their right to rejoin it if they wish, and the status of women who consent to the violation of their human rights for the sake of participation in their traditional culture. A meeting of indigenous women takes place on the margins of the annual meeting of the Permanent Forum on Indigenous Issues (Xanthaki 2011).

States sometimes hold indigenous practices to be illegal on human-rights grounds as a means to control indigenous groups in ways that may violate their individual and collective rights. The international human-rights system may offer least protection to those indigenous peoples who need it most: states that have agreed to adjudication by the Human Rights Committee are those with relatively good human-rights records (Speed and Collier 2000; Thornberry 2002).

A neglected sub-field of indigenous rights consists of the rights of nomadic peoples. Since Locke, theories of property have favoured agricultural rights over those of nomads. The agricultural theory of land ownership provided a basis for the territorial theory of sovereignty and the exclusion of nomads from the protection of international law. In the *Western Sahara* case (1975), however, the International Court of Justice held that nomads in the Western Sahara had rights over land. Some national courts have also recognized nomadic land rights. Some have, however, been reluctant to extend indigenous rights to nomadic peoples. There is scope within the law of non-discrimination, minority and indigenous rights to protect the human rights of nomadic peoples, but this law is not yet fully developed (Gilbert 2007).

The recent movement for indigenous rights has challenged the liberal-democratic basis of human rights. This is not because indigenous groups reject human rights. Some indigenous practices violate human-rights norms, but indigenous groups also sometimes appeal to those norms to support their cause. However, in claiming various forms of autonomy, indigenous groups challenge the concept of the liberal-democratic nation-state with a homogeneous concept of citizens' rights. They do so partly because they have been conquered and exploited by the states of which they are supposed to be citizens, and partly because their experience of liberal-democratic citizens' rights has not been pleasant. The 'international community' of nation-states and its international law were constructed by imperial conquest. Natural law provided a basis for criticizing imperialism, but when it was replaced by positive international law in the nineteenth century, indigenous peoples were coercively included in the system of sovereign states. Liberal democracies form part of this international system and so their moral claim to the loyalty of their indigenous groups has been questioned (Keal 2003). Nevertheless, the rich liberal democracies have been able to afford limited concessions to indigenous peoples, while the 'development imperative' of less developed countries makes such concessions more difficult.

Some have questioned the very idea of 'indigenous rights' without denying that indigenous peoples have been victims of gross injustice. The argument is that it is not 'indigeneity' as such that grounds rights, but historical injustice. Some indigenous groups may be the perpetrators, not the victims, of injustice: the indigenous Fijians may be an example. The right of indigenous peoples to self-determination is, some say, in principle no different from the right of any people to self-determination. Its ground is not indigeneity, but the contingent, though pervasive, historical fact that indigenous peoples have been the victims of gross human-rights violations, and that some form of autonomy is the most appropriate remedy (Buchanan 2004).

The right to self-determination

Both the international human-rights covenants of 1966 state that all peoples have the right to self-determination, but who has this right is controversial. The orthodox view in international law is that it is a right to be free from European imperial rule, and not to be subject to racist domination or alien occupation (Cassese 1995). This view is strongly influenced by particular political phenomena such as the world-wide anti-colonial movement, the campaign against apartheid in South Africa, and opposition to Israeli occupation of Palestinian lands. The right has not been extended to other peoples subject to alien rule, such as the Tibetans. The right to self-determination has been interpreted in international politics for the sake of the stability of the states system. This policy of the 'international community' has not been very successful, since conflicts over self-determination have constituted perhaps the most disorderly feature of the states system in recent years. The international community has given priority to the principle of *territorial integrity* over that of self-determination. This has left minority peoples vulnerable to majority oppression, encouraged secessionist conflicts, provoked state violence and gross human-rights violations, and threatened destabilization of the inter-state order.

Political theorists have proposed various theories of self-determination on the basis of liberal-democratic principles. The most influential is the *remedial theory*. This says that states which respect the human rights of their citizens have a right to their loyalty, and there is therefore no right of secession from such states. There is a right of secession only if there are serious and persistent human-rights violations and no solution other than secession is available (Birch 1984). This theory is *liberal* rather than *nationalist*, for the violation of individual human rights rather than national interests justifies secession, although the theory might support national self-determination if the victims of human-rights violations constituted a nation.

Beran has developed an alternative liberal theory that may be called the *voluntarist theory*. This is based on the liberal value of *individual* self-determination. This entails the right to freedom of association. Any individual who wishes to leave a political community has the right to do so. If the majority in part of a state's territory wishes to secede, they have the right to do so. Human-rights violations are not necessary to this right of secession. Nor is it necessary that the secessionists are a nation (Beran 1984, 1988). The right to secession is subject to two important conditions: (1) secessionists must respect the human rights of everyone living in the new state; (2) they must also recognize the right to secession of the majority of any territory within its borders. This generates what is sometimes called the 'Russian doll' problem. If all territorial majorities have the right to secede, the states-system might split up into ever smaller states, with consequent anarchy. Beran advances four answers to this objection: (1) the risk of war may override the right to secession; (2) war apart, the right to secession overrides concerns about the number of states; (3) excessive secession would be checked by the self-interest of potential secessionists; (4) excessive secession can be checked by enlightened concessions by states to potential secessionists. Theoretically, Beran has difficulty in deriving a *collective* right to self-determination from his *individualist* premises. He says that those with property rights have the right to alter the sovereignty over their property, but, since he has no theory of property rights, this argument is weak. Whether Beran's theory would work in practice is hard to say, since no actual secession has been based on it (Pavković and Radan 2007).

The collective right to self-determination may be derived from *democratic* premises. According to democratic theory, the legitimacy of government derives from the will of the people. The self-determination of nations is, therefore, equivalent to democracy. Since democratic self-government is a collective value, democratic theory may be better suited than liberal individualism to justify a collective right to self-determination.

A collective right to national self-determination can also be derived from *communitarian* premises. Communitarians reject Beran's assumption that national membership is voluntary. Most people are born into their nation; it forms part of their identity. Communitarians argue that, if there is a right to national self-determination, it must be a collective right (Raz 1986: 207–9). Margalit and Raz argue that individuals flourish through culture; culture is maintained by groups; the prosperity of cultural groups is therefore necessary to the well-being of their members; and self-determination is necessary for the protection of groups. Human-rights violations are not necessary to justify the right to national self-determination. The right of groups to self-determination is the weaker, however, the more likely it is that recognizing it would lead to the violation of the rights either of group members or of outsiders (Margalit and Raz 1990). The communitarian right to self-determination is therefore subject to liberal conditions.

David Miller argues that nations are ethical communities and states are the most effective co-ordinating mechanisms for nations. Nation-states are therefore the best available institutions for social justice, and this provides the justification for national self-determination (Miller, D. 1995). This raises several problems. There are problems, for example, in defining nations and in showing that they are 'ethical communities'. The argument also claims only that nation-states are the best institutions to provide justice *for their citizens*. This allows at best only weak obligations on the part of nation-states towards the human rights of foreigners.

Practical discussions of self-determination are more concerned with international order than with human rights. Shehadi argues that, in order to achieve its goal of international order, the international community must balance the principle of the territorial integrity of states with the aspirations of aggrieved nations, and that there should be international institutions with the authority to settle self-determination disputes in accordance with the rule of law rather than the rule of force (Shehadi 1993). This proposal tries to combine principle with pragmatism, but may be too principled to be acceptable to powerful states, and too pragmatic to satisfy the requirements of justice. This shows how difficult it is to implement the right of *peoples* to self-determination in a world of *states*.

There is a consensus among practical scholars that the right to *secession* should rarely be recognized, but that states should recognize forms of self-determination that fall short of secession (Hannum 1990). Many governments, however, fear that self-determination may be the first step to secession. Such fears are often exaggerated, but they are not always. Self-determination problems can be extremely difficult, but their solutions are likely to require, not the abolition of nation-states, but new thinking about the forms that it might take. Some have maintained that the right to self-determination is *the most important* human right or the *precondition* of all other human rights. Some persecuted nations undoubtedly have strong claims to self-determination. However, the idea of a universal human right to the self-determination of peoples raises complex analytical problems and carries great dangers to human rights. It may even be incoherent, as the right to self-determination of one people (say, the Québecois) may conflict with the right to self-determination of another people (say, the Canadians).

The rights of women

According to the World Health Organization 70 per cent of those in extreme poverty are female, two-thirds of those who are illiterate are women, and on average women are paid between 30 and 40 per cent less than men for comparable work (Simmons 2009: 204). Certain forms of the mistreatment of women were objects of international standard-setting by inter-governmental conferences and the ILO before the Second World War. In 1945 feminists succeeded in having the equal rights of men and women written into the UN Charter and in establishing the Commission on the Status of Women (CSW). The prohibition of discrimination against women was included in the UDHR. The CSW, though hampered by underfunding and the opposition of culturally conservative states, was responsible for CEDAW, adopted in 1979. Many states have ratified CEDAW, but it is weakened by numerous reservations. The Committee charged with implementing CEDAW is also under-resourced (Reanda 1992; Jacobson 1992).

Growing dissatisfaction among women's groups and Commission members with the slow pace of progress led to the Decade for Women 1975–85, which included three world conferences, held in Mexico City, Copenhagen and Nairobi. The declarations and programmes of action adopted by these conferences were endorsed by the UN General Assembly. The issues thus officially recognized included political participation, education, employment, health, nutrition, agricultural production and marketing, access to credit, housing, industrial development, and the special vulnerability of refugees, the disabled, the elderly and many others. The Women's Decade led to a shift of emphasis from activities specifically related to women to 'mainstreaming', that is, incorporating women's issues in all UN planning. UN human-rights bodies began to include gender issues in their work, an innovation that was strengthened when Mary Robinson became the High Commissioner for Human Rights (Gaer 2001). It was also recognized that the situation of women would not be improved unless women were empowered through participation in decision-making. Whether this change of strategy has led to much improvement in the everyday lives of women is uncertain (Reanda 1992; Simmons 2009).

Feminists have challenged dominant interpretations of human rights, arguing that they are biased against women, because they address violations by states, and ignore the violations that women suffer at the hands of men in the private sphere. In classical natural-rights theory, natural rights are held by all human beings and entail obligations by all human beings. This theory has been translated into international human-rights law, in which the rights are held by individual human beings, but the obligations not to violate those rights are borne mainly by *states*. This element of the dominant conception of human rights is sometimes justified as necessary to distinguish human-rights violations from ordinary crimes (Donnelly 1999: 85–6).

The UDHR, however, is not so statist, and imposes obligations on states, groups and persons. Article 2(e) of CEDAW imposes on states the obligation to eliminate discrimination against women 'by any person, organization or enterprise'. The Vienna Declaration acknowledged that 'gender-based violence and all forms of sexual harassment and exploitation' were human-rights violations. In 1993 the UN General Assembly unanimously adopted the Declaration on the Elimination of All Forms of Violence Against Women. Article 4 (c) requires states to exercise due diligence to prevent and punish acts of violence against women, 'whether those acts are perpetrated by the State or by private persons'. In 1994 the Commission on Human Rights appointed a Special Rapporteur on Violence Against Women (Joachim 2003: 247–8). Feminists sometimes cite Article 16 (3) of the UDHR, which says that the family is 'the natural and fundamental group unit of society' and is 'entitled to protection by society and the State' in order to show that the Declaration endorses the male-dominated family. Article 16 (3) does not have to be interpreted in this way, however, and there are other provisions of human-rights law that can provide the basis for feminist campaigns.

Liberals can reply to the feminist criticism that, by insisting on a protected private sphere, they protect the violation of women's rights by men, with the argument that liberalism imposes on the state the duty to protect everyone from violation of their rights in the private as well as the public sphere. Feminists argue that the subjection of women in the household often leads to their disempowerment in the public sphere. The distinction between the public domain of the state and the private domain of the family is fallacious, they say, because the family is, in all societies, regulated by the state and its law. Reproduction and child-rearing, usually considered to be private activities *par excellence*, are typically regulated by men to form male and female identities so as to ensure the subordination of women. Some recognized human-rights violations, such as torture, are experienced by women in a distinctive way, for example as sexual violence and/or humiliation. Women suffer much more than men from justifications of the violations of almost all their human rights by appeals to culture. In addition, their access to legal redress is often barred by discriminatory, male-dominated legal systems (Binion 1995; Desai 1999). Some feminists criticize the concept of equality in human-rights discourse on the ground that it fails to recognize the difference of women's experience. It is valid to emphasize the difference of women's experiences, but the critique of equality for the sake of difference may be counter-productive because cultural groups often justify treating women unequally on the ground of cultural difference.

Feminism has energized the cause of women's human rights, and drawn the attention of the UN, governments and human-rights NGOs to the many serious human-rights violations that are suffered exclusively or predominantly by women. This cause was advanced at the fourth World Conference on Women, held in Beijing in 1995, despite opposition from various conservative groups, religious institutions and states. This has certainly been one of the most significant shifts in the interpretation of human rights in international politics since the end of the Cold War. Against the feminist critique of international human-rights law, Fellmeth has pointed out that there about two dozen significant international legal texts aimed at protecting women's rights. The bias against women is much less in international law than in the difficulty of implementing it (Fellmeth 2000: 727–8).

Some feminists, however, complain that the individualism of human rights conceals the structural oppression of women. However, defending the rights of individual women does not entail denying the structural causes of their violation. Nyamu-Musembi argues that the human-rights movement has neglected the rights of women in developing countries, especially those in rural areas. The feminist critique of 'culture' ignores the fact that the state often determines what counts as 'culture'. The rights of these women require political rather than cultural change. Modern political and economic forces may be more harmful to women than traditional culture, which often accorded them land rights that they have lost. Culture can be an emancipatory as well as a repressive force. International human-rights law without legal and social anthropology may be futile or counter-productive (Nyamu-Musembi 2000).

The rights of children

Gross violation of the human rights of children is widespread. Almost one-quarter of the world's youth live in extreme poverty; 250 million children live on the street; 211 million must work to feed themselves and their families; 115 million have never been to school. The UN estimates that some 25 million children are displaced; children are trafficked into slavery; millions are refugees; they are sent abroad for forced marriage or genital mutilation; they suffer many abuses in conflict zones; they are recruited as child soldiers, raped and forced into marriage. It is estimated that, in the first decade of this century, more than two million children were killed, six million permanently disabled or injured, 250,000 exploited as child soldiers, tens of thousands of girls raped and subjected to other forms of sexual violence, and more than 14 million children displaced, in armed conflict (Chikuhwa 2010; Singer 2010; Archard 2012; Bochenek 2015).

Although concern for the welfare of children pre-dates the modern concept of human rights, the human-rights movement was slow to incorporate children into its concerns. The declarations of the American and French Revolutions were silent on children. In the nineteenth century the child-protection movement established orphanages, schools, and juvenile courts. The Geneva Declaration of the Rights of the Child, adopted by the League of Nations in 1924, stated that 'mankind owed to the Child the best that it has to give', and proclaimed a duty to provide the necessary means for normal development, food and medicine, relief in times of distress, protection against exploitation, and socialization to serve others. The UN Declaration of the Rights of the Child, adopted in 1959, also emphasized child protection (Freeman 1997).

Michael D. A. Freeman has distinguished three approaches to child welfare: child protection, children's liberation, and children's rights. The first treats children as objects of concern; the second emphasizes the adolescent's right to self-determination. Freeman proposes a middle way, according to which children both need protection and are capable of making autonomous choices. On this view, children move from requiring protection and nurturance to respect for their autonomy as they grow older. Some adolescents have more capacity than many adults. The value of autonomy is compatible with the practice of compulsion, so that, for example, compulsory education can be justified on the ground that it can develop the child's capacity for autonomy (Freeman 1997).

The middle approach has been taken by the UN, which in 1989 adopted its Convention on the Rights of the Child (CRC) without a vote. The Convention received the 20 ratifications it needed to come into force in less than a year; for comparison, the International Covenant on Civil and Political Rights took ten years to achieve the same result. By June 2016 CRC had been ratified by all UN states except the USA, more than any other human-rights treaty.

Five issues were controversial in the drafting process: freedom of religion; inter-country adoption; the rights of unborn children; traditional practices harmful to children's health; and the duties of children. Article 14 combines the right of children to freedom of religion with the right of parents to guide their children in the exercise of this right, and the right of the state to regulate religion in the public interest. Adoption is not recognized in Islam, and there was Latin American opposition to inter-country adoption on the ground that it might amount to 'exporting children'. Article 21 permits, but does not require, inter-country adoption where it is 'in the best interests of the child' and subject to various legal safeguards. The rights of the unborn are left ambiguous by a combination of the preamble, which states that children need special protection 'before as well as after birth', and Article 1, which defines children as human beings below the age of 18. The Convention is also somewhat ambiguous about traditional practices harmful to children's health, as Article 24 (3) calls on states parties to take 'appropriate' measures to abolish such practices, while the preamble recognizes the importance of traditions and cultural values. Article 29 (1) (c) states that education should include respect for parents. Perhaps the most distinctive element in the Convention is Article 12, which recognizes the right of children to freedom of expression, especially in legal proceedings concerning their welfare. CRC also unifies civil and political rights with economic, social and cultural rights more thoroughly than any other human-rights treaty.

CRC has been criticized because Article 38 permits the recruitment of child soldiers once they have reached the age of 15. However, as a result of an initiative by CRC's committee the issues of child soldiers and the impact of armed conflicts on child civilians have been 'mainstreamed' in the UN Security Council. In 1997 the General Assembly established a special representative of the Secretary-General for children and armed conflict. In 1998 the Coalition to Stop the Use of Child Soldiers – now called Child Soldiers International – was established by a group of leading human-rights organizations. The General Assembly adopted the Optional Protocol to CRC on the Involvement of Children in Armed Conflict in 2000; the protocol had been ratified by 165 countries by August 2016. In 2005 the Security Council established its Working Group on Children and Armed Conflict, and concern for children in armed conflict is increasingly integrated into the international peace and security agenda of the Council. The causes of the child-soldiers problem are complex, but they have little to do with culture, and much to do with social dislocation, poverty, disease, unemployment and the consequent availability of children for recruitment into low-tech, low-cost forms of warfare, often by non-state, 'irregular' forces fighting for control over resources, and resembling ruthless, criminal gangs more than armies (Singer 2010).

Although CRC represents a substantial cross-cultural consensus on the human rights of children, it suffers from many reservations, a weak implementation system, and the lack of the right of individual petition. Its monitoring committee is very under-resourced. Ten years after the Convention came into force, the committee was almost four years behind in considering state reports, and was only saved from a worse situation because 57 states were overdue with their reports. The committee has no investigative capacity, and is reliant on NGOs for information. King argues that CRC fails to address the causes of children's suffering, and that its vague language permits governments to evade their responsibilities (King 2004). This criticism applies to some extent to all international human-rights law, and it has some merit. Article 3 says that the best interests of the child shall be a primary consideration in all actions concerning children. This may seem to be an attractive principle, but it makes CRC susceptible to different interpretations in different cultural contexts. Also, because the best interests of the child are *a* rather than *the* primary consideration, they can be overruled. This is common in immigration cases, where the deportation of adults may be carried out, even when this is not in the best interests of their children (Todres 2004).

Nevertheless, it may be that CRC provides a helpful framework and a form of legitimation for those who campaign for children. CRC and its committee have influenced the European Court of Human Rights and some national courts (Johnson 1992; Fottrell 2000). Some improvements in children's well-being have been attributed to it: child mortality has decreased; children's educational opportunities have improved; the number of child soldiers and child workers has reduced; measures have been taken against child trafficking and exploitation; corporal punishment has declined; children's voices are heard more often (Archard 2012).

Sexual minorities

Hostility to 'sexual minorities' – that is, lesbian, gay, bisexual and transgender (LGBT) persons – exists in every society. Government and other leaders often dehumanize them in language that would be considered unacceptable if applied to racial, ethnic or religious minorities. Punishments for sexual conduct that arouses the disapproval of the authorities is extremely harsh in many countries, including the death penalty. Members of sexual minorities are subjected to a range of serious human-rights violations, including discrimination in education, health care and employment, physical assault, torture and murder (Baisley 2016). In most countries same-sex couples lack the legal economic rights of those who are conventionally married. Concern for the rights of sexual minorities is often said to be a Western cultural peculiarity, but this claim, like all similar East/West claims, is at best an oversimplification. There is prejudice against sexual minorities in the West, and there are 'gay rights' movements outside the West. Appeal is sometimes made to the provision of international human-rights law (for example, in Article 29 of the UDHR) that states have the right and the duty to restrict human rights for the sake of 'public morals'. However, if this (extremely vague) provision is used to persecute sexual minorities, it is part of the problem, not part of the solution. As Donnelly has emphasized, human rights are designed to protect the dignity and freedoms of unpopular minorities (Donnelly 2003).

Nevertheless, there is no international consensus on the rights of sexual minorities (Miller 2009). When international human-rights law was being developed after the Second World War, same-sex sexual activity was illegal in most countries. There were no 'gay rights' even though homosexuals had been explicit targets of Nazi persecution. In more recent times, the rights of sexual minorities have crept into human-rights law. In the 1980s, for example, the European Court of Human Rights held that the criminalization of consensual adult sex between men in private violated the right to privacy. However, gays have been unsuccessful in claiming the right to family life or to non-discrimination in employment benefits in European courts. Amnesty International took up gay issues in 1991; civil-society groups were active on sexual-orientation and gender-identity (SOGI) issues at UN world conferences in 1993, 1994 and 1995. These groups were cross-cultural, and not only Western, but they faced strong opposition from conservative religious groups and governments. A group of NGOs, the Sexual Rights Initiative, has lobbied the UN Human Rights Council since 2006 (Miller 2009: 8; Baisley 2016). In 1993 the International Lesbian, Gay, Bisexual, Trans and Intersex Association (ILGA) became the first lesbian and gay organization with consultative status with the UN Economic and Social Council (ECOSOC). In 1994 the UN Human Rights Committee held, in *Toonen v. Australia*, that a law in Tasmania criminalizing private consensual sex between men violated the right to privacy. Some countries accept persecuted gays, lesbians and transsexuals as refugees. The status of refugee is sometimes granted on the basis of sexual identity, but almost never on the basis of sexual conduct.

A meeting of human-rights experts, held in Yogyakarta, Indonesia, in 2006, adopted the Yogyakarta Principles on the Application of International Human Rights Law in relation to Sexual Orientation and Gender Identity. The experts agreed that these principles affirm binding international legal standards with which all states must comply. The principle of non-discrimination entails that sexual orientation and gender identity should not be a reason for reducing any person's enjoyment of human rights (Yogyakarta Principles 2006). The claim that the principles reflect the existing state of international human-rights law has been questioned (Miller 2009: 11, 22). The principles are morally compelling for those who accept that sexual orientation is integral to human dignity. In July 2010 ECOSOC granted the International Gay and Lesbian Human Rights Commission consultative status, the tenth organization working primarily for LGBT human rights to gain such status. In December 2010 the General Assembly voted to reinsert a reference to sexual orientation into its resolution on extra-judicial killings after its Third Committee had deleted it from the text. In June 2011 the Human Rights Council adopted a resolution presented by 41 countries from all regions, expressing grave concern at acts of violence and discrimination committed against individuals because of their sexual orientation and gender identity. It requested that the High Commissioner arrange a study documenting discriminatory laws and practices and acts of violence against such individuals, and how international human-rights law could be used to end such human-rights violations. A report was submitted to the Council in November 2011, and the Council's Panel on Sexual Orientation and Gender Identity was held in March 2012. Joint statements on SOGI issues have received increasing support at the Council; in 2011 a joint statement was supported by 85 states from all regions (Baisley 2016). On 13 June 2016 the Security Council issued a statement condemning 'in the strongest terms' the terrorist attack in Orlando, Florida, on 12 June 2016, 'targeting persons as a result of their sexual orientation' – the first time the UN's principal security body has acknowledged the existence of LGBT persons. On 30 June 2016 the Human Rights Council adopted by 23 to 18 with six abstentions a resolution creating an independent expert on SOGI-based violence and discrimination.

Baisley has argued that new human-rights norms are more likely to become influential if they can be linked to established norms. As of 2010 UN human-rights treaty bodies had issued decisions or general comments confirming that existing language on non-discrimination applies to LGBT persons; in the same period 17 special-procedures mandate-holders had highlighted the vulnerability of such persons or called for efforts to counter violence and discrimination based on sexual orientation or gender identity. Treaty bodies and special procedures have, however, been inconsistent on SOGI issues, sometimes apparently employing a version of 'the margin of appreciation' to find state discrimination against LGBT persons to be reasonable. In the General Assembly even states opposed to SOGI rights do not deny that sexual minorities have basic human rights. Ban Ki-Moon, the Secretary-General, appealed to the priority of human rights over culture to call for an end to violence and criminal sanctions based on SOGI at a Council event in September 2010. In July 2013 the High Commissioner, Navi Pillay, launched the UN's first global public-education campaign to counter hostility to sexual minorities. Both the Secretary-General and the High Commissioner cited the treaty bodies and special procedures, denying that they were introducing new human rights. Significantly, neither is 'Western'. International SOGI rights are therefore emerging under cover of established human rights. This leaves open particularly controversial issues, such as same-sex marriage (Baisley 2016).

Persons with disabilities

Discrimination against persons with disabilities takes many forms: unemployment; institutionalization; social and political exclusion; violence and abuse; lack of access to essential services. It has been estimated that there are about one billion disabled persons in the world (Sabatello and Schulze 2014; Sabatello 2014a).

Campaigns for improved rights for persons with disabilities can be traced back to the nineteenth century, but they gained increased momentum as part of the 'new social movements' of the 1960s. In 1975 the UN adopted a Declaration on the Rights of Disabled Persons, declared 1981 the International Year of Disabled Persons, 1983 the beginning of the UN Decade of Disabled Persons, and set up the World Programme of Action Concerning Disabled Persons. In 1993 the General Assembly adopted the Standard Rules on the Equalization of Opportunities for Persons with Disabilities. Treaty bodies of the core human-rights conventions began to address human-rights violations of persons with disabilities; in 1994 the Committee on Economic, Social and Cultural Rights adopted a comprehensive General Comment on Persons with Disabilities (Sabatello 2014a). The Convention on the Rights of Persons with Disabilities (CRPD) was adopted by the General Assembly on 13 December 2006, following a global campaign by civil-society disability organizations and national human-rights institutions, and entered into force on 3 May 2008. As of 2 August 2016 there were 166 parties to the convention. The convention prohibits arbitrary discrimination against persons with disabilities and requires 'reasonable accommodation' to equalize opportunities for them. It also calls on governments to undertake public-education campaigns to ensure respect for the disabled. The convention includes civil, political, economic, social and cultural rights; indeed, it is said that the supposed distinction between civil and political rights, on the one hand, and economic, social and cultural rights, on the other hand, makes little sense in this field. The convention also addresses the special problems of women and children. CRPD was not intended to introduce new human rights, but rather to affirm the equal rights of disabled persons and thereby to enrich conceptions of human rights. Implementation of the convention is left to states and NGOs (McCallum 2014; Sabatello 2014b).

The campaign for disability rights has been primarily a campaign of persons with disabilities, who have sought to change the perception that disability is a medical 'defect' that requires a 'remedy' to the claim that it raises issues of citizenship rights. Disability activists claim that their 'disabilities' are political, social and cultural; prejudice and discrimination are the principal barriers to the participation of persons with disabilities in citizenship rights. The definition of 'disability' has, however, proved to be problematic, and is to some extent culturally relative. There are also different approaches within the disability rights movement; for example, some deaf persons affirm this as an identity rather than a disability, but other deaf persons do not share this view. CPRD does not define 'disability' (Sabatello 2014a).

Migrants, refugees, asylum-seekers

Article 13 of the UDHR affirms the right of everyone to 'leave any country', while Article 14 states that everyone has the right 'to seek and to enjoy in other countries' asylum from persecution. The UN Refugee Convention 1951, which had 145 states parties in April 2015, offers protection to refugees who can show a well-founded fear of persecution. The definition of 'persecution' is controversial, although it does include persecution on the ground of sexual orientation. The most distinctive right of refugees is the right to 'non-refoulement', that is the right not to be returned to a jurisdiction where persecution is likely. In practice, many countries discourage asylum-seeking, which is often difficult as asylum-seekers may be unable to prove that they are at risk of persecution. Refugees rescued at sea are often returned to their countries of origin so that the rescuing state can escape its obligation of non-refoulement, contrary to the spirit of the convention. The rights to family life and to non-discrimination in health care, education and employment are also important rights for refugees and for migrant workers; it is argued that these are better protected by human-rights than by refugee law. The recognized rights of refugees vary considerably in different regions of the world. The convention does not recognize as refugees: (1) those fleeing war wherever they are; (2) those fleeing starvation wherever they are; or (3) those fleeing persecution who remain in their own country (Edwards 2005; Aldana 2012).

The UN Refugee Agency (UNHCR) and many NGOs provide assistance to refugees, but their work is hampered by inadequate resources and the strict immigration policies of most developed countries. Poverty, increasing global inequality, improved communications and transportation technologies, human-rights violations and conflict have increased global migration and asylum-seeking. The number of people displaced by war, conflict or persecution reached a record of nearly 65.3 million in 2015. The proportion of women and children among the world's refugees has increased rapidly.

Some migrants benefit from migration, but many others are exploited and suffer from various human-rights violations both during their migration and on arrival at their destination. Women and children migrants are particularly vulnerable to violations of their human rights. Transnational migration brings economic and cultural benefits and costs to the host country, and is consequently politically controversial. This can give rise to anti-immigrant politics with attendant human-rights violations. Migration also creates costs (the 'brain drain') and benefits (for example, remittances) for sending countries. In 2014 developing countries hosted 86 per cent of the world's refugees; the least developed countries provided asylum to 25 per cent of the global total. The International Convention on the Protection of the Rights of All Migrant Workers and Members of Their Families was adopted by the UN General Assembly in 1990; it entered into force in 2003; as of 22 July 2016 it had been ratified by 48 states, almost all those that send migrant workers abroad, almost none of those that receive such workers. The Commission on Human Rights established the mandate of a Special Rapporteur on the Rights of Migrants in 1999, and this has been continued by the Human Rights Council. There is much dissatisfaction with the Refugee Convention on the grounds of its limited coverage, inadequate practical implementation and subordination to immigration policies. Some think it would be more effective to pay more attention to the human rights of refugees and migrants than to rely on the limited protections of refugee and migrant law. The 'persecution' criterion for refugee status keeps alive the distinction between civil-political and socio-economic rights, which does not correspond to the experience of many *de facto* refugees. The denial of the enjoyment of their human rights to refugees, asylum-seekers and other migrants is a major challenge to the claim that human rights are universal. In particular, citizens have more rights than migrants; legal migrants have more rights than illegal migrants (Edwards 2005; Rubio-Marín 2014; Betts 2015).

The concept of 'burden-sharing' is a potentially important, though poorly recognized, concept in the refugee field. Refugees have rights, but who has the corresponding obligations, and when do these burdens become too onerous? Many developed countries claim that they are overwhelmed by too many migrants and refugees, and that the costs of greater generosity to their own citizens would be too high and politically unacceptable. Yet most refugees are in very poor countries. Humanitarian critics say that the developed countries are in gross dereliction of their duty to rescue migrants whose human rights are denied; these countries are constrained by the politics of migration and of democracy (Albahari 2016).

Conclusion

Human rights are, by definition, universal. Theoretically, all human beings have all human rights. The universality of human rights has been proclaimed many times in international law and politics. Yet this claim has been questioned by cultural relativists, communitarians and postmodernists, and by particularist claims, such as those of 'Asian values'. The vulnerability of claims to universalism arise from (1) the lack of consensus about, and plural options for, the philosophical foundations of human rights; and (2) the great, intractable cultural diversity of the world.

The human right to culture is affirmed in the UDHR. International law requires that international human-rights law-making, monitoring and implementation bodies represent different civilizations. UN human-rights agencies have emphasized that human rights should be implemented with respect for local cultures. Human rights are therefore 'culturally inflected' (Healy 2006) at international, regional, national and local levels. The interpretation of human rights will necessarily be influenced by culture when abstract concepts, such as 'degrading treatment', must be made more determinate, and when rights conflict. Human rights can protect culture; human rights can be promoted through cultural practices; but cultures can be obstacles to human-rights implementation. Conflict between human rights and culture are seen especially clearly in relation to vulnerable groups, such as women, children, persons with disabilities, and sexual minorities. Sociologically, modernization and globalization create benefits, costs and insecurities for millions; in these circumstances cultural relativism and communitarianism become attractive alternatives to individual rights. This appeal is strengthened by the belief that human-rights lawyers and activists sometimes lack understanding of cultures that are alien to them. Yet there is empirical evidence that the core values of universal human rights retain strong appeal to the world's poor and oppressed. International human-rights law and institutions may be disappointingly weak, but they can provide valuable support for campaigns against injustice, and not only in the Western world (Tsutsui and Shin 2008).

7
The Politics of Human Rights

The real politics of human rights

The concept of human rights belongs to the *Idealist* tradition in the study of international relations in so far as it sets high ethical standards for governments. The dominant tradition, however, has been that of *Realism*, which assumes that the principal actors in international relations are states, that states are motivated primarily by self-interest, and that self-interest excludes, or at best marginalizes, concern for human rights. Realism can explain the neglect of human rights by *states*, but it can explain neither the introduction nor the increasing influence of human rights in international relations.

We saw, in chapter five, that the concept of human rights can be understood in terms of *regime theory*. International regimes consist of rules and institutions to which states commit themselves. International human rights constitute such a regime, though implementation of the regime is relatively weak. The existence and limited achievements of the regime support the Idealist approach to international relations, whereas its limitations and failures can be explained by Realism. The international human-rights regime not only implements human rights to some extent itself, but also provides the basis for human-rights actions by both governments and non-governmental organizations. The international policies of states are dominated by Realist concerns, whereas NGOs are more Idealistic, but carry less 'clout' in international relations.

The principle and practice of state sovereignty are, therefore, strong barriers to the implementation of international human-rights standards. Another strong barrier is the cultural diversity of the world, and the fact that many cultures legitimate practices that violate human-rights norms. The international human-rights regime is commonly presented as the 'imperialist' imposition of Western values on non-Western societies, but the USA has been reluctant to recognize economic, social and cultural rights, and to ratify human-rights treaties. Despite the problems posed by state sovereignty and cultural difference, the legitimacy of human rights is sufficiently strong that pressures from governments and NGOs can lead to improvements in the human-rights performance of governments, and even to changes of government that lead to improvements. The desire of governments to benefit economically and politically from 'good standing' in the international community may play a role in this process, but Realists would be wrong to insist that the moral appeal of human rights has no effect in international relations.

The growth of international human-rights law since 1945 and the dominance of lawyers in human-rights institutions and academic human-rights study conceal the priority of politics over law in the struggle for human rights. International human-rights law is made by a political process. Political campaigns play an important role in human-rights implementation. Powerful non-governmental economic organizations, such as multinational corporations, are now recognized as important players in the violation and, potentially, in the promotion of human rights, and *political* pressure on these organizations, especially by NGOs, has recently increased. Lawyers and human-rights activists typically assign a central role to legal processes in the protection of human rights, whereas political scientists are more likely to consider them to be marginal. Forsythe points out that the dramatic improvements at the end of the twentieth century in Latin America, in the former Communist societies of central and eastern Europe, and in South Africa, owed little to legal processes, and much to politics. The dominant human-rights problem in the contemporary world is the gap between human-rights ideals and law, on the one hand, and the reality of human-rights violations, on the other hand. The causes of this gap are not primarily legal or cultural, but political and economic (Forsythe 2000).

The human-rights component of foreign policy is, Forsythe maintains, a central feature of international human-rights politics. States set up international human-rights institutions, support and/or resist their efforts to implement human rights, and are the principal targets of those efforts. NGOs have become increasingly important in international human-rights politics, but their importance derives largely from the influence that they have on the human-rights policies of states (Forsythe 2000).

International human-rights politics may seem relatively ineffective if its achievements are contrasted with human-rights ideals, but they may seem more impressive if we remember that there was almost no such politics before the Second World War. After the end of the Cold War, the centre of international action for human rights shifted somewhat from the more legalistic UN institutions to the highly politicized Security Council. The so-called 'second generation' of UN peace-keeping operations has combined politics, human rights and military force. Human-rights enforcement by the Security Council may be relatively legitimate and effective, but, because this body is highly political, agreement on action is likely to be rare and selective. This is due not, as is often said, to the 'weakness' of the UN, but to the real political divisions in the world. Military enforcement of human rights is costly in lives and cash, and may be limited by the unwillingness of public opinion to make such sacrifices. It is also not necessarily well suited to solving the political problems underlying human-rights violations.

Even if governments include the promotion of human rights in their foreign policies, this will be only one among several elements, and will usually be given a much lower priority than defence and trade. Governments are often accused of 'inconsistency' in their human-rights policies; this inconsistency may be caused by changing perceptions of the national interest in a changing world or shifts in public opinion (Forsythe 2000). Governments are not unified actors: they consist of different ministries, subject to different pressure groups, and these will also lead to 'inconsistency' in human-rights foreign policy. In addition, although UN rhetoric says that human rights, peace and economic development are interdependent, in the real world of foreign policy, pursuing these goals consistently may not always be possible. The demand that the promotion of human rights should be a dominant goal of foreign policy is probably unrealistic. Nevertheless, states could probably do more than they do now to promote human rights without damaging the pursuit of other legitimate goals, and contempt for human rights can lead to foreign-policy disasters, as the USA learned in such countries as Iran and the Philippines, and, more recently, arguably, in Iraq. Thus, the strict Realist theory of human rights and foreign policy is false. More accurate is 'the principle of limited sacrifice', which says that some states will sometimes include human rights among their foreign-policy concerns, but will usually be willing to pay only a limited price for implementing them.

Armed conflict is a major cause of human-rights violations. Between 1989 and 2001 there were 57 major armed conflicts in the world. Of these, 54 were internal to states. Most of these were identity-based, and led to massive human-rights violations in such places as Bosnia, Rwanda, Sudan, Liberia, Angola, Tajikistan, Congo, Kosovo, Sierra Leone and East Timor. Some scholars have argued that an emphasis on rights, especially individual rights, can exacerbate group conflicts, thereby producing outcomes in which human-rights violations increase (Marchetti and Tocci 2011; McCrudden and O'Leary 2013).

The boomerang theory

We saw in chapter five that Risse et al. have attempted, with their 'spiral model', to show how governments which violate human rights may be subject to internal and external pressures to conform to human-rights standards, and that they may respond to these pressures from instrumental or principled motives. They may consider concessions, for example, to secure trade advantages, or because they have been 'shamed' for not conforming to the principles of the international community. It is often said that many states pay only 'lip service' to human rights. Risse and Sikkink take lip service seriously. Governments who 'talk the talk' of human rights may find it hard not to 'walk the walk', that is, to back words with actions, for fear of being accused of hypocrisy. If human-rights norms become institutionalized, they may become standard operating procedures (Risse and Sikkink 1999). The dynamic in this model is provided by the 'boomerang effect'. National human-rights NGOs seek transnational support that is converted into international pressure, which, under favourable conditions, strengthens the hands of the national groups. The effectiveness of the boomerang depends on world opinion, but, over time 'norms cascades' have occurred: the influence of human-rights norms has spread and strengthened, so that now there are few hiding-places from human-rights activism (Risse and Sikkink 1999: 18, 21).

The model proposes five phases of change. The first phase consists of repression. Repressive states often seek to prevent news of human-rights violations from leaking out. The spread of such information is necessary for the activation of a human-rights response, and the move to phase two, which consists of 'denial'. This involves not merely the denial that violations took place, but also that external pressure is legitimate. Governments may be able to mobilize nationalist sentiment in their resistance to 'outside interference'. In response, external actors can mobilize a combination of material and normative pressures: economic sanctions, 'shaming' publicity, etc. Repressive governments may 'tough out' this pressure in the hope that it will not be sustained. However, if it is sustained, and even escalated, the 'target' state may enter phase three, which is that of tactical concessions. These can lead in two directions: they may create space for internal pressure groups to bring about further change or they may 'buy off' external pressure. Risse and Sikkink believe that governments often overestimate the extent to which they can control this process, and tactical concessions may lead to 'self-entrapment', in which governments find themselves engaged in moral dialogue with external and/or internal critics (Risse and Sikkink 1999: 22–5, 28).

In the fourth phase, human-rights norms attain 'prescriptive status': governments accept them as legitimate, even though they implement them imperfectly. They ratify human-rights covenants, institutionalize their norms in national constitutions and/or laws, and provide their citizens with remedies for violations. Although violations occur, dialogue about them takes place in terms of human rights. In phase five, compliance with international human-rights standards becomes habitual and enforced, when necessary, by the rule of law.

There is no necessary progress towards the implementation of human rights. Governments may ignore international pressures, and seek to stamp out internal resistance. If they make some concessions to such pressures, they may return to repression when the pressures relax. The main factors that affect the chances of human-rights reform are: (1) the vulnerability of repressive states to external material and moral pressures; (2) the willingness of external actors to sustain these pressures; (3) the presence or absence of class-based, ethno-national or religious forces threatening the territorial integrity or the internal cohesion of the state; (4) the space available for internal NGOs; (5) the strength of the international human-rights regime and transnational NGOs; (6) 'norm resonance', that is, the degree of fit between international norms and national cultures (Risse and Ropp 1999). The authors claim that their model is superior to that of Realism, which cannot explain changes in human-rights policies. Some changes have not been direct consequences of state pressures; in some cases, such as that of the Philippines, internal NGO pressure changed great-power foreign policy (Risse and Sikkink 1999: 35; Risse and Ropp 1999: 268). The 'boomerang' model may not, however, explain such changes in foreign policy as that between the policies of Presidents Bush and Obama. The model is also said to be superior to 'modernization' theory, which has been used to explain both repression and liberalization, and therefore explains neither (Risse and Sikkink 1999: 37; Risse and Ropp 1999: 269–70). The 'boomerang' model provides a framework for analysing human-rights change, but it does not fulfil its promise of explaining variations among different societies. Realism and modernization may be insufficient for this, and the 'boomerang' may add a necessary dimension by relating external to internal pressures on repressive states, but we are left with something less than a full explanation of different human-rights performance in different societies.

Risse and Ropp conclude with ten lessons for human-rights practitioners.

1. Transnational human-rights NGOs have been very influential in recent years.
2. The impact of transnational NGOs is limited by the internal politics of target states, and national NGOs have to play an important role in this arena.
3. Transnational NGOs should direct their efforts both to weakening the resistance of governments to international norms and to supporting national NGOs.
4. Different strategies may be appropriate in different phases: blaming and shaming may be more effective in the repression and denial phases, and dialogue may be more effective in the later phases.
5. Moral and legal ideas are more effective in international politics than Realists recognize.
6. Transnational human-rights NGOs have been correct to rely on international law, for appeals to international law play an important role in effecting human-rights change.
7. In so far as human-rights activists have been anti-statist, they have been mistaken, for the pressure put by liberal states on repressive states forms an important part of the international implementation of human rights.
8. The global implementation of human rights requires the consistent and persistent implementation of human-rights foreign policy by those states that claim to take human rights seriously.
9. Economic and other material sanctions are more likely to be effective in the repression and denial phases, and less likely to be effective in the later phases, especially if the target government can mobilize a nationalist backlash against them.

10. Dialogue or 'constructive engagement' is unlikely to work in the repression and denial phases, but may be appropriate in the later phases (Risse and Ropp 1999: 275–8).

In a follow-up work, Risse and Ropp admit some limitations of the spiral model: it underestimates the significance of limited state capacity; it is best suited to violation of civil and political rights by authoritarian governments, and less suited to economic and social rights, and to human-rights violations by non-state actors (Risse and Ropp 2013). Scott argues that state failures often derive from the gap between state policies and local knowledge and other aspects of local cultures; states, like human-rights activists, may fail to implement human rights from ignorance of local cultures (Scott 1998). The empirical basis of the claim that states fail to fulfil their human-rights obligations because of limited capacity has, however, been questioned (Smith-Cannoy 2012).

The national politics of human rights

The failure of Risse and his colleagues to explain variations in respect for human rights in different societies results from their international-relations approach that does not pay sufficient attention to the *internal* causes of such variations. This requires the approaches of comparative history and comparative political science. In chapter five we examined Claude's argument that national human-rights regimes developed gradually in Britain, France and the USA, on the basis of capitalist economies, popular social movements, and strong states. He doubted whether this could be done when, as is widespread around the contemporary world, rapid economic development is a dominant national priority. Claude's relative pessimism is explained partly by the fact that he was writing during the Cold War, when the international human-rights regime was less effective than it is now.

Donnelly later clarified the relations between economic development and human rights. He identified three trade-offs in these relations: needs, equality and liberty. The needs trade-off sacrificed basic needs for investment. The equality trade-off created inequality in order to provide incentives for economic development. The liberty trade-off restricted civil and political rights to allow economic growth to advance unhindered by protest. Trade-off ideology said that trade-offs would be temporary, and that economic development would eventually meet basic needs, diminish inequality, and promote civil and political rights. Donnelly tested this claim with a comparative study of Brazil and South Korea. Brazil showed that economic development did not necessarily benefit the poor or reduce inequality. The explanation was political not economic: the rich were powerful, and used their power to defend inequality. South Korea achieved more rapid economic growth with less inequality and a relatively good record in the protection of social and economic rights between 1960 and 1980. This refuted the hypothesis that needs and equality trade-offs were necessary for rapid economic development. South Korea's record of civil and political rights during this period was, however, very bad. Political repression commonly accompanied economic development, but it did not necessarily lead to such development. If rapid economic development tended to produce political repression, it did not follow that any particular act of oppression was necessary to development (Donnelly 1989: 163–202).

Gurr sought to explain state repression by concentrating on the way that states responded to challenges. He took into account four general types of factor: (1) the nature of the challenge; (2) the nature of the state and its ideology; (3) the extent of ethnic diversity and inequality in society; and (4) the global environment. He developed numerous hypotheses about the likelihood of state repression (Gurr 1986). These pointed to plausible factors that cause or inhibit human-rights violations, but failed to clarify the interrelations among the factors or the dynamics of rights-violating conflicts.

Foweraker and Landman adopted a social-movement approach to the establishment of rights regimes. Social movements seek rights from the state. States may grant rights in order to increase their legitimacy. Claims for rights may, however, be counter-productive, and lead to greater state repression. The social-movement approach sees rights as outcomes of struggles between subordinate groups and the state (Foweraker and Landman 1997). Whereas Gurr emphasized state *strategies* in dealing with challenges, Foweraker and Landman emphasized the social bases of struggles for rights. They neglected the international dimension of struggles for rights, but they did point out that the concept of 'rights' was well adapted to create solidarity among social groups with different, and even partly incompatible interests, such as ethnic minorities and women.

Explaining human-rights violations: the quantitative approach

Foweraker and Landman used quantitative analysis of four countries to show that social movements have generally been successful in gaining rights. Others have followed the lead of Strouse and Claude in seeking to explain human-rights violations by quantitative methods. The first of these studies found that, even though the US Congress had mandated that US aid be tied to human rights, US foreign policy still ignored human rights. Later, methodologically more developed research showed that human rights played a role in US foreign policy, but were trumped by strategic concerns. Generally, the role of human rights was small. Making aid conditional on human-rights performance might influence recipient governments, but the withdrawal of aid from rights-violating governments could undermine their strength and thereby *increase* violations (Carey and Poe 2004; Poe 2004). Barratt found, similarly, that, in the period 1980–96, human rights had some influence on British aid policy, but only when it had little or no adverse effect on trade (Barratt 2004).

Mitchell and McCormick found that political prisoners and torture were more likely in poor countries, and in countries that were involved in capitalist international trade (Mitchell and McCormick 1988). Henderson found that the less democracy, the more poverty, the greater the inequality, the worse the repression. Contrary to the findings of Strouse and Claude, he found that rapid economic growth was associated with less repression (Henderson 1991). Poe and Tate found that poor states and military governments were more likely to violate civil and political rights in the 1980s. They also found that, where the level of democracy declines, human-rights violations increase. They found only a weak relation between wealth or economic growth rates and human-rights violations. By contrast, the threat of both external and internal war was positively linked with human-rights violations (Poe and Tate 1994).

Cingranelli and Richards sought to investigate whether or not the end of the Cold War had brought improvements in human rights. One view would be that, since Communist regimes were serious human-rights violators, and during the Cold War both superpowers, the USA and the USSR, supported rights-violating regimes, the end of the Cold War would bring considerable improvements in respect for human rights. An alternative view was that, since many violent conflicts had broken out after the end of the Cold War, human-rights violations might have increased. Research had generally shown that democracy was strongly associated with human rights, so that the post-Cold War increase in democracy should have led to human-rights improvements. Fein, however, had found 'more murder in the middle', that is to say that what she called 'life-integrity violations' were most likely to occur in societies that lay in the middle between democracy and authoritarianism. The democratization of authoritarian political systems might, therefore, be dangerous for the protection of human rights (Fein 1995).

Davenport and Armstrong challenged this finding, contending that democracy has no discernible effect on human rights below a certain level, although above this level it improves respect for human rights (Davenport and Armstrong 2004). Landman found that old democracies violate civil and political rights less than new democracies (Landman 2005a: 92, 117–18). Bueno De Mesquita and his colleagues found that elections without multi-party competition and constrained executives can make human rights worse, not better. Political competition leads to governmental accountability, which in turn leads to human-rights protection (Bueno De Mesquita et al. 2005). Davenport found that political competition and participation are more effective than constraints on the executive in decreasing repression. Constraints on the executive are in turn more effective than voting. Democracy is also more effective in reducing state violence than in preventing restrictions on civil liberties (Davenport 2007). The evidence therefore suggests that, although democracy is broadly good for human rights, the relation between the two is complex.

Cingranelli and Richards examined a random sample of 79 countries in the period 1981–96. The level of respect for the rights to be protected from disappearance, extra-judicial killing and torture did not improve by a statistically significant amount. Indeed, the amount of torture in 1996 was more than it had been throughout most of the Cold War. However, the level of respect for the right not to be imprisoned for political reasons nearly doubled after the end of the Cold War. Almost all this improvement occurred immediately after the Cold War ended (1990–3). There was no evidence of improvement in the years 1993–6. They concluded that the strongest explanation for the reduction in political prisoners after the end of the Cold War was the extent of democratization and, to a lesser extent, the increase in participation in the global economy. Neither the substantial increase in internal conflict that occurred after the end of the Cold War nor inter-state conflicts in this period had a significant independent effect on respect for the right not to be imprisoned for political reasons (Cingranelli and Richards 1999). The statistical method tells us nothing about human-rights improvements and failures in particular countries, but it does paint a rather bleak picture of human rights after the Cold War, except for the finding that more democracy means fewer political prisoners. Zanger, in a study of 147 countries from 1977–93, found that violations of life-integrity rights decreased in the year of change from authoritarian to democratic government, but increased in the following year. This suggests that democratization itself produces short-term benefits for these rights, but that the consolidation of democracy may be associated with violations. She also suggested that the use of economic sanctions to improve human rights may be counter-productive, since lowering a country's economic performance is more likely to worsen than improve its respect for human rights (Zanger 2000). Gruen and Klasen found mixed results for post-Communist societies, but generally civil and political rights fared better than economic and social rights (Gruen and Klasen 2012).

Milner, Poe and Leblang found that democracies score better than authoritarian states on economic and social rights, as well as on personal security. In contrast with Cingranelli and Richards, they found that human-rights performance worsened from 1989–92, and improved in 1993. This difference may be the product of different statistical methods, rights studied, time-frames and/or sample of countries. Technical differences in statistical methods can, therefore, lead to different substantive conclusions. The study also lends some support to the thesis that security, subsistence and liberty rights are indivisible and interdependent, and that the need for trade-offs is limited. This finding is preliminary, and further research is needed to test whether trade-offs can be avoided (Milner, Poe and Leblang 1999).

Quantitative studies show that democracies and rich countries are less likely to violate personal integrity rights, and that countries involved in international or civil wars, with large populations, authoritarian regimes and/or previous high levels of repression are more likely to violate such rights. The positive relation between economic development and human rights that exists globally does not, however, hold for Latin America (Landman 2002, 2006). Smith-Cannoy found that countries experiencing debt crises were especially likely to accept oversight of their human-rights records by UN treaty bodies (Smith-Cannoy 2012).

NGOs

These quantitative studies demonstrate *relationships* between various social, economic and political factors and certain types of human-rights behaviour, but, with the exception of the study of Foweraker and Landman, which is confined to only four similar countries, they tell us little or nothing about the effects of *human-rights activism*. In recent years non-governmental organizations have played an increasing role in human-rights politics at local, national and international levels, and, very recently, the serious study of these organizations has begun.

NGOs working for human rights are not new. Following medieval religious and academic networks, the flourishing of liberal ideas in the eighteenth-century Enlightenment encouraged the founding of various humanitarian associations. A society for the abolition of slavery was formed in 1787, the British and Foreign Anti-Slavery Society was established in 1839, and this, the oldest human-rights NGO in the world, exists today as Anti-Slavery International. In the nineteenth century, international societies were active in the struggle against slavery, for the improvement of working conditions, and for the emancipation of women. In 1864 the Swiss humanitarian, Henri Dunant, set up the Red Cross. From the end of the eighteenth century to the end of the nineteenth, numerous international conferences were held with both governmental and non-governmental participants, and these led to a number of international conventions. After the end of the First World War, the International Labour Organization encouraged the participation of NGOs in international standard-setting (Charnovitz 1996–7).

NGOs played an important role in ensuring that the promotion of human rights was included in the UN Charter and in the drafting of the UDHR. Article 71 of the UN Charter, the product of NGO lobbying, states that the Economic and Social Council (ECOSOC) 'may make suitable arrangements for consultations with non-governmental organizations which are concerned with matters within its competence'. In 1948 41 NGOs had consultative status with ECOSOC. In 1992 there were more than 1,000 (Korey 1998). By 2016 there were more than 4,500. It has been estimated that in 1953 there were 33 human-rights international NGOs (INGOs) and in 2000 there were 250 (Keck and Sikkink 1998: 10–11; Claude 2002a: 149).

The organizations that took part in the early years of the UN were religious, business, trade-union and women's associations. During the Cold War, NGOs were not viewed favourably by the Communist or 'third-world' states. Most international NGOs were based in the West, and the very idea of independent citizens' organizations seemed to belong to the Western, liberal-democratic tradition, and was inimical to the authoritarian statism of the Communist and third-world societies (Korey 1998: 77).

Although NGOs played a significant role in the drafting of both the UN Charter and the UDHR, UN human-rights institutions were suspicious of NGOs in the early years, but gradually came to recognize their value as sources of information. Over time, human-rights NGOs developed the scope of their activities, publicizing violations, campaigning to persuade governments to refrain from them, and playing an important role in UN standard-setting and implementation procedures (Wiseberg 1992: 376; Brett 1995: 103–4). NGOs were influential in drafting the two covenants of 1966; Amnesty International played a leading role in the adoption of the Convention Against Torture; and NGOs were very active in the drafting of the Convention on the Rights of the Child. This last Convention was the first human-rights treaty that explicitly allowed NGOs to play a role in monitoring its implementation (Charnovitz 1996–7: 259, 264; Breen 2005: 109). An international campaign of about 1,000 NGOs in 60 countries led to a Convention to ban landmines in 1997 (Wiseberg 2003: 347). Over 200 NGOs participated in drafting the statute of the International Criminal Court. NGOs have also played an increasingly important role in UN conferences. Baehr estimated that 1,500 NGOs attended the Vienna human-rights conference of 1993 (Baehr 1999: 114, 123). Almost 3,000 NGOs were accredited to the 1995 World Conference on Women (Otto 1996: 120). For a long time, the Security Council refused to have anything to do with NGOs, but in 1996 it agreed that members could meet NGOs in their national capacity, and since 1997 most Council members have met NGO representatives frequently (Paul 2001).

NGOs range from one-person organizations to large international bodies, and from the well-intentioned amateur to the highly professional. There are international NGOs, such as Amnesty International and Human Rights Watch, national NGOs, and local NGOs. Some international and national organizations, such as religious bodies and trade unions, which are not primarily concerned with human rights, may play an important role in certain human-rights campaigns. Some of these organizations are genuinely concerned with human rights, but others may use the human-rights cause to further other aims. NGOs are neither opposition groups as such nor political parties, even though they may have genuine concerns for human rights. Some organizations that are apparently non-governmental are actually government-controlled. The greatly increased number of NGOs has given rise to problems of co-operation. There are, in particular, some tensions between Western-based NGOs, some of which are relatively long-established, professionalized and well financed, and NGOs from poorer countries, which are less well resourced, and may have different perspectives on human rights. At the end of the twentieth century, 1,550 NGOs were associated with the UN, of which only 251 were from developing countries (McDonnell 1999: 206). These tensions are not necessarily regrettable, for they can enrich the struggle for human rights. Nevertheless, NGOs can be competitors for scarce resources, and local activists can become over-dependent on the funds and priorities of richer and more experienced INGOs (Baehr 1999: 114–15, 121–4). Forsythe identifies several difficulties in measuring the influence of NGOs. They have undoubtedly made an important contribution to the development of international law and institutions, but the effectiveness of this law and these institutions is uncertain. NGOs may well have raised world consciousness about human rights, but this is difficult to measure. He suggests the following kinds of success: (1) getting human-rights issues on the political agenda; (2) getting serious discussion of the issues; (3) getting procedural or institutional changes; (4) getting policy changes that improve respect for human rights. We cannot measure the effectiveness of NGOs precisely, but nearly everyone familiar with human-rights politics acknowledges their influence, including many governments whom they have criticized, and this suggests that the influence is significant. NGOs can sometimes be shown to have had a direct, positive effect on human rights, but often their impact, if it exists, combines with other factors, such as the media and governmental action, in such a way that the independent causal weight of the NGO is not known (Forsythe 2006: 200–6). There is evidence that, although neither treaty ratifications nor NGOs are sufficient for improved human-rights protection, the two together have a positive effect (Neumayer 2005: 950). An indirect indicator that NGOs are effective is that governments have begun to crack down on them (Sherwood 2015). NGOs should not be romanticized – they can be neither democratic nor wise – but, overall, they act as creative breaks on irresponsible government (Simmons 1998).

It is often said that NGOs work by 'the mobilization of shame' (Baehr 1999: 114). This may be misleading, however, for human-rights violators may feel little shame, but the publicity that NGOs give to the violation of international norms, which the offending governments may have supported publicly through declarations and ratification of covenants, may damage their standing in the international community. From a social-scientific point of view, states may be seen as concerned with their reputation in the community on which they depend for material and non-material benefits, and their responses to NGO pressures may be motivated by the calculation that this is in their national interest (Baehr 1999: 126–7). Smith-Cannoy, however, doubts that reputational concerns play a major role in explaining states' compliance with their human-rights obligations (Smith-Cannoy 2012). The 'boomerang' model suggests that 'shaming' governments may be counter-productive in some circumstances, and there is evidence supporting this hypothesis. Burgerman has argued that the following conditions are necessary, but not sufficient, for international NGOs to change state human-rights policies: (1) no major state opposes this aim; (2) part of the state's elite is concerned with its international human-rights reputation; (3) there is some internal pressure for such changes (Burgerman 1998). There is evidence that shaming can have both positive and harmful effects on human rights (Hafner-Burton 2008).

Perhaps the most important function of international NGOs is the provision of reliable information to governments, inter-governmental organizations, politicians, news media, academics and the general public. UN human-rights institutions are poorly resourced, and very dependent on NGOs for information (Baehr 1999; Brett 1995). Governments lie. NGOs can publicize part of the truth (Brett 1995: 101–3). NGOs have also provided important information to truth commissions and human-rights tribunals, often in methodologically rigorous, statistical form (Wiseberg 2003: 357).

They may also play an important role at national level in the drafting of constitutions and human-rights law (Wiseberg 1992: 376). NGO representatives are sometimes members of official delegations, and some become governmental officials with human-rights responsibilities. NGOs seek to influence governments, but they need to maintain their independence even from relatively co-operative governments. Similarly, NGOs may welcome publicity for human-rights violations by the media, but the media can distort the global human-rights agenda.

NGOs are sometimes referred to as 'grass-roots organizations', but the extent to which they are so is highly variable, and the term is somewhat misleading. Some NGOs consist of small elites of human-rights professionals; others combine professionals with concerned citizens; yet others have roots among the people whose rights they seek to defend. There are thousands of national and local NGOs around the world that combine human-rights, humanitarian and development programmes, providing services that their states do not provide. In a study of Mexico, Colombia, Morocco and India, Ron, Crow and Golden found much more human-rights awareness and activism among elites than others – though with considerable variation – raising the concern that those who needed human rights most had least contact with the human-rights world (Ron, Crow and Golden 2013).

This raises the question of the accountability of NGOs. To whom should they be accountable? Their members? Those they seek to help? Their own governments, law and/or public opinion? The governments, law and/or public opinion of countries they seek to influence? The international community? This raises also the question of the relation between the accountability and the effectiveness of NGOs: it is unclear whether democratic organizations are more effective than those that are elitist, nor which forms of accountability improve effectiveness (Baehr 1999: 115–24). NGOs are idealistic organizations, with considerable influence, working in a non-ideal world of power that gives rise to challenging responsibilities and ethical dilemmas (Blitt 2004; Bell and Coicaud 2007; Lepora and Goodin 2013). In response to this challenge, 11 leading international NGOs signed the international NGO Accountability Charter in 2006.

Bob argues that the NGO world is not simply one of benevolent and beneficent altruists, but also one in which diverse groups compete for scarce attention, sympathy, and money. Rights-claimants have to market themselves to potential benefactors through charismatic leaders, the medium of the English language, and the adoption of dominant political styles. Thus, the global human-rights project 'works' in so far as the victims subordinate themselves to the culture of their INGO 'saviours' (Bob 2002). This is neither entirely mistaken nor entirely fair. The leading INGOs attempt, so far as they are able, to develop and implement impartial, global human-rights policies. They derive their authority from international moral and legal standards, their reputation for truth-telling, and the extent to which they represent and empower the oppressed (Slim 2002). Ron et al. found that Amnesty International's reporting was largely determined by the severity of human-rights violations in a country, although it was shaped also by an emphasis on powerful countries and media interest. Thus human-rights violations in 'unfashionable' countries might be neglected, but Amnesty had to balance the severity of violations with the availability of resources and the prospects for effectiveness (Ron et al. 2005). Gordon argued that the strategies of NGOs may be less important than their social location for their effectiveness. NGOs close to, and respected by, governments may have more influence, but at the cost of collaborating with some human-rights violations. The distinction between the state and civil society can become blurred as they share both personnel and values. More 'radical' or principled groups may have less impact in the short term, but they can 'shame' more moderate groups into more forceful action (Gordon 2008).

NGOs also provide direct help to the victims of human-rights violations through legal aid, medical assistance and financial support. They raise consciousness through human-rights education, which may be formal or informal, independent of or supported by governments, narrowly legal or broadly interdisciplinary in a way that connects the concept of human rights with the practical concerns of the people (Andreopoulos and Claude 1997; Claude 2002b). NGOs provide an important bridge between the remote world of law, politics and bureaucracy, on the one hand, and the actual experience of human-rights violations, on the other. Western-based NGOs can be very professional, and fairly effective, but there is a need for 'the democratization of human rights' through the empowerment of local organizations. Ironically, governments that complain of the Western bias of NGOs often prevent the formation of NGOs in their own countries (Brett 1995: 105–6). There is a considerable gap between UN institutions and genuinely grass-roots NGOs, many of which have few resources to gain access to, or assistance from, these institutions (Smith, Pagnucco and Lopez 1998: 412).

Human-rights NGOs have been criticized on the ground that their legalistic approach, while it may provide some short-term gains in human-rights protection, is both irrelevant to the most serious human-rights violations, such as the genocidal events that have taken place in Burundi, Cambodia, Bosnia and Rwanda, and may obscure the deeper conditions that reproduce those violations, thereby inhibiting efforts to identify and address their root causes (Korey 1998: 308–9, 312–13). There is some truth in this criticism, but it is nonetheless unfair, unless certain facts are taken into account. Firstly, NGOs have sometimes provided early warnings of human-rights disasters, and it has not been their fault that governments have failed to respond. Secondly, NGOs have been willing to adapt to changing human-rights problems: Amnesty International, for example, modified its emphasis on prisoners of conscience to campaign against 'disappearances' in the 1970s. Thirdly, NGOs have very limited resources. NGOs seek to influence governments by appearing 'non-political' and appealing to international law. This is a *politically* rational strategy for improving human rights world-wide, but it has its limits. There is room also for a more robust and confrontational politics of human rights, which will also have its achievements and its limitations. NGOs may also, and to some extent do, take advantage of academic research into the structural causes of human-rights violations, but the practical value of this research should not be exaggerated. The quantitative, empirical literature on human-rights violations tells us that democracy, economic development and peace reduce violations. These are not variables that can be easily manipulated by governments or NGOs.

Human-rights NGOs have also been criticized for being biased towards Western priorities, and emphasizing civil and political rights at the expense of economic, social and cultural rights (Mutua 2001). There is also truth in this criticism, but both Human Rights Watch and Amnesty International have recently extended their mandates beyond their previous exclusive concern with civil and political rights to include economic, social and cultural rights. This move runs the risk of over-extending the limited resources and blurring the focus of these organizations, but has the advantages of embracing the human-rights concerns of non-Western peoples and emphasizing the 'interdependence' of all human rights. Finally, NGOs have been criticized, along with UN agencies, for complicity with sexual assaults on their employees (Laville and Leach 2015).

Conclusion

The international human-rights regime is a political as well as a legal institution. As such, it reflects the balance of power in the world. Since the end of the Cold War, the balance of political and economic power has been held by the West, and consequently the Western human-rights agenda has dominated the international human-rights regime. NGOs with different priorities constitute a social movement that counteracts those of the major state powers, though selectively and with limited resources. International human-rights law has been developed to modify, but not to reject, the statist conception of international society. Some human-rights NGOs operate within that state-centred, human-rights regime; others challenge the 'club of states' as social movements with grass roots; yet others seek to form a bridge between these two, very different worlds. The point of NGOs is to hold states to account; it is not surprising that some states seek to limit their influence in international politics.

8

Globalization, Development and Poverty

Economics and Human Rights

Globalization

Human rights have economic implications, since implementing them requires resources, and economic policies can have massive impacts on human rights. Those concerned with human rights should understand the positive and negative effects of economic forces on human rights, and the economics of the best attainable human-rights outcomes. Economic policies can be evaluated by human-rights standards. Yet human-rights activists and scholars have neglected economics, and most economists are not interested in human rights. This is now changing, slowly.

In the nineteenth and early twentieth centuries capitalism created great wealth and great misery. This led to the creation of welfare states in rich countries, which influenced the principles of the United Nations (UN). The UN Charter proclaims that a principal aim of the organization is to promote better living standards. Article 25 of the Universal Declaration of Human Rights (UDHR) affirms that everyone has the right to an adequate standard of living.

During the Cold War human rights evolved in a world divided between capitalism and socialism. They also had to address the demand of the poor, newly decolonized states for 'development'. In 1974 the UN General Assembly called for a New International Economic Order (NIEO) to rectify the perceived injustices of global inequality. The rich countries rejected the NIEO, and the idea came to nothing. Stagnation of the rich economies generated policies of deregulation and privatization. The free-market ideology of 'neo-liberalism' became the dominant solution to the problems of development. After the Cold War poor states abandoned their suspicion of Western capitalism and sought loans and investment from Western banks and transnational corporations (TNCs). To achieve this they had to reduce state expenditures on social services. The post-war consensus on the welfare state began to collapse just when the human rights movement took off in the 1970s. Many then saw economic 'globalization' as hostile to human rights and participated in 'anti-globalization' protests.

Neo-liberal globalization transfers power from states to private economic actors and thus threatens the international human-rights regime which imposes obligations on states. This tension between 'globalization' and human rights is complicated by the fact that the human-rights movement is part of globalization. Globalization may raise living standards for many while acting as accomplice to human-rights violations. UN human-rights bodies have expressed concern over the impact of globalization on human rights; states may incur economic obligations incompatible with their human-rights obligations. Global economic processes tend to marginalize human rights. Economic globalization and human rights are thus poorly integrated.

Global poverty and inequality

According to the World Bank, in 2013 767 million people – 10.7 per cent of the world's population – lived in extreme poverty (World Bank Group 2016). Children were more than twice as likely as adults to live in extreme poverty: 385 million children – almost one child in five – lived in extreme poverty. These figures are based on the Bank's 'extreme poverty' line of $1.90 a day. Using a higher line of $3.10 a day, measuring 'moderate and extreme poverty', estimates are that 27 per cent of adults and 45 per cent of children live in poverty (World Bank Group and UNICEF 2016). Every day 16,000 children die under the age of five (United Nations Inter-agency Group for Child Mortality Estimation 2015).

Global poverty violates the human rights to life, an adequate standard of living, health, food, water, sanitation and housing. The World Bank claims that global poverty is declining: in 1990 1.85 billion people – or 35 per cent of the world population – were living in extreme poverty (World Bank Group 2016). World Bank poverty measures are controversial. Some experts believe that the number of the global poor is much higher than the World Bank estimates; others calculate that it is lower; still others hold that no one knows how many poor people there are in the world (Anand, Segal and Stiglitz 2009). Disagreements about world poverty statistics may be moral and philosophical rather than economic.

Many economists argue that, far from globalization causing poverty, isolation from the global economy explains development failure. Dissenting economists counter that protectionism can aid development and that political factors such as bad governance and conflict are significant causes of poverty (Wade 2004b; Collier 2007).

Economic and social rights

Civil and political rights are sometimes distinguished from economic and social rights by Kant's distinction between perfect and imperfect duties. Negative rights not to be harmed are said to entail perfect duties not to harm others. Positive rights to benefits entail imperfect duties as no one has a perfect duty to benefit others in the absence of a special relationship. Some argue that economic and social rights are *not* human rights because the corresponding duties are imperfect and can be implemented only through institutions which create *special* not *human* rights. UK citizens have a right to health care because they are UK citizens, not because they are human beings.

Some counter that there is no moral distinction between the right not to be tortured and the right not to starve. Both can be negative rights not to suffer or positive rights to assistance. Civil and political rights entail both perfect and imperfect obligations. For example, the right not to be tortured entails the perfect obligation of everyone not to torture anyone but also imperfect obligations to do what one reasonably can to prevent torture. All rights require institutions to implement them. Economic and social rights entail negative duties and are not necessarily expensive: governments respect the right to housing by not destroying houses. It is now common to distinguish obligations to *respect* rights (not violate them), *protect* rights (ensure that others not violate them), and *fulfil* rights (ensure everyone enjoys them). The obligation to respect is negative for all types of rights; the obligation to fulfil is positive for all types; all three types of obligation may be negative and positive. Several philosophers hold that duties to the poor include the negative duty not to harm and the positive duty to assist.

Some maintain that human rights may entail imperfect duties. The rich may have imperfect duties to the poor, but perfect duties to support institutions that have perfect duties to help the poor. Human rights of all kinds may entail duties that, as a matter of fact, are unlikely to be fulfilled. This does not defeat the case for economic and social rights; rather, it makes the case for criticizing existing institutions. If the enjoyment of economic and social rights is necessary to a life of dignity, the case for these rights is independent of the corresponding duties. On this view rights ground the institutional duties rather than vice versa. Economic and social rights may be necessary to the enjoyment of civil and political rights: a starving person cannot participate effectively in politics. Civil rights may be *components* of social rights: there is a right to a fair hearing in a social dispute.

Economic and social rights are commonly called 'second-generation' rights, but this is unhistorical. Medieval philosophers discussed the right of the needy to assistance from the rich. In modern times economic and social rights were roughly contemporary with political rights. Social rights, especially workers' rights, preceded civil and political rights in international relations, leading to the establishment of the International Labour Organization (ILO) in 1919. In 1944 President Roosevelt called for an economic bill of rights. The Universal Declaration contains economic and social as well as civil and political rights. Economic and social rights were marginalized for a long time. This has changed somewhat. The UN Commission on Human Rights established several special rapporteurs on these rights. Amnesty International and Human Rights Watch have taken them on, and numerous NGOs now specialize in them.

The International Covenant on Economic, Social and Cultural Rights (ICESCR) requires states parties to take steps, using the maximum of available resources, to realize the Covenant rights *progressively*. States must assure the enjoyment of at least the minimum essential levels of these rights by everyone. States have *immediate* obligations to 'take steps' to implement the rights without discrimination. Retrogressive steps must be justified by Covenant rights and available resources. States have a 'minimum core obligation' to fulfil the essential levels. Rich states have an obligation to assist states lacking the resources to implement their Covenant obligations (United Nations Committee on Economic, Social and Cultural Rights 1991: 1–4).

The 'minimum core obligation' raises a problem for human-rights universalism. Is it the same for Chad as for Canada? How is the minimum determined? The obligation of 'progressive realization' is also relative in so far as it depends on available resources. Young has argued that different philosophical bases for economic and social rights – basic needs, autonomy, or dignity – will generate difference conceptions of the minimum. Thus, the minimum core fails to form an agreed bedrock of economic and social rights, but is 'essentially contested' (Young 2008).

There is a rebuttable presumption that every state has sufficient resources to meet its minimum obligations. The Covenant does not clarify how poor states should balance Covenant obligations with legitimate, non-Covenant expenditures, such as those on investment, debt reduction and defence. Budget analysis may, however, show that state expenditure on Covenant rights has fallen as a proportion of GDP or of government spending, that the allocated budget was not all spent, or that it was spent in a discriminatory way (Hofbauer, Blyberg and Krafchik 2004). The conceptual, methodological and data-collection problems of measuring 'progressive realization' of economic and social rights are formidable and as yet unsolved, although progress has been made in tackling them.

Lawyers regard treaty obligations as 'binding', whereas political scientists and economists consider public policy as deciding priorities and making trade-offs. Legally, the obligation of 'progressive realization' applies to economic and social but not to civil and political rights. Donnelly maintains, however, that all human rights are subject to progressive realization (Donnelly 2007). It is therefore not always clear when a failure of progress constitutes a human-rights violation. The obligation of rich and poor states to realize rights progressively is hard to reconcile with the principle of universal equal rights. Economic and social rights also have a relativist element because states are expected to implement these rights in a culturally appropriate way.

The obligations to realize economic and social rights are generally limited to states' own jurisdictions. The obligation to help those outside those jurisdictions is weak. Overseas development aid is still treated as political policy or charity rather as a human-rights obligation.

Economic and social rights are said to be not 'justiciable', that is, they cannot be decided in courts of law. One informed estimate, however, suggests that more than 100,000 such decisions can be found (Langford 2009: 91). Some argue that judges lack the expertise and legitimacy to decide disputes with large budgetary implications. But civil and political rights raise controversial questions, such as the detention of terrorist suspects, and judges often decide cases with huge financial implications. Legislatures often specify economic and social rights in general terms and leave judges to elaborate the law. Thus, the claim that the legalization of economic and social rights illegitimately transfers powers from democratic legislatures to unaccountable judges is not wholly justified. There is conflicting evidence, however, on the question whether the constitutionalization and judicialization of economic and social rights leads to improvements in the enjoyment of these rights (Brinks and Gauri 2012; Bjørnskov and Mchangama 2013). This challenges the simple view that judicialization of these rights improves their enjoyment, but leaves open the question as to which combinations of political mobilization and judicial enforcement are optimal for these rights.

Some worry that economic and social rights discourage individual initiative, but these rights are intended to support, not displace, self-help. The legalization of these rights may have saved and improved many lives, but the combination of political and legal approaches may be optimal for their realization. The consequences for economic development of implementing economic and social rights remain uncertain.

Development

Concern for human rights and development evolved separately for many years. Some said that development was a *precondition* of human rights. It has not, however, been shown that violating human rights is necessary to economic development. Protecting human rights may facilitate development and has an intrinsic value in respecting human dignity. Human rights are also necessary to determine what people really need. The meaning of 'development' is contested, and human rights are necessary to determine what types of development are really beneficial.

In the 1980s many saw 'structural adjustment programmes' as violating human rights for the sake of economic development. Popular protests invoked human rights. In the 1990s the UN Development Programme (UNDP) adopted the concept of 'human development' which partially incorporated human rights into development policy. The World Bank included some human rights in its lending policies.

The 'rights-based approach' to development treats poverty as a human-rights violation and emphasizes the *obligations* of governments. Denial of such human rights as those to food and health are *constitutive* of poverty. Other human rights, such as the right to work, are *instrumental* to eliminating poverty. The right to political participation empowers the poor, which is the first step out of poverty. The rights-based approach emphasizes non-discrimination and accountability (Andreassen 2003; Office of the United Nations High Commissioner for Human Rights 2006). The rights-based approach provides a relatively coherent normative basis for development policy. It has, however, been criticized for conceptual vagueness, lack of systematic practice and failure to evaluate projects rigorously. The rights approach does not always help to determine priorities when resources are scarce. Popular participation is vulnerable to capture by local elites and its effectiveness is uncertain. The human-rights culture is legalistic and individualistic, and is accused of being ill-equipped to address the structural causes of poverty. The rights-based and economic approaches to development have not yet been integrated by human-rights or development specialists (Uvin 2004).

In 2000 the UN General Assembly adopted the Millennium Declaration, which became the basis for eight millennium development goals (MDGs) for the period 2000–15. The MDGs, however, constituted a set of *goals* and *priorities* rather than *rights*. They overlapped with human rights, but fell short of established human rights. Development institutions referred to the MDGs with few references to human rights, while human-rights organizations referred to rights rather than the MDGs. The MDGs had therefore had limited success in integrating development and human rights. In September 2015 a UN summit adopted a set of sustainable development goals (SDGs) for the period 2015–30 to follow up the MDGs. The SDGs cover much of the ground of human rights, but have been criticized both for being too ambitious and for not being ambitious enough. Human-rights commentators worry that the SDGs make no explicit reference to human rights and have been agreed at a time when human rights are under attack in many countries.

The right to development

In 1986 the UN General Assembly adopted the Declaration on the Right to Development. This proclaims that the right is a human right by virtue of which every person and all peoples are entitled to participate in, contribute to, and enjoy economic, social, cultural and political development in which all human rights can be fully realized. The right has been reaffirmed by numerous international meetings.

The primary legal obligation to implement this right is that of states to their citizens. The discourse of the right to development suggests, however, that the primary obligation is that of rich to poor countries, although this obligation is unclear and controversial. It is also unclear whether the right to development is a distinct human right or a combination of pre-existing human rights, and to what it is a right (Donnelly 1985b: 474–5). Sengupta, the UN's independent expert on the right from 1999 to 2004, said that it was more than the pre-existing rights: it was a *vector* of all human rights, including elements of well-being that went beyond human rights (Sengupta 2002).

Donnelly argues that there is no right to development. Individual development is the goal of all human rights. The supposed right to development adds nothing to established human rights and provides an excuse for violating them (Donnelly 1985b). Salomon concludes that the right to development is conceptually unclear and practically useless. It was an attempt to transform the NIEO into the discourse of human rights. It has failed because the rich states deny that it creates any binding obligations (Salomon 2007). Sorell and Landman suggest that the supposed right to development is not a human right because the best-off do not have the right to be better off and may have the obligation to be worse off in order to help the worst-off: there is therefore no *universal* right to development (Sorell and Landman 2006: 393). Charvet and Kaczynska-Nay take a more favourable view of the right to development, arguing that it is both clear and partially implemented. Its merits are that it makes clear the obligation of developed countries to help developing countries to fulfil the human rights of all their citizens, and the obligation of developing countries to fulfil all human rights. It does not create a new right, but sets existing rights in the context of development (Charvet and Kaczynska-Nay 2008). Developing countries' representatives advocate the right to development but reject rights-based development.

Development policy ignores the right. Development in practice often benefits the rich at the expense of the poor, by, for example, the appropriation of poor people's land (Kennedy 2011). The optimal strategy for economic development in the short term may not be the optimal strategy for human rights: development and human rights may be *competitors* for funding (Collier 2007: 121–2).

The causes of development

Three types of factor may explain variations in development and poverty among countries. Geography affects natural resources, health, productivity and trade opportunities. Culture and institutions affect attitudes to economic activity, governance and the rule of law. International politics, trade and law affect development directly or indirectly through the quality of institutions.

Evidence suggests that capital accumulation and technological progress are the proximate causes of economic growth. Research shows, however, that *institutions*, especially the rule of law and protection of property rights, are the primary independent causes. Geography may have some effect on institutions. Trade is an effect of good institutions rather than an independent cause of development. It is not clear how institutions promote development: there are considerable institutional differences among the successful economies. International factors may undermine institutions and inhibit development in poor countries by protecting domestic industries and supporting corrupt dictators (Rodrik, Subrahamian and Trebbi 2004; Sachs 2005: 189–90; Pogge 2005a, 2005c, 2007).

Knowledge of the causes of economic growth and poverty remains partial and it is difficult to infer the best policy for a particular country from cross-country comparisons. Generally, however, the more unequal countries are, the higher the level of poverty. Rapid development may accompany slow poverty reduction because inequality increases. Improving growth does not necessarily improve human rights (Besley and Burgess 2003; Sachs 2005: 165–6).

Is colonialism a cause of global poverty? Many poor countries are former colonies, but some former colonies are not poor: for example, South Korea, Taiwan, Singapore and Hong Kong. Statistical analysis shows that, although colonialism probably obstructed economic growth in the short term, there is no evidence of long-term adverse effects (Sachs 2005: 191).

Democracy is not necessary for economic growth: dictatorships with smart economic policies have produced successful development. Dictatorships in poor countries have, however, had very variable growth rates. Glaeser et al. suggest that human capital may be more important for economic growth than institutions (Glaeser et al. 2004). Culture does not explain development well: 'Asian values', for example, have been associated with development success and failure. Governments may, however, fail to develop human capital for economic, political and/or cultural reasons (Sachs 2005: 72, 315–17).

The World Bank claims that trade liberalization has led to a reduction in extreme poverty since 1980. Some rapid developers, such as China and India, are quite protectionist, however, and free trade has done little to benefit the poorest (Wade 2004a; Sachs 2005: 326).

The contribution of aid to development is controversial and uncertain. Development is possible without aid, as China shows. Aid may fund corrupt and incompetent government, and discourage local initiative and reform. It may fail because poor countries lack the capacity to use it effectively (Wade 2004a; Easterly 2007: 44). Well-targeted aid may, however, improve the capacity of a country to use aid well (Sachs 2005: 274). Easterly argues that aid has failed to eradicate poverty because it has been based on top-down planning whereas bottom-up, market-based initiatives are the source of development. International planners cannot understand the social complexities that underlie economies and are not accountable to the poor. He concedes that aid can contribute to development in democracies with good economic policies, and that aid for health and education has often been successful. Aid is, however, rarely evaluated rigorously so we do not know how effective it is in reducing poverty (Easterly 2007). Much aid fails because it serves the political and commercial interests of donors. Effective aid may conflict with aid to the neediest, and aid for development may compete with aid for human rights (Collier 2007). Aid is often inefficient because there are multiple donors who are poorly co-ordinated. Riddell suggests that aid sometimes works and sometimes doesn't; where it doesn't, this is often the result of non-aid factors (Riddell 2007). Clemens and Moss argue that the commonly cited aid target of 0.7 per cent of rich-country gross national income is fundamentally flawed methodologically and empirically, and that it is extremely difficult to translate the human needs of the global poor into financial assistance from the rich (Clemens and Moss 2005: 18). Kenny suggests that *expenditure* is probably less important for improving the quality of life of the poor than is commonly assumed, which implies that the cost of making such improvements may be considerably lower than is commonly assumed (Kenny 2005).

Development science is underdeveloped. 'Development' and 'poverty' are contested concepts; data and methodologies are problematic; theory is weak. Easterly maintains that development economics has contributed little to development and poverty reduction (Easterly 2009: 28–30). Simple generalizations about human rights and development cannot be justified as we do not know enough.

Trade and investment

The UN founders believed that free trade would raise living standards and thereby promote human rights. Trade can, however, violate human rights in various ways: goods can be harmful to health; they can be produced by means that violate human rights (e.g., child labour); or they can be used for human-rights violations (e.g., police or military equipment sold to dictators).

The World Trade Organization (WTO) was founded in 1994 by the signatories to the General Agreement on Tariffs and Trade (GATT). Most WTO members have ratified the ICCPR and the ICESCR. The WTO is not a UN agency and has no mandate to implement human rights. Trade negotiations and the WTO dispute-settlement procedures are neither transparent nor democratically accountable. The world's poor have almost no capacity to participate in trade negotiations or the WTO. NGOs have less access to the WTO than to many UN agencies. The WTO's impact on human rights and its lack of accountability have provoked popular protests (Benedek 2007).

The WTO can impose sanctions for violations of trade agreements and thereby has more power than any UN human-rights body. However, the developing countries have resisted rich countries' attempts to incorporate human rights in WTO negotiations on the ground that they amount to trade discrimination. The 1996 Singapore Declaration of WTO ministers reaffirmed their commitment to international core labour standards but said that the ILO (a much weaker organization) not the WTO was the body to deal with these (Aaronson 2007).

The WTO Agreement on the Trade-Related Aspects of Intellectual Property Rights (TRIPS) has been especially problematic for human rights. It established pharmaceutical patents limiting the ability of developing countries to address diseases such as HIV/AIDS. The 2001 WTO Doha conference declared that TRIPS does not prevent members from taking measures to protect public health. The Doha Declaration has, however, been by-passed by bilateral and regional deals.

Bilateral investment treaties (BITs) are now common and can have serious implications for human rights. Most BITs prohibit regulations that reduce the value of investments. Investment tribunals have made states pay compensation for regulations implementing their obligations to fulfil economic and social rights. Poor states lack the capacity to contest such compensation claims effectively, and may consequently be reluctant to fulfil these human-rights obligations.

The WTO has never addressed conflicts between trade and human-rights law. GATT allows exceptions to free-trade rules for national security, protection of public morals, human life and health, and prison labour, but it is uncertain whether this permits trade restrictions for human rights. The WTO respects sanctions authorized by the UN Security Council, and legal scholars believe it must respect *jus cogens*, the prohibition of the gravest human-rights crimes. The WTO has allowed trade restrictions on members that do not participate in the Kimberley Certification Scheme to combat trade in diamonds used to finance conflict. It also accepts trade agreements giving developing countries preferential access to rich countries' markets on condition that they meet certain human-rights conditions if these agreements meet the development needs of poor countries (Cottier, Pauwelyn and Bürgi 2005; Pauwelyn 2005).

WTO agreements make commitments to the needs of developing countries but these countries often lack the resources and bargaining power to make these provisions effective. Poor countries exporting to rich countries face tariffs on average four times higher than the barriers applied in trade among rich countries (United Nations Development Programme 2005: 127).

Empirical studies have found both positive and negative relations between foreign direct investment (FDI) and trade, on the one hand, and human rights in developing countries on the other, although most studies find a positive relation, especially with civil and political rights (Mitchell and McCormick 1988; Cingranelli and Richards 1999; Richards, Gelleny and Sacko 2001; Milner 2002). Hafner-Burton found that trade and FDI generally had a positive influence on human rights, but results varied with different economies and different methods (Hafner-Burton 2005a). Evidence also indicates that preferential trade agreements with tough sanctions are more effective than human-rights treaties in implementing human rights, although they are not always effective (Hafner-Burton 2005b, 2009).

Business corporations

The Nuremberg trials of Nazi war criminals after the Second World War convicted several industrialists of grave human-rights crimes. The UDHR implies that corporations have human-rights obligations. Corporations may violate human rights; they may be complicit in state violations; and the privatization of traditional state functions – such as security, prisons, water and health – means that corporations may become quasi-state organizations. The empirical evidence on the impact of transnational corporations (TNCs) on human rights is mixed, depending on the methods used (Meyer 1996; Smith, Bolyard and Ippolito 1999).

The anti-apartheid movement pioneered attempts to get corporations to respect human rights. The Sullivan Principles (1977) proposed a voluntary code for US companies in South Africa. They were supported by more than 125 companies, but were considered ineffectual (Compa and Hinchliffe-Darricarrère 1995).

In 1974 the UN Economic and Social Council (ECOSOC) established the UN Commission on TNCs. The Commission submitted a draft code of conduct to ECOSOC in 1990, providing, among other things, that TNCs should respect human rights. Negotiations on the code collapsed in 1992, victim of the shift by developing countries from hostility to acceptance of TNCs.

In 1976 the Organization of Economic Co-operation and Development (OECD) issued non-binding Guidelines for Multinational Enterprises to protect union rights and prohibit discrimination. They were revised in 2000 to include a general requirement to respect human rights. In 1977 the ILO published a Tripartite Declaration of Principles Concerning Multinational Enterprises and Social Policy, which was amended in 2000. It affirms an obligation to respect the International Bill of Rights. It is voluntary and is considered to be rather ineffective (Compa and Hinchliffe-Darricarrère 1995: 670–1; Murphy 2004–5).

In 1986 the US Anti-Apartheid Act prohibited US companies from doing business in South Africa. The Clinton administration proposed a voluntary code of conduct for US TNCs, which was adopted by several corporations. In 1996 the administration established the Apparel Industry Partnership workplace code of conduct for companies and overseas contractors. Social Accountability 8000 was launched in 1997 by the Council on Economic Priorities and some influential companies as an attempt to compel firms to comply with a set of labour and human-rights standards (Spar 1998: 8–10; Ratner 2001–2: 457–63). Other corporate codes have been proposed for Northern Ireland, the USSR and China, for labour standards and against child labour. Some corporations have adopted codes incorporating human rights and refused to do business with countries where serious violations occurred (Compa and Hinchliffe-Darricarrère 1995: 671–84; Frey 1997: 175–6, 187). Such codes generally include a limited range of rights, and are difficult to implement (Ratner 2001–2: 531).

In 1999 the UN Secretary-General, Kofi Annan, proposed a 'global compact' for TNCs. This is a voluntary agreement by which TNCs undertake to abide by ten human-rights and environmental principles within their 'sphere of influence'. The Global Compact claims participation by 8,000 companies and 4,000 non-business entities. However, its principles are vague and its implementation mechanisms weak.

In 2003 the UN Sub-Commission on the Promotion and Protection of Human Rights approved norms on the responsibilities of TNCs and other business enterprises (OBEs) for human rights within their sphere of influence, and submitted the norms to the Commission on Human Rights. The Commission requested the Office of the High Commissioner for Human Rights (OHCHR) to investigate the responsibilities of TNCs and related business enterprises for human rights, and submit a report to the Commission.

The OHCHR reported that opinion on the Sub-Commission's norms was deeply divided, and that the human-rights obligations of business remained unclear. The Commission requested the UN Secretary-General to appoint a special representative on human rights and TNCs and OBEs. The Secretary-General appointed Professor John Ruggie to clarify the responsibilities of governments, TNCs and OBEs for human rights and business.

Ruggie estimated that there were about 80,000 TNCs with about 800,000 subsidiaries and millions of suppliers. Human-rights violations by some companies had led to demands, some from corporations, for greater corporate responsibility. Unregulated markets were destabilizing and human rights must be central to regulation. The problems of business and human rights varied by sector and type of government. Many of the world's largest companies had, however, adopted human-rights policies and practices. The effects of various initiatives on business and human rights were limited geographically and in the human rights covered. The worst offenders were untouched.

The Sub-Commission's norms incorrectly assumed that international law imposed binding human-rights obligations on companies. Most human-rights obligations were obligations of states. Only the norms specifying the worst human-rights crimes applied directly to corporations. The human-rights obligations of states and corporations should take account of their different social roles. The Sub-Commission had been divisive rather than constructive (United Nations Commission on Human Rights 2006; United Nations Human Rights Council 2010).

Generally, states were not fulfilling their obligations to protect human rights by regulating corporations, although corporations might be liable under national laws for some violations (United Nations Human Rights Council 2007b). Ruggie proposed a 'protect, respect, remedy' framework: states should protect everyone against violations by business; corporations should respect human rights; victims should have access to remedies. The concept of 'sphere of influence' lacked legal definition and failed to make clear who was responsible for what. Corporations do not have obligations to prevent violations by all those over whom they have influence, but to exercise due diligence for the *impact* of their activities. They should carry out human-rights impact assessments when planning ventures with human-rights risks. Access to remedies is least where it is most needed (United Nations Human Rights Council 2007a, 2008a, 2008b).

Ruggie submitted his final report to the Human Rights Council in March 2011, including the Guiding Principles on Business and Human Rights with the aim of implementing the 'protect, respect and remedy' framework. The Council endorsed the Principles in June 2011, and set up a working group on human rights, TNCs and OBEs and a forum on business and human rights.

The Guiding Principles are supported by some NGOs and by business, and some governments, inter-governmental organizations and corporations have begun to implement them (United Nations Human Rights Council 2009, 2010). Some NGOs have criticized Ruggie for not investigating the causes of corporate violations and for not recommending complaint procedures or binding international standards. Ruggie holds that international adjudication of alleged corporate violations would face intractable problems of evidence gathering and due process.

In June 2014 the Council established an open-ended inter-governmental working group whose mandate is to elaborate an international treaty to regulate TNCs and OBEs by international human-rights law. This proposal is, however, very controversial (McBrearty 2016).

International financial institutions

In 1944 the Allies met at Bretton Woods, New Hampshire, and established the World Bank and the International Monetary Fund (IMF) to redevelop Europe and restore global economic stability. These international financial institutions (IFIs) are considered to be UN agencies with mandates to act independently on economic, not political grounds, subject only to the Security Council. They have interpreted this to mean that they have no human-rights obligations, although they claim that they take human rights into account and that their work promotes human rights. They take little note, however, of international human-rights law or UN human-rights bodies. The IFIs have sometimes taken decisions on political or human-rights grounds but they have used the 'non-political' principle to justify financing some of the world's worst human-rights violators. Human-rights NGOs neglected this until recently (Boisson de Chazournes 2007). The World Bank is the world's most important lending institution for development, while the IMF is primarily concerned with financial stability. The two institutions began to converge in the 1980s on 'structural adjustment loans' (SALs) for development with strict conditions. By the mid-1990s almost 120 countries had 'structural adjustment programmes' (SAPs). Critics claimed that, although some 'structural adjustment' might be necessary, SAPs have often been ineffectual, are undemocratic, violate economic and social rights, provoke instability and serve the interests of Western capital at the expense of the global poor (Stiglitz 2002; Sachs 2005; McBeth 2006; Abouharb and Cingranelli 2007: 3–4, 7, 24, 50, 77). Abouharb and Cingranelli, in a study of all countries undergoing structural adjustment from 1981 to 2003, found that, on average, SAPs led to less respect for most types of human rights. This held true when account was taken of the fact that countries seeking IFI help often had poor human-rights records before the IFI intervened (Abouharb and Cingranelli 2007). SAPs were often poorly implemented because of lack of governmental capacity, political opposition and failure of lenders to enforce them (Riddell 2007).

The IMF has been defended on the ground that the crises it addresses threaten human rights; its conditions are necessary to sustain the financial viability of its assistance; it does not always cut social expenditures; it is not competent to make human-rights judgements; financial help to countries where human-rights violations occur is better than refusal to help; and SAPs may improve human rights in the long term (Leite 2001: 2–6; McBeth 2006). In the 1990s the Bank and the Fund included safety nets and compensation in their SAPs.

Between 1968 and 1981 the Bank became concerned with poverty alleviation, accepted the 'basic needs' approach to development, and began to fund health, education, agriculture and housing, and then took up environmental, gender, governance and participation issues. In 1989 the Bank included human rights in its 'good governance' criteria. Both the Bank and the IMF accepted the Millennium Development Goals (Bradlow 1996: 48–89; Riddell 2007; Boisson de Chazournes 2007). The Bank has thus become more open to human rights, though in a limited way. In 1993 it established an Inspection Panel to hear complaints. The Panel can hear only complaints that Bank projects violate Bank policy, not complaints of human-rights violations as such. Borrowing countries resist the influence of NGOs with the Panel, and it has had limited effects (Fox 2002). The IMF has irregular contacts with UN human-rights bodies and informal discussions with NGOs. The IFIs advocate transparency and popular participation for client-states, but have been criticized for not practising what they preach. Popular participation is, however, not necessarily compatible with human rights or development. Some see the Bank as having had a positive effect on a wide range of human rights, especially relating to women and indigenous peoples. However, it has no human-rights policy, and considers human rights only if it thinks them relevant to its mandate. The Bank's encouragement of participation raises the question of protecting the civil and political rights of those who participate. If the IFIs refuse to make loans on human-rights grounds, the would-be borrowers may turn to other sources, even less concerned with human rights. NGOs may influence the Bank through its member governments, especially the USA. The influence of the USA with the IFIs has been criticized for being anti-poor, but it is not always anti-human rights.

In 1996 the Bank and the Fund introduced their Heavily Indebted Poor Countries Initiative (HIPCI). To qualify for HIPCI debt reduction, a government must formulate a Poverty Reduction Strategy Paper (PRSP). PRSPs include human-rights elements and the participation of civil society is required. PRSPs are subject to approval by the IFIs (Tostensen 2007: 186, 197–200, 210). Nearly all poor, highly indebted countries have produced PRSPs. Critics maintain that the power of the IFIs means that PRSPs are not very different from SAPs; civil-society participation is inadequate; insufficient debt relief has been provided to insufficient countries; and consequently they have done little for human rights (Darrow 2003; Stewart and Wang 2005). The World Bank has admitted that NGOs played a major role in its debt reduction programme. Debt reduction has, however, represented a very small proportion of the most heavily indebted countries' debt (Donnelly 2002).

The IFIs are not parties to human-rights treaties, but the states that own them are. The IFIs emphasize their legal obligations to maintain financial soundness and believe that this constrains their commitment to human rights. The main causes of their limited commitment to human rights, however, are the interests of the rich states that dominate them and their economic theories. The IFIs' reluctance to acknowledge systematically that 'development' includes human rights is incompatible with UN development thinking and their own rhetoric.

Climate change

The idea that fossil-fuel combustion might increase concentrations of carbon dioxide (CO_2) in the atmosphere and cause climate warming originated in the nineteenth century. However, it was not until 1979 that the science of 'global warming' entered the political arena when the US National Academy of Sciences warned that increasing CO_2 might substantially increase global average temperatures. In 1988 the UN Environment Programme and the World Meteorological Organization created the Intergovernmental Panel on Climate Change (IPCC). In 1992 the UN Conference on the Environment and Development in Rio adopted the UN Framework Convention on Climate Change (FCCC). In 1995 the IPCC Second Assessment Report said that human activities were having a 'discernible' impact on the climate. In 2001 the IPCC's Third Assessment Report announced new evidence that most recent global warming was attributable to human activities and this was set to continue. The Kyoto Protocol to the UNFCCC was adopted in 1997. It provided for emission reductions by developed countries but none by developing countries. Kyoto would make little impact on climate change, especially since the USA failed to ratify it, and Japan, Canada and Russia refused to continue it after 2012 (Luterbacher and Sprinz 2001; Harvey and Vidal 2011).

The IPCC predicted that global temperature would rise by 1.4–5.8°C and global average sea level by 0.11–0.77 metres by 2100. Such rises would cause storms, floods and droughts, damage food production and cause massive loss of life, livelihoods and property damage. The World Health Organization has estimated that climate change since the 1970s has already caused 140,000 deaths annually. The IPCC predictions did not take account of certain climate catastrophes that it considered improbable but possible. Climate change will benefit some regions in the short term, but those most vulnerable will be those living on low-lying islands or in coastal regions and on arid or semi-arid agricultural land. The poor are most vulnerable to climate change and least able to adapt to it. Although climate science is uncertain,

Stern thinks that we should base policy on it because (1) it is the best knowledge we have, and (2) the risks of ignoring it are enormous. Climate-change and development policy are indivisible because neglecting climate change will harm development (Luterbacher and Sprinz 2001: 4; Stern 2009; Bull 2012).

Who should pay the cost of adapting to, and mitigating, climate change? The favourite principle is probably that 'the polluter pays': the developed countries caused and have benefited from greenhouse gas emissions, so they should pay to rectify the damage. They also have the ability to pay and perhaps an obligation under international human-rights law to assist developing countries to mitigate climate harm. Three counter-arguments are that until recently no one knew that economic activity caused climate change; developing countries have benefited from that activity; and those now alive are not responsible for past emissions. Contrary arguments are that developed countries have done little to mitigate global warming since the science became clear; the global poor have benefited little from climate-damaging progress; and present generations have benefited from past emissions and are responsible for current emissions. It is nevertheless difficult to identify causal links between particular economic activities and particular natural disasters (Paterson 2001: 121–3; Baer 2006).

The developed countries do not accept responsibility for past emissions: the Kyoto Protocol assumed that obligations start now. Recent negotiations recognize that developing countries are increasing emissions and should bear part of the cost. There has been much discussion, but little agreement, on the allocation of 'the right to emit'. Some economists support the right to emit and 'emissions trading' on the ground that a market in this right will allocate it efficiently. Critics argue that emissions trading favours the economically powerful and that trading 'the right to emit' would not necessarily reconcile optimal climate policy with human rights (Hayward 2007: 431–47; International Council on Human Rights Policy 2008).

Climate science is uncertain, which raises the question of how much we should spend now to prevent uncertain harm in future. Some economists believe that we should invest now in economic growth and increase expenditure on climate change slowly as the science becomes more certain and we become richer (Nordhaus 2008). Others believe that this would leave us vulnerable to catastrophic and irreversible change in future which could overwhelm our increased wealth; although current science tells us this is unlikely, it is not impossible (Stern 2009). Economists tend to seek the best-value climate policy *for the world*. They ignore the *distribution* of the costs, and especially the cost to the human rights of the most vulnerable (Gardiner 2004).

Some climate theorists distinguish between survival and luxury emissions: a human-rights approach would prioritize survival emissions. Human rights entail that climate policy respect the human rights of all. Climate change poses challenges to human-rights activists and scholars, however, who are used to thinking about *violations*, not *probabilities* of future harm: causal responsibility for climate harm may be more complex than for familiar violations. It is also difficult to attribute human rights to non-existent persons of distant future generations who may be harmed by climate change (Page 2006; International Council on Human Rights Policy 2008). Caney argues that we must assume that the interests and rights of future generations will probably be similar to ours. Contributing to climate change without due regard to its effect on the human rights of future generations is a grave human-rights violation. Yet the IPCC and the negotiations held under the FCCC have largely ignored human rights (Caney 2006; International Council on Human Rights Policy 2008).

The twenty-first yearly session of the Conference of Parties to the FCCC (COP21) was held in Paris from 30 November to 12 December 2015. Representatives of 196 parties to the Convention agreed to limit their countries' emissions to levels that would increase global warming by 2°C and to 'pursue efforts' to limit it to 1.5°C above pre-industrial levels. They agreed also to take stock in 2023 and every five years thereafter. No detailed timetable or country-specific goals were included in the agreement, in contrast to the Kyoto Protocol. Both developed and developing countries are supposed to curb emissions according to national plans that take account of national circumstances. Finance would be provided to poor nations to help them cut emissions and cope with the effects of climate change. Countries affected by climate-related disasters are to get urgent aid. However, existing commitments to cap emissions could lead to global warming of 2.7–3.0°C above pre-industrial levels; poor countries believe that the funding will be insufficient; and key elements of the agreement are voluntary. The consensus is that COP21 was a considerable diplomatic achievement that may have fallen well short of what is necessary to 'save the planet' (Harvey 2015; Levi 2015; Bawden 2016). As of 6 November 2016, more than 90 countries had ratified the Paris agreement. COP16, held in Cancún, Mexico, in 2010, agreed that parties should, in all actions related to climate change, fully respect human rights (Office of the United Nations High Commissioner for Human Rights 2015). Climate-change mitigation and adaptation measures may violate human rights (Neslen 2015).

Global justice

The theory of human rights says that a government is legitimate only if it respects the human rights of its citizens. Pogge argues that the global economic order is imposed on the world's people and is therefore legitimate only if it respects their human rights. The fact that many people prosper under this order does not make it just if the human rights of many are violated, even if the distribution of poverty depends on local factors. The massive non-fulfilment of economic and social human rights means that the global order falls short of the minimum conditions of global justice (Pogge 2002a: 117, 175, 199; 2005a: 39–40, 42–3; 2007: 23–5, 44–5).

The continuing imposition of the global institutional order constitutes a massive violation of the human right to basic necessities, for which the governments and electorates of the more powerful countries bear primary responsibility. The rich countries have contributed to contemporary global poverty historically and benefit from it (Pogge 2007: 53). The moral value of this order should be judged not by *the rate of decline* of serious human-rights violations but by comparing the *current rate* with the rate that might be achieved by a *feasible* alternative order. Participation in a system in which avoidable human-rights violations occur is itself a massive human-rights violation. Abolishing poverty as defined by the World Bank would cost 1.21 per cent of the gross national incomes of the rich countries (Pogge 2002a: 92, 99, 230 n. 122; 2005c: 60; 2007: 30).

Pogge has been criticized on the ground that he shows neither how much poverty the global order causes nor how much his favoured alternative order would eliminate (Patten 2005: 21–4). His claim that the *electorates* of powerful countries bear *primary* responsibility for massive human-rights violations by the global order has also been questioned (Satz 2005: 50–1; Bleisch 2009: 157–65). Pogge replies that the global order harms the poor through the arms trade, by the borrowing privilege that permits dictators to impose international debts on their people, and the resource privilege which enables rich countries to buy resources that dictators have corruptly obtained. In these ways rich states and international institutions not only collaborate with bad institutions in developing countries but make bad institutions more likely by increasing their incentives and durability. No global institutional order could prevent all human-rights violations but most severe poverty could be avoided if the global order were just. There is considerable empirical uncertainty about the causes of global poverty, but mobilization for a poverty-avoidance design of the global institutional order could eradicate most severe poverty within a few years (Pogge 2005c, 2007: 39–41, 46–53).

Others have emphasized various ways in which the global order harms the poor. For example, the cost to poor countries of rich-country subsidies, tariffs and quotas may be more than rich-country aid. Aid can save lives, and additional aid might have public support (Stiglitz 2002: xii–xv, 61, 269; Riddell 2007). The IFIs have collaborated with violating regimes (Darrow 2003: 95–6). The World Bank estimates that the West has received $500–800 billion in illegal transfers from poor countries since 1990, about ten times all aid (Baker and Joly 2009: 62).

Mathias Risse maintains that the global order not only does not harm the poor but has massively improved human well-being over the past 200 years. The global order is therefore not fundamentally unjust but incompletely just. Pogge assumes that the global order causes oppression and poverty, but oppression and poverty pre-existed this order, and it is hard to say whether that order has made them worse (Risse 2005a: 9–17). Empirical research suggests that the quality of national institutions is the primary explanation of developmental success or failure and that integration into the global economy plays little independent role. Pogge does not prove that the global order causes poverty: he implies that the global order causes poverty because the ideal world would cause none (Risse 2005b).

This argument is flawed. The empirical evidence upon which Risse relies does not show that the global order does not cause poverty but, rather, that national institutions are more important than international trade in explaining development. It does not refute Pogge's claim that international institutions cause some of the defects of national institutions. Pogge does not condemn the global order for not being ideal but for not being just. *Minimal justice* requires that human rights be fulfilled as far as possible. He claims that global rules *avoidably* deny many people enjoyment of their human rights. The cost of abolishing world poverty is affordable (Pogge 2005c: 1–5). The weakness of Pogge's argument is that it depends on an incomplete theory of the causes of global poverty.

Conclusion

The implementation of human rights depends on various economic factors. It is easy to proclaim that everyone has a right to an adequate standard of living; the economics of implementing this right are complicated and controversial. Human-rights activists and scholars have largely ignored economics, although this is beginning to change. Economists have largely ignored human rights. The concept of human rights emphasizes the rights of individuals with little concern for the costs of implementing rights or deciding priorities when resources are scarce. It emphasizes too the obligations of states, but is ill-equipped to address the complex structural causes of human-rights deprivations. Bjørnskov and Mchangama, for example, find that incorporating economic and social rights into law has inflationary effects, so that, while some may benefit, others lose, and the net result may be negative (Bjørnskov and Mchangama 2013). Financial crises, such as that of 2008, may have a greater adverse effect on the enjoyment of human rights than the depredations of many dictators, yet, Dowell-Jones and Kinley complain, the human-rights community has offered little analysis of the human-rights implications of such crises: there has been no 'rights-based approach' to sovereign bond markets, capital adequacy, liquidity, leverage levels, algorithmic trading, risk management, derivatives, financial modelling, procylicality, ratings, or bank supervision, all of which may greatly affect human rights (Dowell-Jones and Kinley 2011). Other economic policies that may have significant indirect effects on human rights are aid, capital account liberalization, and national and international tax policies (Goldin and Reinert 2006; Collier 2007; International Bar Association 2013). Which policies are best for human rights cannot be determined solely by identifying and defining the rights involved. Human-rights policy should be based on sound economics while economic policy should be constrained by respect for human rights as far as possible.

9
Conclusion
Human Rights in the Twenty-first Century

Learning from history

The concept of human rights is now so familiar that we need to remember how new it is. It is true that, according to some scholars, the concept of 'rights' was implicit in ancient cultures: the commandment 'thou shalt not steal', for example, they say, implies the right to property. Other scholars, however, maintain that legal disputes in classical Greece were decided by reference to the common good rather than to the rights of the parties. Fred Miller has nevertheless made a strong case that the concept of *citizens' rights* is found in the political philosophy of Aristotle (Miller, F. 1995). The Stoic philosophers had the concept of universal natural law, but not of natural rights. It was not until the Middle Ages that, within the framework of Christian theology, the concept of universal natural rights could emerge.

There is another way of thinking about the history of the concept of human rights in different cultures. At the core of *our* concept of human rights is the idea of protecting individuals (and perhaps groups) from *the abuse of power*. All human societies have power structures, and many of them have throughout history had some conception of the abuse of power. The concepts of *natural rights* and *human rights* are particular ways of expressing this concern about the abuse of power.

Some say that the concept of human rights derives from the political struggles and the property interests of the bourgeoisie in seventeenth-century England (Donnelly 1989: 89, 104–5). Recent research has, however, shown that there was lively debate, if little systematic theory, about natural rights among late-medieval Christian philosophers and theologians centuries earlier (Tierney 1997). Medieval debates about rights were concerned with property, but not only with property. The Magna Carta of 1215 provided for the right to a fair trial. Medieval Christian natural-rights theory was concerned with, among other things, the right to *subsistence*. In the sixteenth century Las Casas and Vitoria used a Christian conception of natural rights to condemn Spanish imperialism in America, but in the seventeenth century the Dutch jurist Grotius used the concept to defend the commercial interests of the Dutch East India Company (Van Ittersum 2006). Medieval debates were conducted in Latin, and, in Latin, the concept of 'property' refers to what is one's own, and that may include one's life and liberty. We see this late-medieval conception of rights in the political philosophy of Locke, who was the first modern natural-rights thinker, but influenced by medieval conceptions of natural rights. This more complex history of the origins of modern rights theory is relevant to human-rights debates today, because it shows that talk of 'three generations' of rights is unhistorical, and that the distinction between civil and political rights, on the one hand, and economic and social rights, on the other, cannot be derived from the history of the concept, which was concerned, first with the right to subsistence and other (economic) property rights, and then with civil and political rights, because these were thought to be necessary to secure the basic rights to survival and property.

The concept of natural rights in the seventeenth and eighteenth centuries was associated with (1) opposition to absolute monarchy; (2) emergent capitalism; and (3) dissident Protestantism or secularized political thought. These themes burst onto the stage of world history in the English Revolution of 1642–9, and the American and French Revolutions of the late eighteenth century.

The violent disorder of the French Revolution provoked a strong *philosophical* reaction that targeted the concept of natural rights as (1) subversive, and (2) unscientific. The concept of natural rights derived the natural rights of individuals from the supposed will of God and the belief that *reason* could tell us what was right and wrong. The scientific philosophy of the eighteenth and nineteenth centuries undermined the concept of the natural rights of individuals and replaced it with that of the science of society (sociology). Saint-Simon, Comte, Marx, Weber and Durkheim were the leaders of this development. Rights were no longer fundamental moral ideas to regulate political life, but ideological products of social struggle. The social sciences marginalized the concept of rights. When the United Nations, after the Second World War, revived the eighteenth-century concept of the Rights of Man as *human rights* in order to express its liberal-democratic opposition to Fascism, it ignored this social-scientific tradition. Both the concept of human rights and the social sciences have flourished since 1945, but for the most part independently of each other. Recently, the increasing influence of the concept of human rights in international and national politics, especially since the end of the Cold War, has made some social scientists aware of the fact that they have ignored a major social development of the past 50 years. At last, they are applying their distinctive concepts, theories and methods to the real world of human rights and their violation. I have, in this book, offered a review, both sympathetic and critical, of the new social science of human rights in the hope that it will advance the reconciliation of ethical idealism and scientific realism that the academic study of human rights requires.

After the adoption of the Universal Declaration of Human Rights (UDHR) by the UN General Assembly in 1948, the slow process of standard-setting (international human-rights law) and institution-building began. The Cold War blocked progress for human rights, however, as Communist regimes perpetrated gross violations of civil and political rights, and the West was implicated in massive violations, either directly or through support of anti-Communist dictatorships. Worldwide decolonization brought many new states to the UN. At first anti-colonial elites found the concept of human rights helpful to their cause, but, after independence, post-colonial state leaders gave priority to economic development, self-determination and anti-racism, but resisted human-rights criticism from the West and domestic oppositions. Many post-colonial states had terrible records in the violation of civil and political rights, and few were successful in protecting economic and social rights. Nevertheless, the international campaign against apartheid in South Africa established the principle that human-rights violations within one nation-state were properly the object of condemnation and sanctions by the international community.

The progress of human rights since 1948 has a number of significant landmarks: the foundation of Amnesty International (1961); the two UN covenants of 1966; the Helsinki Accords of 1975; the human-rights foreign policy of President Jimmy Carter in the 1970s; the democratization of various Latin American and European countries from the mid-1980s; the Vienna Conference of 1993. The end of the Cold War at the end of the 1980s produced contradictory results: liberalization in many former Communist societies, but violent ethno-nationalist conflict in others. By the end of the twentieth century the concept of human rights had become a 'hegemonic ideology'; there had been a tremendous expansion of human-rights law and institutions; there had been great real advances in many countries; and there were many unsolved political problems in the world that still gave rise to grave human-rights violations. As of 14 August 2016, more than 86,000 civilian casualties of the Syrian civil war have been reported, including more than 15,000 children and 10,000 women (Syrian Observatory for Human Rights 2016). The battle for human rights is far from won.

Human rights may seem like an idea whose time has come, but this proposition must be treated with caution. We should not accept the extreme Idealist view that the concept of human rights is very powerful in international politics: states still resist human-rights pressures from within and outside their societies when they think that their interests are threatened. We should not, however, take the extreme Realist view that the concept makes no significant difference to international politics. Communist human-rights violations may have been brought to an end because the West won the Cold War, but the concept of human rights played a role in that war. The social sciences can clarify the respective roles of ideas and material interests in the politics of human rights, although isolating causal connections in international politics is difficult, and there is still much we do not know about the 'power' of human rights.

Some critics believe that the concept of human rights is too *individualistic* and *legalistic*, so that the *structural* causes of human-rights violations, especially of economic and social rights, are ignored. This view almost certainly underestimates the achievements of the human-rights movement based on human-rights law. The structural approach is nevertheless useful in emphasizing the role played by inequalities of political power and the dynamics of the global economy in the causation of human-rights violations. It is limited by the difficulty of identifying alternative structures that would better protect human rights and are attainable. States, international institutions and transnational corporations are the principal players in international politics. NGOs have played an increasingly important role, but their resources and power are relatively weak. The UN is seriously under-funded. Its weakness can be explained by *the principle of limited sacrifice*. We are human and decent, and so we say that everyone ought to enjoy their human rights. However, human-rights declarations are cheap, whereas human-rights implementation is rather expensive. We are unwilling to pay the bill. We are disappointed at the gap between human-rights ideals and human-rights realities, but we are unwilling to recognize our fault in creating that gap, and find it easier to blame economic structures or supposedly ineffective institutions such as the UN. The weakness of the structural approach is that it fails to locate sources of possible change. The strength of the activist approach is that it emphasizes that we are responsible for the structures that we support. Human-rights activists have, however, begun to tackle the structural sources of human-rights violations, and so the idealist and structuralist approaches may be converging.

The history of the concept of human rights supports the contemporary thesis that human rights are 'indivisible' in that basic human material interests are closely connected with political freedom. This history shows, too, that the concept reaches for the fundamental conditions of human well-being while evolving in response to changing social conditions. The social constructivist theory of human rights advocated by Donnelly emphasizes the changing nature of human rights (Donnelly 1985a: 87). The social sciences can explain these changes, although their achievements in doing so have so far been disappointing. Social constructivism, however, gives us no standard for *evaluating* these changes. The legacy of the history of the concept of human rights is confusion about how ethical, analytical and explanatory approaches are related to each other. Historically, social science attempted, but failed, to replace the ethical approach to human rights. Reconciling the ethics and social science of human rights is a principal challenge of the future.

Objections to human rights

The history of human rights teaches us not only *that* the concept of human rights is controversial, but also rather precisely *why* it is. The principal criticisms that were made in the late eighteenth and early nineteenth centuries of the Rights of Man bite still today. Burke said that the concept ignored the value of national traditions. Bentham argued that it ignored the social nature of moral and legal concepts. Marx complained that it concealed and legitimated exploitative and oppressive social structures. Such arguments are still made today. There is a danger that the success of the concept can induce complacency and dogmatism. In the face of relativist objections to human-rights universalism for being 'imperialistic', human-rights advocates would do well to recall the origin of the concept in the revulsion against Nazism. They would do well to remember the victims of genocide in Cambodia and Rwanda. The contemporary appeal and influence of the concept of human rights provide reasons to subject it to critical theoretical (philosophical) and practical (political, economic and cultural) scrutiny. The rhetoric of human rights is universal; the scope of human rights is not: there is a human right to food, but millions starve. In this book I have tried to show both the moral power of the concept, and the difficult theoretical and practical problems that it raises.

Beyond human-rights law

We cannot know the future of human rights, but the social sciences can throw some light on the darkness ahead. Risse et al., for example, have argued that human-rights advances are brought about by a combination of external and internal pressures on rights-violating states (Risse, Ropp and Sikkink 1999). The Vienna Conference of 1993 reinforced the commitment of the international community in principle to universal human rights. Most governments are formally committed to human rights, and the number and effectiveness of human-rights NGOs have greatly increased in recent years. Unashamed human-rights-violating states are now much rarer than they were 30 years ago. Yet serious violations continue, especially against vulnerable groups, such as women, children, indigenous peoples, minorities, migrant workers, and asylum seekers. Here the limits of law and the need for social science are clear. Human-rights scholars have begun to recognize that the global economy and the global climate may have massive implications for human rights. This takes us beyond law to a number of technical disciplines that have until recently not appeared on the human-rights radar; the impact of new technologies on human rights, for example, has recently appeared on the agenda (Murphy 2009). The state–individual model of human rights, which international human-rights law inherited from Locke, must be expanded to address the complex causes of human-rights violations.

The socialist critique of capitalism has been replaced by a more diffuse concern with 'globalization'. We saw in chapter eight that the concept of human rights has a complex relation with globalization, for it claims global validity while criticizing several powerful global institutions. Donnelly emphasizes the persistence of state sovereignty as a barrier to human-rights advance (Donnelly 1998: 152–3). This is true, but not the whole truth in at least two important respects. The first is that states are not the only abusers of human rights: transnational corporations and international financial institutions that are partly independent of states can be human-rights violators. The second is that states do what certain human agents decide that they should do, and the relation between sovereignty and human rights can be changed in the future, as it has been changed in the past.

State sovereignty obstructs the implementation of human rights, partly because state leaders have an interest in violating human rights, and partly because ordinary people have a limited willingness to make sacrifices to defend the human rights of others. However, even if we can summon the will to defend human rights, it may be very difficult to do so. In 1994 the international community stood by while genocide was committed in Rwanda. In response the doctrine of 'the responsibility to protect' was developed to affirm that sovereignty entailed the obligation to protect human rights and that, if a state failed to fulfil this responsibility, the international community might intervene. In 1999 NATO intervened by bombing Serbia to halt the ethnic cleansing of Albanians from Kosovo without the authority of the UN Security Council, and thus apparently illegally. After 9/11, the USA led an international intervention in Afghanistan to topple the government of the Taliban and then, in 2003, an invasion of Iraq. All these interventions removed rights-violating regimes; all killed innocent civilians; all left human rights changed but facing an uncertain future. The international community expressed concern about gross human-rights violations in Darfur, Sudan – some even calling them 'genocide' – but 'intervened' only with inadequate humanitarian aid and peace-keeping operations. The 'responsibility to protect' was failing to protect millions whose human rights were being flagrantly violated. The legal conception of human rights is inadequate for understanding this political complexity. It helps to identify the problem, but says rather little about the solution.

There is much talk in academic and political circles about the need for 'early warning' of human-rights disasters. This raises another difficult problem. We now have fairly good social-scientific knowledge about the early-warning signs of human-rights disasters. Relatively small-scale, but persistent and systematic human-rights violations are often the precursors of much greater ones. The Nazi genocide of the Jews was preceded by several years of *relatively* minor human-rights violations, such as discrimination in employment. Although effective human-rights pressure from governments and NGOs, and skilful conflict-resolution diplomacy may both improve the human-rights situation and reduce the risk of disaster, this may leave a difficult question of *when* to intervene. The problem is that the concept of 'early warning' suggests early intervention, but early intervention may easily be disproportionate and counter-productive. The international human-rights movement may help to prevent human-rights violations from becoming human-rights catastrophes, but the concept of 'early warning' does not resolve all the dilemmas of intervention.

Concluding remarks

Since the end of the Cold War, Western policy-makers have presented human rights, democracy, and market economies as a package. The relations between markets and human rights are, however, complex, problematic and not fully understood. The relations between democracy and human rights are also problematic, because, although democracies generally respect human rights better than authoritarian regimes do, democracies can violate human rights, and the protection of human rights may require limitations on democracy. In practice, the Western powers have interpreted 'democracy' to mean free and fair elections, and, desirable though these are, they are not only not sufficient conditions for the protection of human rights, but sometimes accompany, and perhaps even cause, the deterioration of human rights. In many recent cases, this has been because elected governments have pursued market-based economic policies that have not only worsened the protection of economic and social rights for the most vulnerable sections of society (especially women, children and disabled persons), but also provoked disorder that has led to restrictions on civil and political rights. We must also distinguish between *democracy* and *democratization*, the process of political change that has a problematic relation to human rights for somewhat different reasons. The transition from authoritarianism to democracy may be a change from imposed order to regulated conflict. Where there is little or no tradition of democratic politics, and also economic hardship and/or ethnic divisions, the restraints that democracy places on conflict may break down. The results may resemble the human-rights catastrophes of Rwanda or Yugoslavia, in both of which countries the processes of democratization were involved in the ensuing human-rights tragedies.

The twenty-first century began with the future of human rights uncertain. Great advances have been made since 1945, not only in 'standard-setting' (international and national laws) and 'institution-building' (human-rights commissions, committees, courts, etc.), but also in freedom and well-being for many people in many countries. There are still many countries in which civil and political rights are trampled on. Progress towards the recognition of economic and social rights has been slow, and largely rhetorical. Worse, neo-liberal economic policies reduced the protection of these rights for millions of people around the world who enjoy them least, although there has been some recognition (again, perhaps rhetorical more than practical) that liberal economics should be accompanied by 'safety nets' for the most vulnerable.

Human-rights academics tend to devote excessive attention to the UN system of commissions and committees. These may be important, but they are certainly not the only important institutions that affect human rights in the world, and they are probably not the most important. The concept of human rights is centrally concerned with the misuse of power. The social-scientific study of human rights should give priority to the primary centres of power and to the possible sources of resistance. This entails that human-rights studies should attend more to the G7, the G20, IFIs, the WTO and the foreign policy of the USA. The study of human rights should be integrated with political economy, development economics, conflict studies and the politics of democratic transition. The political theory of human rights has, since Locke, accorded to the rule of law a central place in the protection of human rights. This is correct. Nevertheless, both the theory and practice of human rights have suffered from being excessively legalistic. The kind of economics practised by Amartya Sen and the kind of applied moral philosophy developed by Martha Nussbaum may have more to contribute to the advance of human-rights knowledge than refined legal analysis of human-rights texts (Nussbaum and Sen 1993).

Donnelly has said that the struggle for human rights will be won or lost at the national level (Donnelly 1994: 117). This is only a partial truth. It is true that, notwithstanding globalization, the nation-state is still an important field of power. It is also true that, for many people, the single most important power that affects their human rights is their state and its institutions, especially its legal and law-enforcement agencies. It is also true, however, that, for many others, the structures and processes of the global economy and of global politics are more important. We should recall that many private corporations are richer and more powerful than many states. Risse and his colleagues rightly argue that a complex and finely judged mix of states and NGOs, of internal and external actors, provide the best hope for human rights in the coming years. We have seen that human-rights NGOs have increased greatly in number in recent years, not least in poor countries. Important distinctions are emerging between *international* NGOs, *national* NGOs and *grass-roots* or *community-based* NGOs. Observers have noted tensions among these different types of NGO, especially between those from the rich North and those from the poor South. I have suggested that these tensions may be healthy because they entail *the democratization of the human-rights movement*, that is, the bridging of the gap between the discourse and practices of UN diplomats and human-rights lawyers, on the one hand, and the ordinary people of the world, to protect whose dignity, freedom and well-being the UDHR was adopted. Anthropology may make a special contribution to understanding this aspect of human rights, for it can link the concept of human rights to the cultural understandings of real people in real situations. In addition, a kind of applied human-rights anthropology is being carried out by various projects of human-rights education, formal and informal, around the world (Andreopoulos and Claude 1997; Mihr and Schmitz 2007). The social sciences have, after too long a delay, begun to take human rights seriously. We should hope that this welcome development will be accompanied by human-rights activists taking social science seriously.

References

Aaronson, S. A. 2007: Seeping in slowly: how human rights concerns are penetrating the WTO. *World Trade Review*, 6 (3), 413–49.

Abizadeh, A. 2007: Cooperation, pervasive impact, and coercion: on the scope (not site) of distributive justice. *Philosophy and Public Affairs*, 35 (4), 318–58.

Abouharb, M. R. and Cingranelli, D. 2007: *Human Rights and Structural Adjustment*. New York: Cambridge University Press.

Albahari, M. 2016: *Crimes of Peace: Mediterranean migrations at the world's deadliest border*. Philadelphia, PA: University of Pennsylvania Press.

Aldana, R. 2012: The international rights of migrants. In T. Cushman (ed.), *Handbook of Human Rights*. Abingdon: Routledge, 508–23.

Alston, P. 1992: The Commission on Human Rights. In P. Alston (ed.), *The United Nations and Human Rights: a critical appraisal*. Oxford: Clarendon Press, 126–210.

Alston, P. 1994: The UN's human rights record: from San Francisco to Vienna and beyond. *Human Rights Quarterly*, 16 (2), 375–90.

Alston, P. and Crawford, J. (eds) 2000: *The Future of UN Human Rights Treaty Monitoring*. Cambridge: Cambridge University Press.

American Anthropological Association Executive Board 1947: Statement on human rights. *American Anthropologist*, New Series, 49 (4), 539–43.

Amnesty International 1993: *Getting Away With Murder: political killings and 'disappearances' in the 1990s*. London: Amnesty International Publications.

Anand, S., Segal, P. and Stiglitz, J. (eds) 2009: *Debates on the Measurement of Global Poverty*. Oxford: Oxford University Press.

Andreassen, B. A. 2003: Development, capabilities, rights: what is new about the right to development and a rights approach to development? In M. Bergsmo (ed.), *Human Rights and Criminal Justice for the Downtrodden: essays in honour of Asbjørn Eide*. Leiden: Martinus Nijhoff, 211–32.

Andreopoulos, G. J. and Claude, R. P. (eds) 1997: *Human Rights Education for the Twenty-First Century*. Philadelphia, PA: University of Pennsylvania Press.

An-Na'im, A. A. 1992: Toward a cross-cultural approach to defining international standards of human rights: the meaning of cruel, inhuman, or degrading treatment or punishment. In A. A. An-Na'im (ed.), *Human Rights in Cross-Cultural Perspectives: a quest for consensus*. Philadelphia, PA: University of Pennsylvania Press, 19–43.

Archard, D. 2012: Children's rights. In T. Cushman (ed.), *Handbook of Human Rights*. Abingdon: Routledge, 324–32.

Arnould, V. 2016: Rethinking what ICC success means at the Bemba trial. *OpenDemocracy, Global Rights*, 14 September, https://www.opendemocracy.net/openglobalrights/valerie-arnould/rethinking-what-icc-success-means-at-bemba-trial.

Ashcraft, R. 1986: *Revolutionary Politics and Locke's Two Treatises of Government*. Princeton, NJ: Princeton University Press.

Ashford, E. 2006: The inadequacy of our traditional conception of the duties imposed by human rights. *Canadian Journal of Law and Jurisprudence*, 19 (2), 217–35.

Baehr P. R. 1999: *Human Rights: universality in practice*. Basingstoke: Macmillan.

Baer, P. 2006: Adaptation: who pays whom? In W. N. Adger, J. Paavola, S. Huq and M. J. Mace (eds), *Fairness in Adaptation to Climate Change*. Cambridge, MA: MIT Press, 131–53.

Baghramian, M. 2010: A brief history of relativism. In M. Krausz (ed.), *Relativism: a contemporary anthology*. New York: Columbia University Press, 31–50.

Bailyn, B. 1992: *The Ideological Origins of the American Revolution*. Cambridge, MA: Harvard University Press, enlarged edition.

Baisley, E. 2016: Reaching the tipping point: emerging international human rights norms relating to sexual orientation and gender identity. *Human Rights Quarterly*, 38 (1), 134–63.

Baker, K. M. 1994: The idea of a declaration of rights. In D. Van Kley (ed.), *The French Idea of Freedom: the Old Regime and the Declaration of Rights of 1789*. Stanford, CA: Stanford University Press, 154–96.

Baker, R. and Joly, E. 2009: Illicit money: can it be stopped? *New York Review of Books*, 56 (19), 3–16 December, 61–4.

Barnett, C. R. 1988: Is there a scientific basis in anthropology for the ethics of human rights? In T. E. Downing and G. Kushner (eds), *Human Rights and Anthropology*. Cambridge, MA: Cultural Survival, 21–6.

Barnett, H. G. 1948: On science and human rights. *American Anthropologist*, New Series, 50 (2), 352–5.

Barratt, B. 2004: Aiding or abetting: British foreign aid decisions and recipient country human rights. In S. C. Carey and S. C. Poe (eds), *Understanding Human Rights Violations: new systematic studies*. Aldershot: Ashgate, 43–62.

Barria, L. A. and Roper, S. D. 2005: How effective are international criminal tribunals? An analysis of the ICTY and the ICTR. *International Journal of Human Rights*, 9 (3), 349–68.

Barry, B. M. 2001: *Culture and Equality: an egalitarian critique of multiculturalism*. Cambridge: Polity.

Bauer, J. and Bell, D. (eds) 1999: *The East Asian Challenge for Human Rights*. Cambridge: Cambridge University Press.

Bawden, T. 2016: COP21: Paris deals far too weak to prevent devastating climate change, academics warn. *Independent* online, 8 January.

Becker, C. 1966: *The Declaration of Independence: a study in the history of political ideas*. New York: Alfred A. Knopf.

Beitz, C. R. 2009: *The Idea of Human Rights*. Oxford: Oxford University Press.

Bell, D. A. and Coicaud, J.-M. (eds) 2007: *Ethics in Action: the ethical challenges of international human rights nongovernmental organizations*. Cambridge: Cambridge University Press and United Nations University.

Bellah, R. N. 1983: The ethical aims of social inquiry. In N. Haan, R. N. Bellah, P. Rabinow and W. M. Sullivan (eds), *Social Science as Moral Inquiry*. New York: Columbia University Press, 360–81.

Benedek, W. 2007: The World Trade Organization and human rights. In W. Benedek, K. De Feyter and F. Marrella (eds), *Economic Globalisation and Human Rights*. Cambridge: Cambridge University Press, 137–69.

Beran, H. 1984: A liberal theory of secession. *Political Studies*, XXXII (1), 21–31.

Beran, H. 1988: More theory of secession: a response to Birch. *Political Studies*, XXXVI (2), 316–23.

Bernasconi, R. 2005: Why do the happy inhabitants of Tahiti bother to exist at all? In J. K. Roth (ed.), *Genocide and Human Rights: a philosophical guide*. Basingstoke: Palgrave Macmillan, 139–48.

Besley, T. and Burgess, R. 2003: Halving global poverty. *Journal of Economic Perspectives*, 17 (3), 3–22.

Betts, A. 2015: The normative terrain of the global refugee regime. *Ethics & International Affairs*, 29 (4), 363–75.

Binion, G. 1995: Human rights: a feminist perspective. *Human Rights Quarterly*, 17 (3), 509–26.

Birch, A. H. 1984: Another liberal theory of secession. *Political Studies*, XXXII (4), 596–602.

Bjørnskov, C. and Mchangama, J. 2013: Do social rights affect social outcomes? Economics Working Papers 2013–18, Department of Economics and Business, Aarhus University, http://econ.au.dk/fileadmin/site_files/filer_oekonomi/Working_Papers/Economics/2013/wp13_18.pdf.

Blasi, G. J. and Cingranelli, D. L. 1996: Do constitutions and institutions help protect human rights? In D. L. Cingranelli (ed.), *Human Rights and Developing Countries*. Greenwich, CT: JAI Press, vol. 4, 223–37.

Bleisch, B. 2009: Complicity in harmful action: contributing to world poverty and duties of care. In E. Mack, M. Schramm, S. Klasen and T. Pogge (eds), *Absolute Poverty and Global Justice: empirical data – moral theories – initiatives*. Farnham: Ashgate, 157–66.

Blitt, R. C. 2004: Who will watch the watchdogs? Human rights nongovernmental organizations and the case for regulation. *Buffalo Human Rights Law Review*, 10, 261–398.

Bob, C. 2002: Merchants of morality. *Foreign Policy*, March/April, 36–45.

Bochenek, M. G. 2015: Children's rights as human rights. *Ethics & International Affairs*, 29 (4), 473–88.

Boisson de Chazournes, L. 2007: The Bretton Woods institutions and human rights: converging tendencies. In W. Benedek, K. De Feyter and F. Karrella (eds), *Economic Globalisation and Human Rights*. Cambridge: Cambridge University Press, 210–42.

Bradlow, D. D. 1996: Social justice and development: critical issues facing the Bretton Woods system: the World Bank, the IMF, and human rights. *Transnational Law and Contemporary Problems*, 6, 47–90.

Breay, C. 2002: *Magna Carta: manuscripts and myths*. London: The British Library.

Breen, C. 2005: Rationalising the work of UN human rights bodies or reducing the input of NGOs? The changing role of human rights NGOs at the United Nations. *Non-State Actors and International Law*, 5 (2), 101–26.

Brett, A. S. 2003: *Liberty, Right and Nature*. Cambridge: Cambridge University Press.

Brett, R. 1995: The role and limits of human rights NGOs at the United Nations. *Political Studies*, XLIII, special issue 'Politics and Human Rights', 96–110.

Brinks, D. M. and Gauri, V. 2012: The law's majestic equality? The distributive impact of litigating social and economic rights. Washington, DC: World Bank, Development Research Group, Policy Research Working Paper 5999, March.

Brunsma, D. L., Iyall Smith, K. E. and Gran, B. K. (eds) 2015: *Expanding the Human in Human Rights: toward a sociology of human rights*. Boulder, CO: Paradigm Publishers.

Brysk, A. 2000: *From Tribal Village to Global Village: Indian rights and international relations in Latin America*. Stanford, CA: Stanford University Press.

Brysk, A. 2013: *Speaking Rights to Power: constructing political will*. New York: Oxford University Press.

Buchanan, A. 2004: *Justice, Legitimacy, and Self-determination: moral foundations for international law*. Oxford: Oxford University Press.

Buchanan, A. 2010: The egalitarianism of human rights. *Ethics*, 120 (4), 679–710.

Buchanan, A. 2014: *The Heart of Human Rights*. New York: Oxford University Press.

Bueno De Mesquita, B., Downs, G. W., Smith, A. and Cherif, F. M. 2005: Thinking inside the box: a closer look at democracy and human rights. *International Studies Quarterly*, 49 (3), 439–57.

Bull, M. 2012: What is the rational response? *London Review of Books*, 34 (10), May, 3–6.

Burgerman, S. D. 1998: Mobilising principles: the role of transnational activists in promoting human rights principles. *Human Rights Quarterly*, 20 (4), 905–23.

Caney, S. 1992: Liberalism and communitarianism: a misconceived debate. *Political Studies*, XL (2), 273–89.

Caney, S. 2006: Cosmopolitan justice, rights and global climate change. *Canadian Journal of Law and Jurisprudence*, 19 (2), 255–78.

Cardenas, S. 2009: Mainstreaming human rights: publishing trends in political science. *PS: Political Science & Politics*, 42, 161–6.

Cardenas, S. 2014: *Chains of Justice: the global rise of state institutions for human rights*. Philadelphia, PA: University of Pennsylvania Press.

Carey, S. C. and Poe, S. C. 2004: Human rights research and the quest for human dignity. In S. C. Carey and S. C. Poe (eds),

Understanding Human Rights Violations: new systematic studies. Aldershot: Ashgate, 3–15.

Carozza, P. G. 2003: From conquest to constitutions: retrieving a Latin American tradition of the idea of human rights. *Human Rights Quarterly*, 25 (2), 281–313.

Carr, E. H. 1949: The Rights of Man. In UNESCO (ed.), *Human Rights: comments and interpretations.* Westport, CT: Greenwood Press (1973 reprint), 19–23.

Cassese, A. 1992: The General Assembly: historical perspective 1945–1989. In P. Alston (ed.), *The United Nations and Human Rights: a critical appraisal.* Oxford: Clarendon Press, 25–54.

Cassese, A. 1995: *Self-determination of Peoples: a legal reappraisal.* New York: Cambridge University Press.

Chaplin, J. 1993: How much cultural and religious pluralism can liberalism tolerate? In J. Horton (ed.), *Multiculturalism and Toleration.* Basingstoke: Macmillan, 39–46.

Charnovitz, S. 1996–7: Two centuries of participation: NGOs and international governance. *Michigan Journal of International Law*, 18, 183–286.

Charvet, J. and Kaczynska-Nay, E. 2008: *The Liberal Project and Human Rights: the theory and practice of a new world order.* Cambridge: Cambridge University Press.

Chase, A. 2006: The tail and the dog: constructing Islam and human rights in political context. In A. Chase and A. Hamzawy (eds), *Human Rights in the Arab World.* Philadelphia, PA: University of Pennsylvania Press, 21–36.

Chase, A. 2007: The transnational Muslim world, the foundations and origins of human rights, and their ongoing intersections. *The Muslim World Journal of Human Rights*, 4 (1), 1–14.

Chikuhwa, T. W. 2010: The evolution of the United Nations' protection agenda for children: applying international standards. In S. Gates and S. Reich (eds), *Child Soldiers in the Age of Fractured States.* Pittsburgh, PA: University of Pittsburgh Press, 37–51.

Cingranelli, D. L. and Richards, D. L. 1999: Respect for human rights after the end of the Cold War. *Journal of Peace Research*, 36 (5), 511–34.

Clark, D. A. 2005: The capability approach: its development, critiques and recent advances. ESRC Global Policy Research Group Working Paper No. 32. Oxford: Economic and Social Research Council, Global Policy Research Group.

Claude, R. P. 1976: The classical model of human rights development. In R. P. Claude (ed.), *Comparative Human Rights.* Baltimore, MD: Johns Hopkins University Press, 6–50.

Claude, R. P. 2002a: *Science in the Service of Human Rights*. Philadelphia, PA: University of Pennsylvania Press.

Claude, R. P. 2002b: Personal communication.

Clemens, M. A. and Moss, T. J. 2005: Ghost of 0.7%: origins and relevance of the international aid target. Center for Global Development, Working Paper Number 68, September.

Cole, W. M. 2012: Human rights as myth and ceremony? Re-evaluating the effectiveness of human rights treaties, 1981–2007. *American Journal of Sociology*, 117 (4), 1131–71.

Coleman, J. 1993: Medieval discussions of human rights. In W. Schmale (ed.), *Human Rights and Cultural Diversity*. Goldbach, Germany: Keip Publishing, 103–20.

Collier, P. 2007: *The Bottom Billion: why the poorest countries are failing and what can be done about it*. Oxford: Oxford University Press.

Compa, L. and Hinchliffe-Darricarrère, T. 1995: Enforcing international rights through corporate codes of conduct. *Columbia Journal of Transnational Law*, 33, 663–89.

Cottier, T., Pauwelyn, J. and Bürgi, E. 2005: Introduction: linking trade regulation and human rights in international law: an overview. In T. Cottier, J. Pauwelyn and E. B. Bonanomi (eds), *Human Rights and International Trade*. Oxford: Oxford University Press, 1–26.

Coulthard, G. S. 2014: *Red Skin, White Masks: rejecting the colonial politics of recognition*. Minneapolis, MN: University of Minnesota Press.

Cranston, M. 1973: *What are Human Rights?* London: The Bodley Head.

Dagger, R. 1989: Rights. In T. Ball, J. Farr and R. L. Hanson (eds), *Political Innovation and Conceptual Change*. Cambridge: Cambridge University Press, 292–308.

Dahl, R. 1989: *Democracy and its Critics*. New Haven, CT: Yale University Press.

Darrow, M. 2003: *Between Light and Shadow: the World Bank, the International Monetary Fund and international human rights law*. Oxford: Hart.

Davenport, C. 2007: *State Repression and the Domestic Democratic Peace*. Cambridge: Cambridge University Press.

Davenport, C. and Armstrong, D. A. II 2004: Democracy and the violation of human rights: a statistical analysis from 1976 to 1996. *American Journal of Political Science*, 48 (3), 538–54.

Desai, M. 1999: From Vienna to Beijing: women's human rights activism and the human rights community. In P. Van Ness (ed.),

Debating Human Rights: critical essays from the United States and Asia. London: Routledge, 184–96.

De Waal, A. 2008: Why Darfur intervention is a mistake. http://news.bbc.co.uk/1/hi/world/africa/7411087.stm, 21 May.

Dickinson, H. T. 1977: *Political Ideology in Eighteenth-Century Britain*. London: Methuen.

Donnelly, E. A. 2002: Proclaiming Jubilee: the debt and structural adjustment network. In S. Khagram, J. V. Riker and K. Sikkink (eds), *Restructuring World Politics: transnational social movements, networks, and norms*. Minneapolis, MN: University of Minnesota Press, 155–80.

Donnelly, J. 1982: Human rights as natural rights. *Human Rights Quarterly*, 4 (3), 391–405.

Donnelly, J. 1985a: *The Concept of Human Rights*. London: Croom Helm.

Donnelly, J. 1985b: In search of the unicorn: the jurisprudence and politics of the right to development. *California Western International Law Journal*, 15 (3), 473–509.

Donnelly, J. 1989: *Universal Human Rights in Theory and Practice*. Ithaca, NY: Cornell University Press.

Donnelly, J. 1993: Third generation rights. In C. Brölmann, R. Lefeber and M. Zieck (eds), *Peoples and Minorities in International Law*. Dordrecht: Martinus Nijhoff, 119–50.

Donnelly, J. 1994: Post-Cold War reflections on the study of international human rights. *Ethics and International Affairs*, 8, 97–117.

Donnelly, J. 1998: *International Human Rights*. Boulder, CO: Westview Press, second edition.

Donnelly, J. 1999: The social construction of international human rights. In T. Dunne and N. J. Wheeler (eds), *Human Rights in Global Politics*. Cambridge: Cambridge University Press, 71–102.

Donnelly, J. 2003: *Universal Human Rights in Theory and Practice*. Ithaca, NY: Cornell University Press, second edition.

Donnelly, J. 2007: *International Human Rights*. Boulder, CO: Westview Press, third edition.

Doughty, P. L. 1988: Crossroads for anthropology: human rights in Latin America. In T. E. Downing and G. Kushner (eds), *Human Rights and Anthropology*. Cambridge, MA: Cultural Survival, 43–71.

Dowell-Jones, M. and Kinley, D. 2011: Minding the gap: global finance and human rights. *Ethics & International Affairs*, 25 (2), 183–210.

Downing, T. E. 1988: Human rights research: the challenge for anthropologists. In T. E. Downing and G. Kushner (eds), *Human*

Rights and Anthropology. Cambridge, MA: Cultural Survival, 9–19.

Downing, T. E. and Kushner, G. 1988: Introduction. In T. E. Downing and G. Kushner (eds), *Human Rights and Anthropology*. Cambridge, MA: Cultural Survival, 1–8.

Dworkin, R. 1978: *Taking Rights Seriously*. London: Duckworth, second, corrected impression.

Dworkin, R. 1996: *Freedom's Law: the moral reading of the American Constitution*. Cambridge, MA: Harvard University Press.

Easterly, W. R. 2007: *The White Man's Burden: why the West's efforts to aid the Rest have done so much ill and so little good*. Oxford: Oxford University Press.

Easterly, W. 2009: The anarchy of success. *New York Review of Books*, 56 (15), 8–21 October, 28–30.

Edwards, A. 2005: Human rights, refugees, and the right 'to enjoy' asylum. *International Journal of Refugee Law*, 17 (2), 293–330.

Eide, A. 1992: The Sub-commission on Prevention of Discrimination and Protection of Minorities. In P. Alston (ed.), *The United Nations and Human Rights: a critical appraisal*. Oxford: Clarendon Press, 211–64.

Engle, K. 2001: From skepticism to embrace: human rights and the American Anthropological Association from 1947–1999. *Human Rights Quarterly* 23 (3), 536–59.

Evans, M. D. 2006: International law and human rights in a pre-emptive era. In M. Buckley and R. Singh (eds), *The Bush Doctrine and the War on Terrorism: global responses, global consequences*. London: Routledge, 189–99.

Fein, H. 1995: More murder in the middle: life-integrity violations and democracy in the world, 1987. *Human Rights Quarterly*, 17 (1), 170–91.

Fellmeth, A. X. 2000: Feminism and international law: theory, methodology, and substantive reform. *Human Rights Quarterly*, 22 (3), 658–733.

Finnis, J. 1980: *Natural Law and Natural Rights*. Oxford: Clarendon Press.

Flikschuh, K. 1999: Freedom and constraint in Kant's Metaphysical Elements of Justice. *History of Political Thought*, 20 (2), 250–71.

Flint, J. and de Waal, A. 2008: This prosecution will endanger the people we wish to defend in Sudan. *Observer*, 13 July, 41.

Forsythe, D. P. 1983: *Human Rights and World Politics*. Lincoln, NE: University of Nebraska Press.

Forsythe, D. P. 1989: *Human Rights and World Politics*. Lincoln, NE: University of Nebraska Press, second edition.

Forsythe, D. P. 2000: *Human Rights in International Relations*. Cambridge: Cambridge University Press.

Forsythe, D. P. 2006: *Human Rights in International Relations*. Cambridge: Cambridge University Press, second edition.

Forsythe, D. P. 2012: *Human Rights in International Relations*. Cambridge: Cambridge University Press, third edition.

Fottrell, D. 2000: One step forward or two steps sideways? Assessing the first decade of the United Nations Convention on the Rights of the Child. In D. Fottrell (ed.), *Revisiting Children's Rights: 10 years of the UN Convention on the Rights of the Child*. The Hague: Kluwer Law International, 1–14.

Foweraker, J. and Landman, T. 1997: *Citizenship Rights and Social Movements: a comparative and statistical analysis*. Oxford: Oxford University Press.

Fox, J. 2002: Transnational civil society campaigns and the World Bank Inspection Panel. In A. Brysk (ed.), *Globalization and Human Rights*. Berkeley, CA: University of California Press, 171–200.

Franklin, D. Roosevelt Presidential Library and Museum, Annual Message to Congress, January 6, 1941, The 'Four Freedoms' speech, http://www.fdrlibrary.marist.edu/4free.html.

Freeman, M. A. 1980: *Edmund Burke and the Critique of Political Radicalism*. Oxford: Basil Blackwell.

Freeman, M. D. A. 1997: *The Moral Status of Children: essays on the rights of the child*. The Hague: Martinus Nijhoff.

Frey, B. A. 1997: The legal and ethical responsibilities of transnational corporations in the protection of international human rights. *Minnesota Journal of Global Trade*, 6, 153–88.

Frezzo, M. 2015: *The Sociology of Human Rights: an introduction*. Cambridge: Polity.

Futamura, M. 2008: *War Crimes Tribunals and Transitional Justice: The Tokyo Trial and the Nuremberg Legacy*. London: Routledge.

Gaer, F. D. 2001: Mainstreaming a concern for the human rights of women. In M. Agosín (ed.), *Women, Gender and Human Rights: a global perspective*. New Brunswick, NJ: Rutgers University Press, 98–122.

Gaer, F. D. and Broecker, C. L. (eds) 2014: *The United Nations High Commissioner for Human Rights: conscience for the world*. Leiden: Martinus Nijhoff.

Gandhi, M. 1949: A letter addressed to the Director-General of UNESCO. In UNESCO (ed.), *Human Rights: comments and interpretations*. Westport, CT: Greenwood Press (1973 reprint), 18.

Gardiner, S. M. 2004: Ethics and global climate change. *Ethics*, 114, 555–600.

Garre, M. 1999: *Human Rights in Translation: legal concepts in different languages*. Copenhagen: Copenhagen Business School Press.

Gewirth, A. 1981: The basis and content of human rights. In J. R. Pennock and J. W. Chapman (eds), *Human Rights*. New York: New York University Press, 121–47.

Gewirth, A. 1982: *Human Rights: essays on justification and applications*. Chicago, IL: University of Chicago Press.

Gewirth, A. 1996: *The Community of Rights*. Chicago, IL: University of Chicago Press.

Gilabert, P. 2010: Kant and the claims of the poor. *Philosophy and Phenomenological Research*, 81 (2), 382–418.

Gilbert, J. 2007: Nomadic territories: a human rights approach to nomadic peoples' land rights. *Human Rights Law Review*, 7 (4), 681–716.

Glaeser, E. L., La Porta, R., Lopez-De-Silanes, F. and Shleifer, A. 2004: Do institutions cause growth? *Journal of Economic Growth*, 9 (3), 271–303.

Glover, J. 1999: *Humanity: a moral history of the twentieth century*. London: Jonathan Cape.

Goldin, I. and Reinert, K. 2006: *Globalization for Development: trade, finance, aid, migration, and policy*. Washington, DC and Basingstoke: World Bank and Palgrave Macmillan.

Goodale, M. 2006a: Introduction to 'Anthropology and Human Rights in a New Key'. *American Anthropologist*, 108 (1), 1–8.

Goodale, M. 2006b: Ethical theory as social practice. *American Anthropologist*, 108 (1), 25–37.

Goodale, M. 2009: *Surrendering to Utopia: an anthropology of human rights*. Stanford, CA: Stanford University Press.

Goodman, R. and Jinks, D. 2003: Measuring the effects of human rights treaties. *European Journal of International Law*, 14 (1), 171–83.

Gordon, N. 2008: Human rights, social space and power: why do some NGOs exert more influence than others? *International Journal of Human Rights*, 12 (1), 23–39.

Griffin, J. 2008: *On Human Rights*. Oxford: Oxford University Press.

Griffin, J. 2010: Questions of aim and approach. *Ethics*, 120 (4), 741–60.

Gruen, C. and Klasen, S. 2012: Has transition improved well-being? *Economic Systems*, 36 (1), 11–30.

Gurr, T. R. 1986: The political origins of state violence and terror: a theoretical analysis. In M. Stohl and G. A. Lopez (eds), *Government Violence and Repression: an agenda for research*. New York: Greenwood Press, 45–71.

Hafner-Burton, E. M. 2005a: Right or robust? The sensitive nature of government repression in an era of globalization. *Journal of Peace Research*, 42 (6), 679–98.

Hafner-Burton, E. M. 2005b: Trading human rights: how preferential trade agreements influence government repression. *International Organization*, 59 (3), 2005, 593–629.

Hafner-Burton, E. M. 2008: Sticks and stones: naming and shaming the human rights enforcement problem. *International Organization*, 62 (4), 689–716.

Hafner-Burton, E. M. 2009: *Forced to be Good: why trade agreements boost human rights*. Ithaca, NY: Cornell University Press.

Hafner-Burton, E. M. and Tsutsui, K. 2005: Human rights in a globalizing world: the paradox of empty promises. *American Journal of Sociology*, 110 (5), 1373–1411.

Hafner-Burton, E. M. and Tsutsui, K. 2007: Justice lost! The failure of international law to matter where needed most. *Journal of Peace Research*, 44 (4), 407–25.

Hannum, H. 1990: *Autonomy, Sovereignty and Self-determination: the accommodation of conflicting rights*. Philadelphia, PA: University of Pennsylvania Press.

Harvey, F. 2015: Paris climate change agreement: the world's greatest diplomatic success. *Guardian* online, 14 December.

Harvey, F. and Vidal, J. 2011: Green groups still fear catastrophe for planet. *Guardian*, 12 December, 12.

Hathaway, O. A. 2002: Do human rights treaties make a difference? *Yale Law Journal*, 111, 1935–2042.

Hawkins, D. G. 2002: *International Human Rights and Authoritarian Rule in Chile*. Lincoln, NE: University of Nebraska Press.

Hayner, P. B. 2011: *Unspeakable Truths: transitional justice and the challenge of truth commissions*. New York: Routledge, second edition.

Hayward, T. 2007: Human rights versus emissions rights: climate justice and the equitable distribution of ecological space. *Ethics & International Affairs*, 21 (4), 431–50.

Healy, P. 2006: Human rights and intercultural relations: a hermeneutico-dialogical approach. *Philosophy and Social Criticism*, 32 (4), 513–41.

Hegarty, A. and Fridlund, H. 2016: Taking stock – the Universal Periodic Review's achievements and opportunities. *OpenDemocracy*, 12 August.

Henderson, C. W. 1991: Conditions affecting the use of political repression. *Journal of Conflict Resolution*, 35 (1), 120–42.

Hill, D. W. 2010: Estimating the effects of human rights treaties on state behaviour. *Journal of Politics*, 72 (4), 1161–74.

Hinshelwood, B. 2013: The Carolinian context of John Locke's theory of slavery. *Political Theory*, 41 (4), 562–90.

Hirschman, A. O. 1983: Morality and the social sciences: a durable tension. In N. Haan, R. N. Bellah, P. Rabinow and W. M. Sullivan (eds), *Social Science as Moral Inquiry*. New York: Columbia University Press, 21–32.

Hirschmann, N. J. and McClure, K. M. 2007: Introduction: Johnny, we hardly knew ye. In N. J. Hirschmann and K. M. McClure (eds), *Feminist Interpretations of John Locke*. University Park, PA: Pennsylvania State University Press, 3–15.

Hofbauer, H., Blyberg, A. and Krafchik, W. 2004: Dignity counts: a guide to using budget analysis to advance human rights. Mexico City: Fundar – Centro de Análisis e Investigación, International Budget Project, International Human Rights Internship Program.

Holt, J. C. 1965: *Magna Carta*. Cambridge: Cambridge University Press.

Hopgood, S. 2013: *The Endtimes of Human Rights*. Ithaca, NY: Cornell University Press.

Howard, R. E. 1986: *Human Rights in Commonwealth Africa*. Totowa, NJ: Rowman and Littlefield.

Hynes, P., Lamb, M., Short, D. and Waites, M. (eds) 2011: *Sociology and Human Rights: new engagements*. London: Routledge.

Ignatieff, M. 1999: Human rights: the midlife crisis. *New York Review of Books*, 46 (9), 20 May, 58–62.

International Bar Association 2013: *Tax Abuses, Poverty and Human Rights: a report of the International Bar Association's Human Rights Institute Task Force on Illicit Financial Flows, Poverty and Human Rights*. London: International Bar Association.

International Council on Human Rights Policy 2008: *Climate Change and Human Rights: a rough guide*. Versoix, Switzerland: International Council on Human Rights Policy.

Iriye, A. and Goedde, P. 2012: Introduction: human rights as history. In A. Iriye, P. Goedde and W. I. Hitchcock (eds), *The Human Rights Revolution: an international history*. Oxford: Oxford University Press, 3–24.

Jacobson, R. 1992: The Committee on the Elimination of Discrimination against Women. In P. Alston (ed.), *The United Nations and Human Rights: a critical appraisal*. Oxford: Clarendon Press, 444–72.

Jetschke, A. and Liese, A. 2013: The power of human rights a decade after: from euphoria to contestation? In T. Risse, S. C. Ropp and K. Sikkink (eds), *The Persistent Power of Human Rights: from commitment to compliance*. Cambridge: Cambridge University Press, 26–42.

Joachim, J. 2003: Framing issues and seizing opportunities: the UN, NGOs, and women's rights. *International Studies Quarterly*, 47 (2), 247–74.

Johnson, D. 1992: Cultural and regional pluralism in the drafting of the UN Convention on the Rights of the Child. In M. Freeman and P. Veerman (eds), *The Ideologies of Children's Rights*. Dordrecht: Martinus Nijhoff, 95–114.

Jones, D. 2014: *Magna Carta: the making and legacy of the Great Charter*. London: Head of Zeus.

Jones, P. 1994: *Rights*. Basingstoke: Macmillan.

Keal, P. 2003: *European Conquest and the Rights of Indigenous Peoples: the moral backwardness of international society*. Cambridge: Cambridge University Press.

Keck, M. E. and Sikkink, K. 1998: *Activists Beyond Borders: advocacy networks in international politics*. Ithaca, NY: Cornell University Press.

Keith, L. C. 1999: The United Nations International Covenant on Civil and Political Rights: does it make a difference in human rights behaviour? *Journal of Peace Research*, 36, 95–118.

Keith, L. C. 2002: Constitutional provisions for individual human rights (1977–1996): are they more than mere 'window dressing'? *Political Research Quarterly*, 55 (1), 111–43.

Kennedy, D. 2011: Commentary on anti-eviction and development in the global South. In L. E. White and J. Perelman (eds), *Stones of Hope: how African activists reclaim human rights to challenge poverty*. Stanford, CA: Stanford University Press, 41–50.

Kenny, C. 2005: Why are we worried about income? Nearly everything else that matters is converging. *World Development*, 33 (1), 1–19.

King, M. 2004: Children's rights as communication: reflections on autopoietic theory and the United Nations Convention. In M. D. A. Freeman (ed.), *Children's Rights*. Aldershot: Dartmouth, 311–27.

Kleingeld, P. 2012: *Kant and Cosmopolitanism: the philosophical ideal of world citizenship*. Cambridge: Cambridge University Press.

Korey, W. 1998: *NGOs and the Universal Declaration of Human Rights: 'a curious grapevine'*. Basingstoke: Macmillan.

Kristof, N. D. 2006: Genocide in slow motion. *New York Review of Books*, 53 (2), 9 February, http://www.nybooks.com/articles/archives/2006/feb/09/genocide-in-slow-motion.

Kymlicka, W. 1989: *Liberalism, Community and Culture*. Oxford: Clarendon Press.

Kymlicka, W. 1995: *Multicultural Citizenship: a liberal theory of group rights*. Oxford: Clarendon Press.

Kymlicka, W. 2001: Human rights and ethnocultural justice. In W. Kymlicka, *Politics in the Vernacular: nationalism, multiculturalism and citizenship*. Oxford: Oxford University Press, 69–90.

Kymlicka, W. 2007: *Multicultural Odysseys: navigating the new international politics of diversity*. Oxford: Oxford University Press.

Kymlicka, W. 2011: Beyond the indigenous/minority dichotomy? In S. Allen and A. Xanthaki (eds), *Reflections on the UN Declaration on the Rights of Indigenous Peoples*. Oxford: Hart, 183–208.

Landman, T. 2002: Comparative politics and human rights. *Human Rights Quarterly*, 24 (4), 890–923.

Landman, T. 2005a: *Protecting Human Rights: a comparative study*. Washington, DC: Georgetown University Press.

Landman, T. 2005b: Review article: the political science of human rights. *British Journal of Political Science*, 35 (3), 549–72.

Landman, T. 2006: *Studying Human Rights*. London: Routledge.

Langford, M. 2009: Domestic adjudication and economic, social and cultural rights: a socio-legal review. *Sur: International Journal on Human Rights*, 6 (11), 91–121.

Laville, S. and Leach, A. 2015: Female workers reveal the hidden scale of sexual assaults within aid agencies. *Guardian*, 19 October, 15.

LeBor, A. 2006: *'Complicity with Evil': the United Nations in the age of modern genocide*. New Haven, CT: Yale University Press.

Leite, S. P. 2001: Human rights and the IMF. *Finance and Development*, 38 (4), http://www.imf.org/external/pubs/ft/fandd/2001/12/leite.htm.

Lepora, C. and Goodin, R. E. 2013: *On Complicity and Compromise*. Oxford: Oxford University Press.

Levi, M. 2015: Two cheers for the Paris Agreement on Climate Change. Council on Foreign Relations, 12 December, http://blogs.cfr.org/sivaram/2015/12/12/two-cheers-for-the-paris-agreement-on-climate-change.

Locke, J. [1689] 1970: *Two Treatises of Government*. Cambridge: Cambridge University Press.

Luterbacher, U. and Sprinz, D. F. (eds) 2001: *International Relations and Global Climate Change*. Cambridge, MA: MIT Press.

McBeth, A. 2006: Breaching the vacuum: a consideration of the role of international human rights law in the operations of international financial institutions. *International Journal of Human Rights*, 10 (4), 385–404.

McBrearty, S. 2016: The proposed business and human rights treaty: four challenges and an opportunity. *Harvard International Law Journal*, 57, online symposium, 11–14.

McCallum, R. C. 2014: Preface. In M. Sabatello and M. Schulze (eds), *Human Rights and Disability Advocacy*. Philadelphia, PA: University of Pennsylvania Press, xv–xvi.

McCrudden, C. and O'Leary, B. 2013: *Courts and Consociations: human rights versus power-sharing*. Oxford: Oxford University Press.

Macdonald, M. 1963: Natural rights. In P. Laslett (ed.), *Philosophy, Politics and Society*. Oxford: Basil Blackwell, 35–55.

McDonnell, T. M. 1999: Introduction. In *Human Rights and Non-state Actors. Pace International Law Review*, 11 (1), 205–7.

McGrade, A. S. 1974: *The Political Thought of William of Ockham: personal and institutional principles*. Cambridge: Cambridge University Press.

MacIntyre, A. 1981: *After Virtue*. Notre Dame, IN: University of Notre Dame Press.

Mack, M. 2003: *German Idealism and the Jew: the inner anti-Semitism of philosophy and German Jewish responses*. Chicago, IL: University of Chicago Press.

McNally, D. 1989: Locke, Levellers and liberty: property and democracy in the thought of the first Whigs. *History of Political Thought*, X (1), 17–40.

Macpherson, C. B. 1962: *The Political Theory of Possessive Individualism*. Oxford: Clarendon Press.

Maliks, R. 2014: *Kant's Politics in Context*. Oxford: Oxford University Press.

Marchetti, R. and Tocci, N. (eds) 2011: *Civil Society, Conflicts and the Politicization of Human Rights*. Tokyo: United Nations University Press.

Margalit, A. and Raz, J. 1990: National self-determination. *Journal of Philosophy*, LXXXVII (9), 439–61.

Maritain, J. 1949: Introduction. In UNESCO (ed.), *Human Rights: comments and interpretations*. Westport, CT: Greenwood Press (1973 reprint), 9–17.

Mayer, A. E. 2007: *Islam and Human Rights: tradition and politics*. Boulder, CO: Westview Press, fourth edition.

Mazower, M. 2004: The strange triumph of human rights, 1933–1950. *The Historical Journal*, 47 (2), 379–98.

Melton, J. and Hazell, R. 2015: Introduction: Magna Carta... Holy Grail. In R. Hazell and J. Melton (eds), *Magna Carta and its Modern Legacy*. New York: Cambridge University Press, 3–19.

Méndez, J. E. 1997: Accountability for past abuses. *Human Rights Quarterly*, 19 (2), 255–82.

Merry, S. E. 2006: *Human Rights and Gender Violence: translating international law into local justice*. Chicago, IL: University of Chicago Press.

Mertus, J. 2005: *The United Nations and Human Rights*. London: Routledge.

Messer, E. 1993: Anthropology and human rights. *Annual Review of Anthropology*, 22, 221–49.

Meyer, W. H. 1996: Human rights and MNCs: theory versus quantitative analysis. *Human Rights Quarterly*, 18 (2), 368–97.

Mihr, A. and Schmitz, H. P. 2007: Human rights education (HRE) and transnational activism. *Human Rights Quarterly*, 29 (4), 973–93.

Milgram, S. 1974: *Obedience to Authority: an experimental view*. New York: Harper & Row.

Miller, A. M. 2009: *Sexuality and Human Rights*. Versoix, Switzerland: International Council on Human Rights Policy.

Miller, D. 1995: *On Nationality*. Oxford: Clarendon Press.

Miller, F. Jr 1995: *Nature, Justice, and Rights in Aristotle's Politics*. Oxford: Clarendon Press.

Milner, W. T. 2002: Economic globalization and rights: an empirical analysis. In A. Brysk (ed.), *Globalization and Human Rights*. Berkeley, CA: University of California Press, 77–97.

Milner, W. T., Poe, S. C. and Leblang, D. 1999: Security rights, subsistence rights and liberties: a theoretical survey of the empirical landscape. *Human Rights Quarterly*, 21 (2), 403–43.

Mitchell, N. J. and McCormick, J. M. 1988: Economic and political explanations of human rights violations. *World Politics*, 40 (4), 476–98.

Mitsis, P. 1999: The Stoic origin of natural rights. In K. Ierodiakonou (ed.), *Topics in Stoic Philosophy*. Oxford: Clarendon Press, 153–77.

Moravcsik, A. 1995: Explaining international human rights regimes: liberal theory and Western Europe. *European Journal of International Relations*, 1 (2), 157–89.

Morris, L. 2013: *Human Rights and Social Theory*. Basingstoke: Palgrave Macmillan.

Morsink, J. 1999: *The Universal Declaration of Human Rights: origins, drafting, and intent*. Philadelphia, PA: University of Pennsylvania Press.

Moyn, S. 2010: *The Last Utopia: human rights in history*. Cambridge, MA, and London: The Belknap Press of Harvard University Press.

Mulhall, S. and Swift, A. 1996: *Liberals and Communitarians*. Oxford: Blackwell, second edition.

Murphy, S. D. 2004–5: Taking multinational corporate codes of conduct to the next level. *Columbia Journal of Transnational Law*, 43 (2), 389–433.

Murphy, T. (ed.) 2009: *New Technologies and Human Rights*. Oxford: Oxford University Press.

Muthu, S. 2003: *Enlightenment Against Empire*. Princeton, NJ: Princeton University Press.

Mutua, M. 2001: Human rights international NGOs: a critical evaluation. In C. E. Welch, Jr. (ed.), *NGOs and Human Rights: promise and performance*. Philadelphia, PA: University of Pennsylvania Press, 151–63.

Mutua, M. 2008: *Human Rights: a political and cultural critique*. Philadelphia, PA: University of Pennsylvania Press.

Nash, K. 2015: *The Political Sociology of Human Rights*. Cambridge: Cambridge University Press.

Neslen, A. 2015: 'Green' dam linked to killings of six indigenous people in Guatemala. *Guardian*, 26 March.

Neumayer, E. 2005: Do international treaties improve respect for human rights? *Journal of Conflict Resolution*, 49 (6), 925–53.

Newman, F. and Weissbrodt, D. 1996: *International Human Rights: law, policy, and process*. Cincinnati, OH: Anderson Co, second edition.

Nickel, J. W. 1993: How human rights generate duties to provide and protect. *Human Rights Quarterly*, 15 (1), 77–86.

Nickel, J. W. 2007: *Making Sense of Human Rights*. Malden, MA: Blackwell, second edition.

Nordhaus, W. D. 2008: *A Question of Balance: weighing the options on global warming policies*. New Haven, CT: Yale University Press.

Normand, R. and Zaidi, S. 2008: *Human Rights at the UN: the political history of universal justice*. Bloomington, IN: Indiana University Press.

Nussbaum, M. C. 1993: Commentary on Onora O'Neill: justice, gender, and international boundaries. In M. Nussbaum and A. Sen (eds), *The Quality of Life*. Oxford: Clarendon Press, 324–35.

Nussbaum, M. C. 2016: Women's progress and women's human rights. *Human Rights Quarterly*, 38 (3), 589–622.

Nussbaum, M. C. and Sen, A. (eds) 1993: *The Quality of Life*. Oxford: Clarendon Press.

Nyamu-Musembi, C. 2000: How should human rights and development respond to cultural legitimization of gender hierarchy in developing societies? *Harvard International Law Journal*, 41 (2), 381–418.

Office of the United Nations High Commissioner for Human Rights 2006: *Principles and Guidelines for a Human Rights Approach to Poverty Reduction Strategies*. New York and Geneva: United Nations.

Office of the United Nations High Commissioner for Human Rights 2015: Joint statement by UN Special Procedures on the occasion of World Environment Day (5 June 2015): climate change and human rights.

Oliner, S. P. and Oliner, P. M. 1988: *The Altruistic Personality: rescuers of Jews in Nazi Europe*. New York: The Free Press.

O'Neill, O. 1993: Justice, gender, and international boundaries. In M. Nussbaum and A. Sen (eds), *The Quality of Life*. Oxford: Clarendon Press, 303–23.

O'Neill, O. 2005: Agents of justice. In A. Kuper (ed.), *Global Responsibilities: who must deliver on human rights?* New York: Routledge, 37–52.

Opsahl, T. 1992: The Human Rights Committee. In P. Alston (ed.), *The United Nations and Human Rights: a critical appraisal*. Oxford: Clarendon Press, 369–443.

Othman, N. 1999: Grounding human rights arguments in non-Western culture: Shari'a and the citizenship rights of women in a modern Islamic state. In J. A. Bauer and D. A. Bell (eds), *The East Asian Challenge for Human Rights*. Cambridge: Cambridge University Press, 169–92.

Otto, D. 1996: Non-governmental organizations in the United Nations system: the emerging role of international civil society. *Human Rights Quarterly*, 18 (1), 107–41.

Pagden, A. 1982: *The Fall of Natural Man: the American Indian and the origins of comparative ethnology*. Cambridge: Cambridge University Press.

Page, E. A. 2006: *Climate Change, Justice and Future Generations*. Cheltenham: Edward Elgar.

Paine, T. 1988: *The Rights of Man*. London: Penguin Books.

Paterson, M. 2001: Principles of justice in the context of global climate change. In U. Luterbacher and D. F. Sprinz (eds), *International Relations and Global Climate Change*. Cambridge, MA: MIT Press, 119–26.

Patten, A. 2005: Should we stop thinking about poverty in terms of helping the poor? *Ethics and International Affairs*, 19 (1), 19–27.

Paul, J. A. 2001: A short history of the NGO Working Group. Global Policy Forum, http://www.globalpolicy.org/security/ngowkgrp/history.htm.

Pauwelyn, J. 2005: Human rights in WTO dispute settlement. In T. Cottier, J. Pauwelyn and E. B. Bonanomi (eds), *Human Rights and International Trade*. Oxford: Oxford University Press, 205–31.

Pavković, A. and Radan, P. 2007: *Creating New States: theory and practice of secession*. Aldershot: Ashgate.

Penner, J. 2010: The state duty to support the poor in Kant's *Doctrine of Right*. *British Journal of Politics and International Relations*, 12 (1), 88–110.

Philp, M. 1989: *Paine*. Oxford: Oxford University Press.

Piccone, T. J. 2012: *Catalysts for Change: how the UN's independent experts promote human rights*. Washington, DC: Brookings Institution Press.

Poe, S. C. 2004: The decision to repress: an integrative theoretical approach to the research on human rights and repression. In S. C. Carey and S. C. Poe (eds), *Understanding Human Rights Violations: new systematic studies*. Aldershot: Ashgate, 16–38.

Poe, S. C. and Tate, C. N. 1994: Repression of human rights to personal integrity in the 1980s: a global analysis. *American Political Science Review*, 88 (4), 853–72.

Pogge, T. W. 2002a: *World Poverty and Human Rights: cosmopolitan responsibilities and reforms*. Cambridge: Polity.

Pogge, T. W. 2002b: Can the capability approach be justified? *Philosophical Topics*, 30 (2), 167–228.

Pogge, T. W. 2005a: Human rights and human responsibilities. In A. Kuper (ed.), *Global Responsibilities: who must deliver on human rights?* New York: Routledge, 3–35.

Pogge, T. W. 2005b: World poverty and human rights. *Ethics and International Affairs*, 19 (1), 1–7.

Pogge, T. W. 2005c: Severe poverty as a violation of negative duties: reply to the critics. *Ethics and International Affairs*, 19 (1), 55–83.

Pogge, T. W. 2007: Severe poverty as a human rights violation. In T. W. Pogge (ed.), *Freedom from Poverty as a Human Right: who owes what to the very poor?* Oxford: UNESCO and Oxford University Press, 11–53.

Pogge, T. W. 2008: *World Poverty and Human Rights*. Cambridge: Polity, second edition.

Pogge, T. W. 2009: Shue on rights and duties. In C. R. Beitz and R. E. Goodin (eds), *Global Basic Rights*. Oxford: Oxford University Press, 113–30.

Posner, E. A. 2014: *The Twilight of Human Rights Law*. New York: Oxford University Press.

Pritchard, K. 1989: Political science and the teaching of human rights. *Human Rights Quarterly*, 11 (3), 459–75.

Ratner, S. R. 2001–2: Corporations and human rights: a theory of legal responsibility. *Yale Law Journal*, 111, 443–546.

Rawls, J. 1999: *The Law of Peoples.* Cambridge, MA: Harvard University Press.

Raz, J. 1986: *The Morality of Freedom.* Oxford: Clarendon Press.

Raz, J. 2010: Human rights without foundations. In S. Besson and J. Tasioulas (eds), *The Philosophy of International Law.* Oxford: Oxford University Press, 321–37.

Reanda, L. 1992: The Commission on the Status of Women. In P. Alston (ed.), *The United Nations and Human Rights: a critical appraisal.* Oxford: Clarendon Press, 265–303.

Reeves, E. 2006: Quantifying genocide in Darfur (Part I), 28 April, http://www.sudanreeves.org/Article102.html.

Reeves, E. 2008: Darfur: millions of vulnerable civilians sliding closer to starvation. *Dissent*, 15 June, http://sudanreeves.org/2008/06/15/darfur-millions-of-vulnerable-civilians-sliding-closer-to-starvation.

Ribohn, U. 2002: 'Human rights and the multiparty system have swallowed our traditions': conceiving women and culture in the new Malawi. In H. Englund (ed.), *A Democracy of Chameleons: politics and culture in the new Malawi.* Uppsala: Nordiska Afrikainstitutet, 166–77.

Richards, D. L., Gelleny, R. D. and Sacko, D. H. 2001: Money with a mean streak? Foreign economic penetration and government respect for human rights in developing countries. *International Studies Quarterly*, 45 (2), 219–39.

Riddell, R. C. 2007: *Does Foreign Aid Really Work?* Oxford: Oxford University Press.

Ripstein, A. 2009: *Force and Freedom: Kant's legal and political philosophy.* Cambridge, MA: Harvard University Press.

Risse, M. 2005a: Do we owe the global poor assistance or rectification? *Ethics and International Affairs*, 19 (1), 9–18.

Risse, M. 2005b: How does the global order harm the poor? *Philosophy & Public Affairs*, 33 (4), 349–76.

Risse, T. and Ropp, S. C. 1999. International human rights norms and domestic change: conclusion. In T. Risse, S. C. Ropp and K. Sikkink (eds), *The Power of Human Rights: international norms and domestic change.* Cambridge: Cambridge University Press, 234–78.

Risse, T. and Ropp, S. C. 2013: Introduction and overview. In T. Risse, S. C. Ropp and K. Sikkink (eds), *The Persistent Power of Human Rights: from commitment to compliance.* Cambridge: Cambridge University Press, 3–25.

Risse, T. and Sikkink, K. 1999: The socialization of international human rights norms into domestic practices: introduction. In T. Risse, S. C. Ropp and K. Sikkink (eds), *The Power of Human Rights: international norms and domestic change*. Cambridge: Cambridge University Press, 1–38.

Risse, T. and Sikkink, K. 2013: Conclusions. In T. Risse, S. C. Ropp and K. Sikkink (eds), *The Persistent Power of Human Rights: from commitment to compliance*. Cambridge: Cambridge University Press, 275–95.

Risse, T., Ropp, S. C. and Sikkink, K. (eds) 1999: *The Power of Human Rights: international norms and domestic change*. Cambridge: Cambridge University Press.

Risse, T., Ropp, S. C. and Sikkink, K. (eds) 2013: *The Persistent Power of Human Rights: from commitment to compliance*. Cambridge: Cambridge University Press.

Robertson, A. H. and Merrills, J. G. 1996: *Human Rights in the World: an introduction to the study of the international protection of human rights*. Manchester: Manchester University Press.

Rodman, K. 2008: Darfur and the limits of legal deterrence. *Human Rights Quarterly*, 30 (3), 529–60.

Rodrik, D., Subrahamian, A. and Trebbi, F. 2004: Institutions rule: the primacy of institutions over geography and integration in economic development. *Journal of Economic Growth*, 9, 131–65.

Ron, J., Crow, D. and Golden, S. 2013: The struggle for a truly grassroots human rights movement. *OpenGlobalRights*, 18 June.

Ron, J., Ramos H. and Rodgers, K. 2005: Transnational information politics: NGO human rights reporting, 1985–2000. *International Studies Quarterly*, 49 (3), 557–87.

Rorty, R. 1993: Human rights, rationality, and sentimentality. In S. Shute and S. Hurley (eds), *On Human Rights: the Oxford Amnesty Lectures 1993*. New York: Basic Books, 111–34.

Rose, P. L. 1992: *German Question/Jewish Question: revolutionary anti-Semitism in Germany from Kant to Wagner*. Princeton, NJ: Princeton University Press.

Roshwald, R. 1959: The concept of human rights. *Philosophy and Phenomenological Research*, 19, 354–79.

Rousseau, J.-J. 1968: *The Social Contract*. Harmondsworth: Penguin Books.

Rubio-Marín, R. 2014: Introduction: human rights and the citizen/non-citizen distinction revisited. In R. Rubio-Marín (ed.), *Human Rights and Immigration*. Oxford: Oxford University Press, 1–18.

Rudolph, C. 2001: Constructing an atrocities regime: the politics of war crimes tribunals. *International Organization*, 55 (3), 655–91.

Rummel, R. J. 1994: *Death by Government*. New Brunswick, NJ: Transaction Publishers.

Sabatello, M. 2014a: A short history of the international disability rights movement. In M. Sabatello and M. Schulze (eds), *Human Rights and Disability Advocacy*. Philadelphia, PA: University of Pennsylvania Press, 13–24.

Sabatello, M. 2014b: The new diplomacy. In M. Sabatello and M. Schulze (eds), *Human Rights and Disability Advocacy*. Philadelphia, PA: University of Pennsylvania Press, 239–58.

Sabatello, M. and Schulze, M. 2014: Introduction. In M. Sabatello and M. Schulze (eds), *Human Rights and Disability Advocacy*. Philadelphia, PA: University of Pennsylvania Press, 1–12.

Sachs, J. 2005: *The End of Poverty: how we can make it happen in our lifetime*. London: Penguin Books.

Salomon, M. E. 2007: *Global Responsibility for Human Rights: world poverty and the development of international law*. Oxford: Oxford University Press.

Sangiovanni, A. 2015: Why there cannot be a truly Kantian theory of human rights. In R. Cruft, M. S. Liao and M. Renzo (eds), *Philosophical Foundations of Human Rights*. Oxford: Oxford University Press, 671–89.

Satz, D. 2005: What do we owe the global poor? *Ethics and International Affairs*, 19 (1), 47–54.

Schirmer, J. 1997: Universal and sustainable human rights? Special tribunals in Guatemala. In R. A. Wilson (ed.), *Human Rights, Culture and Context: anthropological perspectives*. London: Pluto Press, 161–86.

Scott, James C. 1998: *Seeing Like A State: how certain schemes to improve the human condition have failed*. New Haven, CT: Yale University Press.

Sen, A. 2005: Human rights and capabilities. *Journal of Human Development*, 6 (2), 151–66.

Sengupta, A. 2002: The theory and practice of the right to development. *Human Rights Quarterly*, 24 (4), 837–89.

Shachar, A. 1999: The paradox of multicultural vulnerability: individual rights, identity groups, and the states. In C. Joppke and S. Lukes (eds), *Multicultural Questions*. Oxford: Oxford University Press, 87–111.

Shehadi, K. S. 1993: *Ethnic Self-determination and the Break-up of States*. London: Brassey's.

Sherwood, H. 2015: Human rights groups face global crackdown 'not seen in a generation'. *Guardian*, 26 August.

Shue, H. 1996: *Basic Rights: subsistence, affluence, and U.S. foreign policy*. Princeton, NJ: Princeton University Press, second edition.

Sikkink, K. and Walling, C. B. 2007: The impact of human rights trials in Latin America. *Journal of Peace Research*, 44 (4), 427–45.

Simmons, A. J. 2001: Human rights and world citizenship: the universality of human rights. In A. J. Simmons, *Justification and Legitimacy: essays on rights and obligations*. Cambridge: Cambridge University Press, 179–96.

Simmons, B. A. 2009: *Mobilizing for Human Rights: international law in domestic politics*. New York: Cambridge University Press.

Simmons, B. A. 2013: From ratification to compliance: quantitative evidence on the spiral model. In T. Risse, S. C. Ropp and K. Sikkink (eds), *The Persistent Power of Human Rights: from commitment to compliance*. Cambridge: Cambridge University Press, 43–59.

Simmons, P. J. 1998: Learning to live with NGOs. *Foreign Policy*, 112, 82–96.

Singer, P. W. 2010: The enablers of war: causal factors behind the child soldier phenomenon. In S. Gates and S. Reich (eds), *Child Soldiers in the Age of Fractured States*. Pittsburgh, PA: University of Pittsburgh Press, 93–107.

Slim, H. 2002: *By What Authority? The legitimacy and accountability of non-governmental organisations*. Geneva: International Council on Human Rights Policy.

Smith, J., Bolyard, M. and Ippolito, A. 1999: Human rights and the global economy: a response to Meyer. *Human Rights Quarterly*, 21 (1), 207–19.

Smith, J., Pagnucco, T. and Lopez, G. A. 1998: Globalizing human rights: the work of transnational human rights NGOs in the 1990s. *Human Rights Quarterly*, 20 (2), 379–412.

Smith-Cannoy, H. 2012: *Insincere Commitments: human rights treaties, abusive states, and citizen activism*. Washington, DC: Georgetown University Press.

Snyder, J. and Vinjamuri, L. 2003–4: Trials and errors: principle and pragmatism in strategies of international justice. *International Security*, 28 (3), 5–44.

Sorabji, R. 1993: *Animal Minds and Human Morals: the origins of the Western debate*. London: Duckworth.

Sorell, T. and Landman, T. 2006: Justifying human rights: the roles of domain, audience, and constituency. *Journal of Human Rights*, 5 (4), 383–400.

Spar, D. L. 1998: The spotlight and the bottom line: how multinationals export human rights. *Foreign Affairs*, 77 (2), 7–12.

Speed, S. and Collier, J. F. 2000: Limiting indigenous autonomy in Chiapas, Mexico: the state government's use of human rights. *Human Rights Quarterly*, 22 (4), 877–905.

Stammers, N. 1999: Social movements and the social construction of human rights. *Human Rights Quarterly*, 21 (4), 980–1008.

Steiner, H. 1994: *An Essay on Rights*. Oxford: Blackwell.

Stern, N. 2009: *The Global Deal: climate change and the creation of a new era of progress and prosperity*. New York: PublicAffairs.

Stewart, F. and Wang, M. 2005: Poverty reduction strategy papers within the human rights perspective. In P. Alston and M. Robinson (eds), *Human Rights and Development: towards mutual reinforcement*. Oxford: Oxford University Press, 447–74.

Stiglitz, J. E. 2002: *Globalization and Its Discontents*. London: Penguin Books.

Stoll, D. 1997: To whom should we listen? Human rights activism in two Guatemalan land disputes. In R. A. Wilson (ed.), *Human Rights, Culture and Context: anthropological perspectives*. London: Pluto Press, 187–215.

Strouse, J. C. and Claude, R. P. 1976: Empirical comparative rights research: some preliminary tests of development hypotheses. In R. P. Claude (ed.), *Comparative Human Rights*. Baltimore, MD: Johns Hopkins University Press, 51–67.

Syrian Observatory for Human Rights 2016: About 430 thousands were killed since the beginning of the Syrian revolution, http://www.syriahr.com/en/?p=50612.

Talbott, W. J. 2005: *Which Rights Should Be Universal?* New York: Oxford University Press.

Tasioulas, J. 2010: Taking rights out of human rights. *Ethics*, 120 (4), 647–78.

Thompson, J. 2002: *Taking Responsibility for the Past: reparation and historical injustice*. Cambridge: Polity.

Thornberry, P. 2002: *Indigenous Peoples and Human Rights*. Manchester: Manchester University Press.

Tierney, B. 1988: Villey, Ockham and the origin of individual rights. In J. Witte, Jr. and F. S. Alexander (eds), *The Weightier Matters of the Law: essays on law and religion. A tribute to Harold J. Berman*. Studies in Religion 51. Atlanta, GA: Scholars Press, 1–31.

Tierney, B. 1989: Origins of natural rights language: texts and contexts, 1150–1250. *History of Political Thought*, 10 (4), 615–46.

Tierney, B. 1992: Natural rights in the thirteenth century: a quaestio of Henry of Ghent. *Speculum*, 67 (1), 58–68.

Tierney, B. 1997: *The Idea of Natural Rights: studies on natural rights, natural law and church law 1150–1625*. Atlanta, GA: Scholars Press.

Todres, J. 2004: Emerging limitations on the rights of the child: the U.N. Convention on the Rights of the Child and its early case law. In M. D. A. Freeman (ed.), *Children's Rights*. Aldershot: Ashgate Dartmouth, volume II, 139–80.

Tostensen, A. 2007: The Bretton Woods institutions: human rights and the PRSPs. In M. E. Salomon, A. Tostensen and W. Vandenhole (eds), *Casting the Net Wider: human rights, development and new duty-bearers*. Antwerp: Intersentia, 185–210.

Tsutsui, K. and Shin, H.-J. 2008: Global norms, local activism, and social movement outcomes: global human rights and resident Koreans in Japan. *Social Problems*, 55 (3), 391–418.

Tuck, R. 1979: *Natural Rights Theories: their origin and development*. Cambridge: Cambridge University Press.

Tully, J. 1980: *A Discourse on Property: John Locke and his adversaries*. Cambridge: Cambridge University Press.

Tully, J. 1993: *An Approach to Political Philosophy: Locke in contexts*. Cambridge: Cambridge University Press.

Tully, J. 1995: *Strange Multiplicity: constitutionalism in an age of diversity*. Cambridge: Cambridge University Press.

Turner, B. S. 1993: Outline of a theory of human rights. *Sociology*, 27 (3), 489–512.

United Nations Commission on Human Rights 2006: Interim Report of the Special Representative of the Secretary-General on the Issue of Human Rights and Transnational Corporations and Other Business Enterprises, 22 February, E/CN.4/2006/97.

United Nations Committee on Economic, Social and Cultural Rights 1991: General Comment 3, the nature of States parties' obligations. U.N. Doc. E/1991/23, annex III at 86.

United Nations Development Programme 2005: *Human Development Report 2005: international co-operation at a crossroads – aid, trade and security in an unequal world*. New York: United Nations Development Programme.

United Nations Human Rights Council 2007a: Human rights impact assessments – resolving key methodological questions. Report of the Special Representative of the Secretary-General on the Issue of Human Rights and Transnational Corporations and Other Business Enterprises, 5 February, A/HRC/4/74.

United Nations Human Rights Council 2007b: Business and Human Rights: mapping international standards of responsibility and accountability for corporate Acts. Report of the Special Representative of the Secretary-General on the Issue of Human Rights and Transnational Corporations and Other Business Enterprises, John Ruggie, 9 February, A/HRC/4/035.

United Nations Human Rights Council 2008a: Protect, respect and remedy: a framework for business and human rights. Report of the Special Representative of the Secretary-General on the

Issue of Human Rights and Transnational Corporations and Other Business Enterprises, John Ruggie, 7 April, A/HRC/8/5.

United Nations Human Rights Council 2008b: Clarifying the concepts of 'sphere of influence' and 'complicity'. Report of the Special Representative of the Secretary-General on the Issue of Human Rights and Transnational Corporations and Other Business Enterprises, John Ruggie, 15 May, A/HRC/8/16.

United Nations Human Rights Council 2009: Business and human rights: towards operationalizing the 'Protect, Respect and Remedy' framework. Report of the Special Representative of the Secretary-General on the Issue of Human Rights and Transnational Corporations and Other Business Enterprises, John Ruggie, 22 April, A/HRC/11/13.

United Nations Human Rights Council 2010: Business and human rights: further steps toward the operationalization of the 'protect, respect and remedy' framework. Report of the Special Representative of the Secretary-General on the Issue of Human Rights and Transnational Corporations and Other Business Enterprises, John Ruggie, 9 April, A/HRC/14/27.

United Nations Inter-agency Group for Child Mortality Estimation 2015: *Levels & Trends in Child Mortality: report 2015*. New York: United Nations Children's Fund.

Uvin, P. 2004: *Human Rights and Development*. Bloomfield, CT: Kumarian Press.

Van Ittersum, M. 2006: *Profit and Principle: Hugo Grotius, natural rights theories and the rise of Dutch power in the East Indies, 1595–1615*. Leiden: Brill.

Verdirame, G. 2011: *The UN and Human Rights: who guards the guardians?* Cambridge: Cambridge University Press.

Vincent, R. J. 1986: *Human Rights and International Relations*. Cambridge: Cambridge University Press.

Vitoria, F. de 1991: On the American Indians. In A. Pagden and J. Lawrance (eds), *Vitoria: political writings*. Cambridge: Cambridge University Press.

Wade, R. H. 2004a: On the causes of increasing world poverty and inequality, or why the Matthew Effect prevails. *New Political Economy*, 9 (2), 163–88.

Wade, R. H. 2004b: Is globalization reducing poverty and inequality? *World Development*, 32 (4), 567–89.

Waldron, J. (ed.) 1987: *'Nonsense Upon Stilts': Bentham, Burke and Marx on the Rights of Man*. London: Methuen.

Waldron, J. 1988: *The Right to Private Property*. Oxford: Clarendon Press.

Waldron, J. 1992: Superseding historic injustice. *Ethics*, 103, 4–28.

Waldron, J. 1993: A rights-based critique of constitutional rights. *Oxford Journal of Legal Studies*, 13 (1), 18–51.

Waltz, S. 2001: Universalizing human rights: the role of small states in the construction of the Universal Declaration of Human Rights. *Human Rights Quarterly*, 23 (1), 44–72.

Waltz, S. 2004: Universal human rights: the contribution of Muslim states. *Human Rights Quarterly*, 26 (4), 799–844.

Washburn, W. E. 1987: Cultural relativism, human rights, and the AAA. *American Anthropologist*, 89 (4), 939–43.

Waters, M. 1996: Human rights and the universalisation of interests: towards a social constructionist approach. *Sociology*, 30 (3), 593–600.

Weeramantry, C. G. 1997: *Justice Without Frontiers: furthering human rights*. The Hague: Kluwer Law International, volume 1.

Weinrib, E. J. 2002–3: Poverty and property in Kant's system of rights. *Notre Dame Law Review*, 78 (3), 795–828.

Weiss, T. G. 2004: The sunset of humanitarian intervention? The responsibility to protect in a unipolar era. *Security Dialogue*, 35 (2), 135–53.

Weissbrodt, D. 2011: United Nations Charter-based procedures for addressing human rights violations. In G. Gilbert, F. Hampson and C. Sandoval (eds), *The Delivery of Human Rights: essays in honour of Professor Sir Nigel Rodley*. Abingdon: Routledge, 13–38.

Welch, C. B. 1984: *Liberty and Utility: The French idéologues and the transformation of liberalism*. New York: Columbia University Press.

Wellman, C. 2011: *The Moral Dimensions of Human Rights*. Oxford: Oxford University Press.

Wiebelhaus-Brahm, E. 2010: *Truth Commissions and Transitional Societies: the impact on human rights and democracy*. Abingdon: Routledge.

Wiles, M. and Santer, M. (eds) 1977: *Documents in Early Christian Thought*. Cambridge: Cambridge University Press.

Wilson, R. A. 1997a: Human rights, culture and context: an introduction. In R. A. Wilson (ed.), *Human Rights, Culture and Context: anthropological perspectives*. London: Pluto Press, 1–27.

Wilson, R. A. 1997b: Representing human rights violations: social contexts and subjectivities. In R. A. Wilson (ed.), *Human Rights, Culture and Context: anthropological perspectives*. London: Pluto Press, 134–60.

Wilson, R. A. 2011: *Writing History in International Criminal Trials*. Cambridge: Cambridge University Press.

Wiseberg, L. S. 1992: Human rights non-governmental organizations. In R. P. Claude and B. H. Weston (eds), *Human Rights in the World Community: issues and action*. Philadelphia, PA: University of Pennsylvania Press, second edition, 372–83.

Wiseberg, L. 2003: The role of non-governmental organizations (NGOs) in the protection and enforcement of human rights. In J. Symonides (ed.), *Human Rights: international protection, monitoring, enforcement*. Paris: UNESCO, 347–72.

Woodiwiss, A. 1998: *Globalisation, Human Rights and Labour Law in Pacific Asia*. Cambridge: Cambridge University Press.

Woodiwiss, A. 2005: *Human Rights*. London: Routledge.

World Bank Group 2016: *Poverty and Shared Prosperity 2016: taking on inequality*. Washington, DC: World Bank.

World Bank Group and UNICEF 2016: *Ending Extreme Poverty: a focus on children*. Washington, DC: World Bank and UNICEF.

Xanthaki, A. 2011: The UN Declaration on the Rights of Indigenous Peoples and collective rights: what's the future for indigenous women? In S. Allen and A. Xanthaki (eds), *Reflections on the UN Declaration on the Rights of Indigenous Peoples*. Oxford: Hart, 413–31.

Yogyakarta Principles 2006: The Yogyakarta Principles: the application of international human rights law in relation to sexual orientation and gender identity, http://yogyakartaprinciples.org.

Young, K. G. 2008: The minimum core of economic and social rights: a concept in search of content. *Yale Journal of International Law*, 33, 113–75.

Zanger, S. C. 2000: A global analysis of the effect of political regime changes on life integrity violations, 1977–93. *Journal of Peace Research*, 37 (2), 213–33.

Index

Afghanistan, 58–9
agency, 74–5
aid, 193–4, 207
Al-Qaeda, 58–9, 117–18
American Anthropological
    Association, 90, 120–1
American Declaration of
    Independence, 27, 63
Amnesty International, 180–1
Arab Spring, 60
Aristotle, 17, 21, 67, 210
Ashford, E., 83
Asian values, 121, 193
asylum, 45, 158
autonomy, 69, 73, 76–7, 110,
    134–5, 150–1

Barry, B., 136–8
Bentham, J., 33–4
Beran, H., 144
bilateral investment
    treaties, 195
boomerang theory, *see* spiral
    model
Brazil, 103, 170
Burke, E., 33
business corporations,
    196–200

Caney, S., 205
capabilities, 70–2
Carr, E. H., 66
Carter, Jimmy, 51–2
child soldiers, 152
children's rights, 150–3,
    184–5
Chile, 107
Christianity, 18–19, 21,
    210–11
citizens' rights, 210
civil rights, 20
Claude, R., 101–2, 169
climate change, 203–6
Cold War, 48, 172–3, 175,
    183–4, 212–3
collective rights, 21, 46, 69,
    121, 135, 138, 140–1,
    144–5
colonialism, 42–3, 193
Commission on Human
    Rights, 41–3, 48–50, 60,
    187, 198
Commission on the Status of
    Women, 146–7
common good, 25
communitarianism, 86, 145
compossibility, 5–6, 84

concept of human rights, 3, 5,
  15–16
  legal, 4, 6–8, 11, 18
  moral, 8–9, 15
  political, 9–11
conflicts of rights, 84
consensus, 63, 67–70, 75–7,
  89, 93
Convention on the Elimination
  of Discrimination against
  Women (CEDAW), 146–8
Convention on the Rights of
  Persons with Disabilities,
  157
Convention on the Rights of
  the Child, 151–3
corporate codes of conduct,
  197–8
costs of rights, 82–4, 208
cultural relativism, 49, 54, 90,
  112, 120–1, 125–7,
  131–2, 141, 148–9, 151,
  153–4, 156, 158, 161,
  163, 188
culture, 126, 136–7, 145,
  149, 193

Dahl, R., 78
Darfur, 1–2, 13, 117, 217
democracy, 77–9, 126–7,
  144–5, 160, 173, 193,
  218–9
democratization of human
  rights, 181, 220
derogation, 83–4
desert, 80
development, 189–94, 196,
  200–2, 204, 208
disability rights, 156–8
Donnelly, J., 103, 115–16,
  122, 138, 154, 169–70,
  188, 191, 215–16
duties, 47, 186
Dworkin, R., 69, 78

early warning, 217–18
Economic and Social
  Council, 41, 48–9, 175,
  197
economic and social
  rights, 28, 36, 46–7,
  53–4, 61, 71, 77–8, 81–4,
  108, 152, 169, 174, 182,
  185–8, 195, 200, 206,
  211, 214, 218
economics, 82, 183–4,
  208–9
ethnic cleansing, 41–2, 56

feminism, 147–9
foreign direct investment,
  196
Forsythe, D., 64–5, 114–15,
  163–4, 177
Foweraker, J. and Landman,
  T., 104, 170–1
freedom of expression, 46
freedom of religion, 46
French Revolution, 27–8,
  211–12

Gandhi, M., 66
Gewirth, A., 65–6, 72–3
Global Compact, 198
globalization, 183–4, 216
global justice, 81, 206–8
global poverty, 184–5, 192–3,
  204, 206–9
global warming, 203
Griffin, J., 73, 76–7
Grotius, H., 22, 211
Guiding Principles on Business
  and Human Rights, 199
Gurr, T. R., 103–4, 170

Hawkins, D. G., 107
Heavily Indebted Poor
  Countries Initiative, 202
Helsinki Final Act, 53

High Commissioner for
Human Rights, 57, 156,
198
Hobbes, T., 22
Howard, R. E., 109
human development, 189
human dignity, 70, 122–3,
131, 138, 155
human nature, 75–6
Human Rights Committee,
51, 141
Human Rights Council, 60–1,
155, 199–200
human rights education,
220–1

Idealism, 162, 213
ideal theory, 65
illicit financial transfers,
207
imperialism, 22, 26, 122–6,
142–3, 163
indigenous rights, 21, 27,
112, 135, 138–43, 202
Intergovernmental Panel on
Climate Change
(IPCC), 203, 205
International Covenant on
Civil and Political
Rights, 50–1, 130, 132
International Covenant on
Economic, Social and
Cultural Rights, 50–1,
82, 187–8
International Criminal
Court, 56, 95–6, 176
International Criminal
Tribunal for the Former
Yugoslavia, 56
international criminal
tribunals, 95–6
international financial
institutions, 200–2, 207,
216–7

International Labour
Organization (ILO), 139,
175, 186–7, 195, 197
International Monetary Fund
(IMF), 200–2
Iraq, 55, 59
ISIS, 59
Islam, 54, 58, 122, 127–9,
151

Jones, P., 85
justice, 80–1
justiciability, 188–9

Kant, I., 29–31
Kosovo, 56
Kymlicka, W., 134–7, 141
Kyoto Protocol, 203–4

Landman, T., 104–5
Las Casas, B. de, 21, 211
League of Nations, 36–7, 40,
132
legalization of human
rights, 91, 97, 188–9,
220
legal positivism, 11, 113
Levellers, 23
liberal democracy, 133–8,
142–3, 175–6, 212
liberalism, 43, 110, 133–7,
144–5, 148, 175
Locke, J., 11, 24–7, 43–4,
133, 141, 211, 216, 220

Macdonald, M., 67
MacIntyre, A., 6–7, 16
Magna Carta, 19–20, 23, 25,
211
mainstreaming, 57, 117, 147
margin of appreciation,
126–7, 156
Maritain, J., 66
marriage, 45

Marx, K., 35
migrants, 158–60
millennium development
    goals, 190, 201
minimum core obligations,
    187
minorities, 40, 132–8, 140,
    143
Moyn, S., 15
multiculturalism, 134
multinational corporations,
    see transnational
    corporations

national emergencies, 83–4
national human rights
    institutions, 100–1
natural law, 18, 20, 22–4, 70,
    210
Nazism, 40, 43–5, 67–8, 126,
    132, 154, 196, 215, 218
needs, 74
neo-liberalism, 184, 219
New International Economic
    Order, 184, 191
Nickel, J., 82
nomadic peoples, 141–2
non-governmental
    organizations (NGOs), 6,
    8, 10, 36, 40, 48–9, 51–3,
    58, 104, 106, 154, 162–4,
    167–8, 174–82, 187, 195,
    199–202, 214, 216, 218,
    220

Obama, Barack, 59–60
objections to human
    rights, 85–6
obligations, 81
O'Neill, O., 82–3
Organization for Economic
    Co-operation and
    Development
    (OECD), 197

Paine, T., 31–2
Paris conference on climate
    change 2015, 205–6
patriarchalism, 110
personhood, 73
Pogge, T., 83, 206–8
polluter pays, 204
poverty, 189–90, 192–4, 201,
    206–7
poverty reduction strategy
    papers, 202
power, abuse of, 210, 219–20
preferential trade
    agreements, 196
progressive realization, 187–8
property, 46, 50, 90, 211
prosecutions of human-rights
    violators, 99
Protestantism, 211

Rawls, J., 76
Realism, 8, 101, 162–3, 165,
    167–8, 213
refugees, 158–60
regime theory, 115–16, 162
Resolution 1235, 49–50, 52
Resolution 1503, 49–50
responsibility to protect, 116–
    17, 217
right of humanitarian
    intervention, 116
rights-based approach to
    development, 189–91
rights-based moralities, 80
rights inflation, 6, 86
right to culture, 47, 130, 132,
    138–9
right to development, 53,
    190–2
right to self-determination, 47,
    49–50, 53, 139–46,
    212–13
right to subsistence, 211
Risse, T., 105–6

Roosevelt, F. D., 39
Rorty, R., 64
Rousseau, J.-J., 133
Ruggie, J., 198–200
Rwanda, 217

Saudi Arabia, 42
scientific positivism, 90, 101,
    119, 212
secession, 143–6
secularization, 22, 26–8, 32,
    63, 71
sexual minorities, 153–6
Shue, H., 76, 82
Simmons, B. A., 107
slavery, 27–8, 45
socialism, 34–6, 46
South Africa, 41–2, 197,
    213
South Korea, 103, 170
sovereignty, 10, 41, 48–9, 61,
    126, 163, 216–7
Spanish conquest of
    America, 21, 211
special procedures, 52–3
spiral model, 105–6, 165–9
statistics, 3
Steiner, H., 84
Stoics, 18, 210
structural adjustment
    programmes, 189, 200–1
sustainable development
    goals, 190
Syria, 60–1, 213

territorial integrity, 143, 145
thematic procedures, 52
third-generation rights, 53–4
trade, 194–6
Trade-Related Aspects of
    Intellectual Property
    Rights (TRIPS), 195
transitional justice, 81,
    97–8

transnational corporations,
    82–3, 163, 197–200,
    216–7, 220
trumps, rights as, 69
truth commissions, 97–9
Tully, J., 136
Turner, B. S., 107

UN Charter, 4, 39–41, 146,
    175, 183
UN Development
    Programme, 189
UN Framework Convention
    on Climate Change, 203,
    205
United Nations, 4–5, 10–13,
    15, 39–40, 48, 55, 57–8,
    61, 63–4, 67, 117, 147,
    181, 183, 212, 214
Universal Declaration of
    Human Rights, 4–6,
    11–12, 20, 41–8, 50–1,
    54, 61, 65–6, 68–9, 76,
    80, 82, 84, 120–2, 124,
    128, 130, 132–3, 136,
    146, 148, 154, 158, 176,
    183, 187, 196, 212
universalism, 121–2, 125–6,
    131–2, 187–8, 215–6
UN norms on the
    responsibilities of
    transnational corporations
    and other business
    enterprises, 198–9
UN Security Council, 57–8,
    152, 155, 164, 176, 195,
    200
UN Sub-Commission on the
    Promotion and Protection
    of Human Rights, 198–9
USA, 51–2, 58–9, 117–18,
    163, 202–3
Utilitarianism, 34, 36, 40,
    84–5

utilitarianism of rights,
84–5

Vienna conference and
declaration, 57, 77–8,
120–1, 130, 148, 176,
216
Vincent, R. J., 115
Vitoria, F. de, 21, 211

Waldron, J., 78
war on terror, 59, 118
William of Ockham, 20

Woodiwiss, A., 109–10
women's rights, 26–8, 36, 46,
69–70, 82–3, 86, 95, 108,
110, 128, 130–1, 141,
146–9, 202
World Bank, 184–5, 189, 193,
200–2, 207
World Health Organization,
203
World Trade Organization,
194–6

Yugoslavia, 55–6